New York Versus

ALSO BY BILL MORALES

Farewell to the Last Golden Era:
The Yankees, the Pirates and the 1960 Baseball Season (McFarland 2009)

New York Versus New York, 1962

The Birth of the Yankees-Mets Rivalry

BILL MORALES

McFarland & Company, Inc., Publishers

Jefferson, North Carolina, and London

In Memoriam
Rubil Morales (1920–1996)
Rosa Vázquez (1922–1997)

All photographs are from National Baseball
Hall of Fame Library, Cooperstown, New York

LIBRARY OF CONGRESS CATALOGUING-IN-PUBLICATION DATA

Morales, Bill, 1950–
    New York versus New York, 1962 : the birth of the
Yankees-Mets rivalry / Bill Morales.
        p.   cm.
    Includes bibliographical references and index.

    ISBN 978-0-7864-7090-7
    softcover : acid free paper ∞

        1. New York Yankees (Baseball team)— History.   2. New
York Mets (Baseball team)— History.   3. Sports rivalries—
New York (State)— New York — History.   I. Title.
GV875.N4M64   2012
796.357'64097471—dc23   2012030083

BRITISH LIBRARY CATALOGUING DATA ARE AVAILABLE

On the cover: Detail from linen postcards of old Yankee Stadium
and the Polo Grounds

Manufactured in the United States of America

McFarland & Company, Inc., Publishers
Box 611, Jefferson, North Carolina 28640
www.mcfarlandpub.com

Table of Contents

Acknowledgments

I would like to thank the following people for their help with this book: Farley Chase, Tim Wiles, Freddy Berowski, John Horne, Mark Artschuler, Bill Burke, Sidney Birnback, Phil Dolce, Ann Wallenhorst, Bob Wiater, Karen Buonsignore, Sally D'Aloisio, Ron Goldfarb, Karen Hays, Eric Perkins, Mary Ann Wilkin, and Tom Wilkin. As always, this work would not have been possible without the love, encouragement, and good humor of my wife, Joann La Perla.

Preface

The View from
the Macombs Dam Bridge

In May 1964, three New York Yankees players, Mickey Mantle, Ralph Terry, and Jim Bouton, were driving together from their New Jersey homes for a ballgame at the Stadium. As their car crossed the McCombs Dam Bridge (which spans the Harlem River between Manhattan and the Bronx), the players spied the half-dismantled hulk of what had been the Polo Grounds, the late home of the New York Mets. Terry hadn't been pitching well of late, and Mantle, surveying the wreckage of the famous horseshoe-shaped ballpark, turned to Terry and quipped, "Ralph, it looks like one of your games."[1] Not so many years before, the view from the span had been quite different. Between October 1961 and October 1962, the Yankees and the Mets shared the city for the first time, their front offices located on opposite sides of Fifth Avenue in mid-town Manhattan, and their playing fields—Yankee Stadium and the Polo Grounds— situated on opposite sides of the Macombs Dam Bridge. This book tells the story of the first year of their life together as New York City rivals.

The emerging rivalry between the New York Yankees and the New York Mets was about more than just games won or money earned. As personified by Mets manager Casey Stengel and Yankees right-fielder Roger Maris, it was also a struggle over the future of the game. Between October 1961 and October 1962, baseball's prospects were the subject of intense debate around the country. The Yankees and Mets, teams with very different levels of talent and contrasting personalities, were at the center of this debate. By the early 1960s, there was a growing concern that Major League Baseball was losing its status as the National Pastime. Professional football was gaining fast in popularity, while baseball's, despite the "M&M Boys'" chase of Babe Ruth's home run record in 1961, was declining in attendance. Rightly or wrongly, for many people Casey Stengel represented everything that was good about baseball; Roger Maris represented much of what was bad with the game. The return

1

of Casey, baseball's greatest salesman, was received like a breath of fresh air in October 1961. With his raspy voice and mangled syntax, the "Ol' Perfessor" was a throwback to a more colorful era. By contrast, the diffident and blunt-speaking Maris, who days earlier had hit his 61st home run, seemed for many to embody everything distasteful about the modern ball player: outsized salary demands, player endorsement deals, a distancing from the average fan. While Stengel was the genuine article, combining "baseball genius" with a gift for clowning, Maris seemed somehow artificial to his critics in both personality and achievement. And so it would continue in 1962: Stengel seemingly reinvented tradition, evoking the glory of a more heroic age in baseball; Maris struggled under the burden of his sudden fame, resisting the mythologizing of a hero-hungry press and fandom.

The rivalry that emerged with the two New York City teams between October 1961 and October 1962 had the sense of a world turned upside down. It was the lowly Mets, not the championship Yankees, who earned the ticker tape parade down the Canyon of Heroes; it was the Mets around whom the press created legends. But the sense of a world turned upside down wasn't limited to the Mets and Yankees. It extended to other aspects of the game: the rising demands for equality by black players against institutionalized racism; and the increasing assertion of the Players' Association versus the owners in its fight for better working conditions. Outside Yankee Stadium and the Polo Grounds, beyond the Macombs Dam Bridge, the New York City metropolitan area was also being turned upside down. The most casual observer could see that the metropolitan area was undergoing vast changes between October 1961 and October 1962: Yankee players and fans residing in New Jersey crossed over on the new lower deck of the George Washington Bridge; the imminent completion of the Verrazano-Narrows Bridge would connect Staten Island fans with Brooklyn, and ultimately, to the Mets' future home in Queens; and Pennsylvania Station, the rendezvous point for the now infrequent Yankees and Mets train rides, was doomed to destruction, making way for a new Madison Square Garden complex. The Yankees and Mets, many of them residing in Bergen County, New Jersey, and Nassau County, New York, were part of the urban exodus to suburbia and the burgeoning consumer culture embodied by Roosevelt Field and Paramus Mall. This book, then, is an elegy to a time (the early 1960s), a place (New York City), and indeed a *game* long since gone.

I try to be as faithful to the times as possible, especially with regard to contemporary words and expressions. Although the words "offense" and "defense" are scattered throughout, I avoid using phrases such as "the offense" and "the defense," which weren't part of the baseball vocabulary of the times. In this vein, I also refer to "Latins" or "Spanish" players, rather than "Latinos" or "Hispanics." However, I try to avoid the contemporary "Negro," substituting "black" instead.

Prologue

"The Newest New York Club"

For twenty-eight hours—between 1 P.M. Friday, February 3, and five P.M. Saturday, February 4, 1961—the New York metropolitan area was blanketed by 17.4 inches of snow. Seventy mile per hour winds created drifts three feet deep and left motorists stranded on the major arteries stretching from Manhattan to the outer boroughs and adjoining suburbs. Mayor Robert F. Wagner declared a state of emergency as 12,000 city workers, wielding 2,500 pieces of motorized equipment, ventured out in zero degree weather to do battle with Mother Nature. The storm, the third major one in six weeks, wreaked havoc on transportation, work and school schedules. In a break with tradition, Mayor Wagner announced that the city's 986,000 school children would be forced to attend classes on Washington's birthday, February 22.

Thirty-five miles north of New York City, someone else's "holiday" was about to be interrupted. At mid-morning of Washington's birthday, the telephone rang at the Greenwich, Connecticut, home of George Weiss, the former long time general manager of the New York Yankees. The voice at the other end of the unlisted telephone number was that of M. Donald Grant, president of the Metropolitan Baseball Club, the National League's new expansion team in New York City. Michael Donald Grant was the managing partner in the Wall Street firm of Fahnestock and Company, and a former member of the board of directors of the New York Giants baseball team. The previous October, Grant assumed temporary leadership of a new ballclub, which, to date, had no nickname, logo, players, manager, or corporate sponsors. Team owner Joan Payson at the suggestion of New York lawyer Bill Shea, first sought out Branch Rickey to guide the new organization. It was an astute choice. Rickey, popularly known as "the Mahatma," had created the farm system with the St. Louis Cardinals in the 1920s and brought Jackie Robinson to the Brooklyn Dodgers in 1947. But when Payson balked at his terms (complete control over the organization), the 79-year-old Mahatma declined the offer. And so Grant

3

placed the call to Greenwich. Would Weiss, he asked, be willing to assume the presidency of the Metropolitan Baseball Club?

Flattered by the offer, Weiss agreed to meet with Grant that evening at the Savoy Hilton Hotel in Manhattan. The Savoy Hilton, located at Fifth Avenue and 58th Street, had been acquired five years earlier by the Conrad Hilton Empire and renovated to the tune of 1.8 million dollars. Weiss knew it all too well. Four months earlier, it had been the site of the infamous press conference in which the Yankee owners, Dan Topping and Del Webb, announced the firing of manager Casey Stengel. It was also where two weeks later, the Yankee owners announced the (forced) retirement of Weiss as general manager. Now, over dinner at the very place where his career and Casey's had come to an end, Weiss listened as Grant continued to press him to take charge of the new National League expansion team in New York.

George Martin Weiss was born in New Haven, Connecticut, on June 23, 1894. Following his father's death, he dropped out of Yale to operate the family grocery business, but soon became involved in minor league baseball. In the 1920s, Weiss ran the New Haven entry in the Eastern League and the Baltimore Orioles of the International League. In 1932, New York Yankees owner Colonel Jacob Ruppert hired him to develop a minor league farm system for his club. Weiss soon fashioned one of the best farm systems in baseball (the Newark Bears were legendary) and, in 1947, he replaced Larry MacPhail as the Yankees' general manager. Under Weiss' stewardship, the Yankees operation grew from three suites overlooking Bryant Park on 42nd Street (adjacent to the New York Public Library) to an entire floor of offices at 745 Fifth Avenue. In 13 years on the job, Weiss oversaw a club that won ten pennants and eight world championships. This amazing run came to an end when he and Casey Stengel were dismissed following the 1960 World Series loss to the Pittsburgh Pirates.

But would he take the job? Living comfortably at his 100-year-old Colonial–style home with his wife Hazel, surrounded by the memorabilia of 40 years in baseball, the 66-year-old Weiss— known as "Lonesome George"— didn't need the money. The Yankees had provided him with a generous profit-sharing retirement plan, and he stood to make $35,000 a year as a consultant to the ballclub through 1965. Still, there was no question that Weiss was intrigued by Grant's offer. His consultant's job was mere window dressing; he no longer had any say in the Yankees' operation. Here was a golden opportunity to get back into the game in the very city where he had made his reputation. Soon after the meeting at the Savoy Hilton, Weiss packed his bags and headed for Florida to escape the icy grip of the northeastern winter. In fact, he would do more than just bask in the sun. While in Florida, he began to systematically scout the National League teams— the future opponents of the Metropolitan Baseball Club.

On March 1, 1961, the weather was in the 70s and clear, as Roger Maris, the American League's Most Valuable Player in 1960, and his fellow Yankees ran onto Miller Huggins Field in St. Petersburg, Florida. It was the first time in thirteen years that the Bombers had taken the field without Casey Stengel. Ralph Houk, who replaced Stengel as the team manager the previous October, divided his charges into two squads. In one were veteran stars like Maris, Mickey Mantle, and Whitey Ford. The other consisted of rookie hopefuls, such as shortstop Tom Tresh, outfielder Joe Pepitone, and pitchers Roland Sheldon and Jim Bouton. Also on hand was the team's reigning literary figure, Lawrence Peter Berra. The 35-year-old catcher-outfielder had just published his autobiography. Titled *Yogi*, the book was fairly bland stuff compared to NBC broadcaster Joe Garagiola's witty *Baseball Is a Funny Game*, and *The Long Season*, a thoughtful, often biting diary written by Cincinnati Reds pitcher Jim Brosnan. Both had been published the previous year. Yogi, however, did offer some simple rules on negotiating baseball salaries, based on his 15-year relationship with the notoriously stingy George Weiss. One, when you make up your mind "on a rock bottom-figure," stick to it. Two, "never accept their first offer."[1] While Yogi and his teammates were limbering up on the West Coast of Florida, Weiss was some 200 miles to the southeast and about to negotiate a contract of his own with the owners of the Metropolitan Baseball Club.

In the early 1950s, Florida's Gold Coast underwent an unprecedented building expansion. Developers invested hundreds of millions of dollars in real estate along the 62 miles from Palm Beach Island to the lower reaches of Collins Avenue in Miami Beach. Each winter, caravans of cars with out-of-state plates crawled down Route A1A. Wide-eyed tourists gawked at the sights along the way — taking in everything from small seaside communities dotted with tiny motels, to the spectacular $13 million Fontainebleau Hotel at Miami Beach. Away from the fray, at the northern end of the Gold Coast, was the exclusive beach community of Hobe Sound. Located about 25 miles above Palm Beach, it was a longtime hideaway for millionaires, yachtsmen, debutantes, and statesmen. Hobe Sound was also the winter home of M. Donald Grant. One of his neighbors was the Metropolitan Baseball Club's principal owner, Joan Whitney Payson.

Joan Payson was the sister of John Hay Whitney, the owner of the *New York Herald Tribune*, and granddaughter of John Hay, a former secretary of state. An avid sports enthusiast, in the 1950s Joan Payson had been on the board of directors of the New York Giants. She and Donald Grant were the lone dissenters when Giants owner Horace Stoneham decided to join Walter O'Malley's Brooklyn Dodgers on the West Coast, starting in 1958. When the National League expanded to ten teams for the 1962 season, Grant and Joan

Payson joined forces to acquire the new club. The two were old friends. She called him "Donnie," and delighted in his rendition of old songs like *Jimmy Cracked Corn*, which he sang with endless verses. But on March 1, 1961, Payson and Grant had more serious matters in mind. They met George Weiss at the Payson estate and convinced him to take the reins of the new National League entry. The terms of a deal were ironed out. Weiss agreed to assume the position of president with a five-year contract paying $100,000 per annum. Grant would move upstairs as chairman of the board. The official announcement was made at a press conference at Miami Beach on March 14. Weiss, a notoriously shy man, stood uncomfortably with Grant and National League president Warren Giles, as the press peppered them with questions. Who, he was asked, would be the field manager of the Metropolitan Baseball Club? Wearing a pained expression on his face, Weiss dismissed the question, saying it was "no time to talk about it."[2]

The year 1961 was a turning point in the history of race relations in Major League Baseball. For the first time, every major league club would have at least one black player on its opening day squad. The first generation of black players like Jackie Robinson, Larry Doby, Luke Easter, and Don Newcombe was retired, and a new crop of youngsters was emerging from the minors to take its place. At two extremes were first baseman Donn Clendenon, signed out of Morehouse State for a mere $500, and outfielder Tommie Agee of Grambling College, acquired by the Cleveland Indians for a reported $60,000 bonus. As the general manager of the New York Yankees, George Weiss had not been very aggressive in pursuing black talent. The first black to wear Yankee pinstripes was catcher Elston Howard, who made his debut in 1955 — eight years after the breaking of the color line. Thus, while the return of George Weiss was hailed in the mainstream press as a major step forward in the fortunes of the Metropolitan Baseball Club, the black press saw his hiring as a possible step backward.

During Weiss' yearlong absence from baseball, the battle for racial equality in the National Pastime had moved on to another front. During the winter of 1961, columnist Wendell Smith had written a series of articles in the *Pittsburgh Courier* chronicling the growing discontent among black players regarding their second-class status in Florida training camps. Black stars like Hank Aaron were "tired of being a first class citizen during the season and a second class citizen during the spring." A white rookie was welcome to stay at the Serano Hotel, the Yankees' longtime spring training residence in St. Petersburg, but black veterans like Elston Howard and Héctor López were forced to find lodgings elsewhere. Returning from road trips, the team bus would drop off the black players in the "colored" section of town, before proceeding to the hotel. But change was in the air. The Reverend Ralph Wimbish, the head of the St. Petersburg NAACP, and Howard's landlord during spring training, announced that he would no longer "aid the cause of Jim Crow" by providing living quarters for Howard and his family. It was "not logical," said Wimbish, "to battle for integration of lunch counters with one hand and to further the cause of segregation by arranging separate housing with the other."[3]

The problem dropped into the lap of the Yankees' managing partner, Dan Topping. Born in Greenwich, Connecticut, on June 11, 1912, Daniel Reid Topping was the scion of a tin plate fortune, amateur golf champion, and man about town. Tall and handsome, with a perpetual tan, he was married to six different women, including Olympic skating champion Sonia Henie. Topping's first foray into sports ownership was not in baseball. In the 1930s, he bought the Brooklyn Dodgers football team, but left it to fight with the Marines in the Pacific during World War II. Following the war, Topping purchased the New York Yankees for $2.8 million in partnership with Larry MacPhail and Del Webb. Two years later, he and Webb bought out MacPhail's interest in the club, and hired George Weiss as the team's general manager. As Yankee general manager, Weiss had shown no inclination to challenge Southern mores. In February 1961 Topping, feeling the pressure from below, took on the Jim Crow South. He announced his desire to have all Yankees players living and eating "under one roof." However, when Topping asked the Soreno Hotel to accommodate Howard, López, and rookie Jesse Gonder, owner C.H. Alberding "politely" refused. The Yankees were "welcome guests on a status quo basis." Otherwise they "should look for other hotels."[4] On March 21, Topping announced that the Yankees would be moving their spring training base to Ft. Lauderdale, beginning in 1962. The black press showered Topping with praise for his "one roof" policy. The Yankees weren't the first team to create integrated facilities. The Branch Rickey Dodgers had created an integrated facility in a converted U.S. naval base at Vero Beach in 1948, called "Dodgertown." But no one else followed their lead. With the Yankees' announcement, a new era in race relations in Major League Baseball had begun. Several club owners, such as Bill Veeck of the Chicago White Sox, began making new living arrangements for their players.

Having lost the Yankees to Ft. Lauderdale, the St. Petersburg city fathers cast about for a suitable replacement. Shortly after Topping's announcement, they concluded a five-year agreement with the Metropolitan Baseball Club. The new club would train at the Bombers' old home, Miller Huggins Field, beginning in 1962. This new development was a cause for worry in the black press. The *Pittsburgh Courier* ran an article by Wendell Smith titled, "Newest New York Club to Carry Bias to Florida." Smith, who believed Weiss' hiring to be "regrettable," feared the renewal of a "segregation pact" between the new National League club and the city of St. Petersburg. New Yorkers should be forewarned, said Smith: their taxes, used to fund the new Flushing Meadows Stadium, would now also subsidize racial discrimination in spring training.[5] Would Weiss resist integration? Only time would tell.

Ironically, George Weiss, so distrusted by blacks, inherited a front office staff created by Branch Rickey during the latter's short-lived stint as head of the Continental League. The staff included Charles Hurth, Rickey's son-in-law, as general manager; Matt Burns, cost and scheduling officer; Lou Niss, director of promotion and public relations; Margaret Regetz, private secretary; and Judy Wilpond, receptionist. They would be housed at the Canada House, a 27-story limestone-sided structure located at 680 Fifth Avenue, next to St. Thomas Church. Weiss moved into the corner office formerly occupied by the Mahatma. The man who had built the famous Yankee machine regarded the scouting system as the backbone of any baseball operation. He hired Rogers Hornsby, the Hall of Fame second baseman, to scout new talent in the Midwest. At this point, however, the question of pursuing talent — of any color — was superceded by a more important one: who would Weiss hire as field manager of the Metropolitan Baseball Club?

On May 8, 1961, the Kennedy administration was still enduring the fallout from the Bay of Pigs invasion, the CIA–planned operation that three weeks earlier had failed to topple Fidel Castro's communist regime in Cuba. The New York Yankees were in second place in the American League pennant race, two and a half games behind the Detroit Tigers. Mickey Mantle was leading the league in home runs and RBIs, but Roger Maris had yet to crack the top five in either category. That same day, the Metropolitan Baseball Club held a press conference at the Savoy Hilton Hotel to announce the new club's official nickname.

The club had submitted a list of ten names to the public: the Continentals, the Burros, the Mets, the Skyliners, the Skyscrapers, the Bees, the Rebels, the NYBS, the Avengers, and the Jets. Joan Payson had been said to favor the Meadowlarks (the team would be playing in the yet to be built Flushing Meadows Stadium). A majority of the 9,613 respondents picked the Mets, and then went outside the list for their second and third choices: the Islanders and the Empires. The final choice was Payson's. Donald Grant thought the new nickname, Mets, was quite appropriate, since a team called the Metropolitans had played in New York from 1883 to 1888. An Associated Press photo, taken at the time, shows Joan Payson wielding a Stan Musial model bat and "christening" the new team by gently whacking a wine bottle nestled in Grant's gloved hand. Witnessing the "birth" of the Mets were Major League Baseball Commissioner Ford Frick, National League president Warren Giles, and George Weiss.

At the All-Star Game break, the Yankees were still in second place, a half game behind the Tigers. Roger Maris had emerged from his early season slump and had 33 round trippers, putting him 13 games ahead of Babe Ruth's 1927 pace, when the Bambino set the fabled record of 60 home runs. Mickey Mantle had 29. The first All-Star Game of the season (two games were played each year from 1959 to 1962), took place at San Francisco's Candlestick Park on July 11, 1961. The National League won, 5–4, with Roberto Clemente of the Pittsburgh Pirates driving in the Giants' Willie Mays with the winning run in the 11th inning. Neither Maris nor Mantle homered for the Americans. The game was marred by seven errors as the swirling bay winds played havoc with players and fans alike.

Two spectators at the game had something more important in mind than the swirling winds. Casey Stengel was at Candlestick Park to throw out the ceremonial first pitch. Earlier, George Weiss, who was also present at the All-Star Game, had collared Casey and sounded him out on the idea of managing the New York Mets. Before falling victim to the Yankees' "youth program" on October 18, 1961, the 70-year-old Charles Dillon Stengel had earned a reputation of being something of a "baseball genius." His Yankee teams had won ten pennants and seven world championships in 12 years. If not universally beloved by his players, the Old Perfessor was the darling of New York sportswriters as well as countless fans who reveled in his mangled English and colorful personality. On a team that would be stocked with aging stars, journeymen, and untried rookies, Stengel's box office appeal was undeniable, and, in fact, urgently needed if the new club was to compete for the entertainment dollar with the mighty Yankees. But like Weiss, Stengel did not need the job. After his sacking, he had gone back to his home in Glendale, California, at the eastern end of the San Fernando Valley, where he had lived with his wife Edna since 1924, and taken the job of vice-president and director of the Valley National Bank. (His job, he quipped, was to guard the vault). It would take some more convincing to bring him back.

On September 29, 1961, at Yankee Stadium, Roger Maris, playing center field in place of the injured Mickey Mantle, and struggling with the unrelenting media pressure, went hitless against the Boston Red Sox. He would have just two more chances to break Babe Ruth's record of 60 home runs. A Sacramento man had offered $5,000 to the fan who caught the 61st homer. The same day, George Weiss called a press conference at the Mets' Fifth Avenue offices to announce what many writers already suspected: Casey Stengel had agreed to manage the team in its inaugural season in 1962. It had not been an easy decision for Stengel. He had been up all night, leaning one way and then the other before finally making up his mind at six A.M., Pacific Coast time. In the end, Stengel was persuaded to return for three reasons. One was loyalty to Weiss. Lonesome George had been calling every day since September

20, telling Casey that he needed a manager in place before the start of the
expansion players' draft on October 10. Second was the "good will" of Joan

Payson and Donald
Grant, who also placed
calls to California ask-
ing him to return. And
third, he had some-
thing to prove after
the way he had been
cashiered by Dan Top-
ping and Del Webb.
He'd show them who
really "knew the busi-
ness."[6]

Casey Stengel was
at the Los Angeles Air-
port with Edna on
Sunday   afternoon,
October 1, getting ready
to board a plane for
New York, when he
learned that Roger
Maris had hit his 61st
home   run   against
Boston Red Sox right-
hander Tracy Stallard,
breaking Babe Ruth's
hallowed record. For
the Yankees it was just
another day at the
office; they won the
game, 1–0, in a swift
1:57. Maris reluctantly

Casey Stengel at his farewell dinner, held at the Waldorf
Astoria Hotel, New York City, October 19, 1960. On October 3, 1961, at the Savoy Hilton Hotel in New York, former
Yankee general manager George Weiss, now the Mets
president, introduced Casey as the manager of the new
National League expansion club. "I want to help baseball," said Casey. For countless fans and media observers,
the Old Perfessor represented everything that was good
about the game.

took a bow (it was the first time in his career he'd won a 1–0 game with a home
run). The business-like Bombers may not have had much flair for promotion
in these pre–YES Network days. But the Mets did. In fact, while the baseball
world was settling into the offseason "Hot Stove League," the Mets, led by Casey
Stengel, were making their first pitch for the hearts, minds, and pocketbooks
of New York area fans.

Part I: Inventing Tradition

1

"I Want to Help Baseball"

While the New York Yankees were in the Bronx, tuning up for the next day's opening World Series game against the Cincinnati Reds on October 3, Casey Stengel was being officially introduced as the manager of the New York Mets. Flanking him at the press conference in the Crystal Room of the Savoy Hilton Hotel were his two new coaches, Solly Hemus and Cookie Lavagetto, both former major league managers. Utilizing his convoluted English to the fullest, the Old Perfessor held court before the bedazzled reporters. He revealed that he had turned down five or six managerial jobs before accepting the Mets' offer. "Mr. Weiss influenced me," he said, "by getting on the phone too often." Asked if he was too old for the baseball diamond, Stengel responded, "I'm still healthy above the shoulders.... If I can't help, I'll walk out and no one will have to tell me." Why, Casey was asked, would he want to jeopardize his reputation as a managerial "genius" by agreeing to take over what was destined to be a second-division club? His answer: "I want to help baseball."[1]

Stengel's response could be taken as mere egotism, but the truth was that baseball sorely needed his salesmanship. Despite the addition of two new teams in the American League and the excitement generated by the "M&M Boys'" home run chase, the major leagues had suffered a 5 percent decline in total attendance in 1961. Only the Yankees, Reds, Detroit Tigers, and Minnesota Twins (the former Washington Senators) had seen an increase at the gate. The previous February, the Baseball Hall of Fame had opened its doors to its first black member, Jackie Robinson, and the game boasted the most diverse group of athletes in American team sports. But moral decency did not necessarily count at the turnstile. As Casey was flying across the country on October 1, the New York Giants were helping the Washington Redskins inaugurate their new District of Columbia Stadium before a crowd of 36,767, the largest ever to attend a sporting event in the nation's capital. The Redskins, under the ownership of the old patriarch George Preston Marshall, had never had a black player. This deplorable fact did not detract from professional football's emergence as the true National Pastime — or from Marshall bragging about it. Later that fall he published an article in the *Saturday Evening Post* that was titled, "Baseball Isn't Our National Sport." A sport that needs an automobile to bring relief pitchers into the game, Marshall taunted, presented no challenge to the NFL. What's more, as Robert Daley pointed out in an article in *Esquire*, "people *talked* about [baseball]" in the good old days; now the subject around the water cooler was football.[2]

No one was more troubled by the "constantly growing interest in football" than the publisher of *The Sporting News*, J.G. Taylor Spink. It was, he lamented, "a blow to the pride of baseball." Spink was especially alarmed at the continuing decline in major league attendance, particularly in September when most teams had been eliminated. Indeed, if not for Mantle and Maris, the 1961 season would have been a "financial disaster." To arrest the decline, Spink proposed "radical changes" in the major league schedule.

1. Reduce the schedule to 154 games. Each team would play each other 17 times, with one extra game against a "natural rival."
2. End the season by Labor Day, trimming playing dates by increasing the number of doubleheaders.
3. Eliminate the second All-Star Game and replace it with a post-season All-Star Tour, including players from all teams, except those playing in the World Series.
4. Schedule All-Star Tour games in all major league cities, except those involved in the World Series, with two games in each city.
5. Guarantee a certain amount of money to the players ($1,500–$2,500), with any extra monies going to the players' pension fund.[3]

Letters to *The Sporting News*, or at least the ones it printed, agreed with Spink. Changes were needed. Correspondents pointed out other problems with baseball: longer games, higher ticket prices, and more entertainment and leisure choices. Yet, at the same time, there was also a sense that the game was changing too much and too fast. C. Hal James of Dallas, Texas, noted that while baseball was not a contact sport like football, "fans came out to see Ty Cobb, John McGraw, Frank Frisch, and others of that type get in the umpire's hair. Now the player can't even toss his hat in the air." This unhappiness with the modern player informed much of the criticism of Roger Maris during his drive to break Babe Ruth's fabled home run record. Oliver Kuechle complained in the *Milwaukee Journal* that Maris was too ordinary looking physically to be a record-breaker. And he was "colorless" and "surly." Added Kuechle, "There just isn't anything deeply heroic about the man and the

American public loves its heroes, particularly a record breaker of something as old as the Babe's mark, to be of heroic mold."[4]

Predictably, Spink's proposal didn't get very far with the conservative-minded people in charge of the game. A year earlier league presidents Warren Giles and Joe Cronin had been brought kicking and screaming to accept expansion. Only the challenge of Branch Rickey and Bill Shea's Continental League, coupled with the threat of anti-trust legislation by Congress, had spurred them to action. Spink's proposal was simply too drastic a departure from tradition. Instead of exploiting Roger Maris' breaking of Ruth's record for publicity purposes, baseball Commissioner Ford Frick was downplaying the feat; he decreed that an asterisk should be attached to the number 61, because Maris had failed to break the record within the 154–game schedule.

By contrast, professional football, under the energetic and innovative leadership of NFL Commissioner Pete Rozelle and AFL boss Joe Foss, had little regard for its leather-helmeted days. The year before, CBS had broadcast a documentary, *The Violent World of Sam Huff*. Narrated by Walter Cronkite, it featured Huff, the New York football Giants' ferocious middle linebacker. The program combined the gridiron's orchestrated brutality with television's technical innovation in a way that riveted millions of viewers around the United States. On another front, the NFL was also about to end its segregationist practices; George Preston Marshall was put on notice by Congress to hire black players for his new federally-funded stadium. In short, while football committed itself wholly to the future, the National Pastime wavered, looking both forward and backward. Casey Stengel and Roger Maris, each in his own way, symbolized the Janus-faced nature of major league baseball.

Coming on the heels of one of the most exciting October Classics in baseball history, the 1961 World Series was a rather lackluster affair. The New York Yankees defeated Fred Hutchinson's Cincinnati Reds in five games—only two of which were played at Yankee Stadium. Roger Maris's ninth inning homer in game three proved to be the turning point. It was Maris' 62nd round tripper, tying Babe Ruth's 1927 combined regular season/World Series total. Whitey Ford broke Babe Ruth's Series record for consecutive scoreless innings, but otherwise there was little drama. Down three games to one, on October 9 the Cincinnati players made a pragmatic decision. They packed a bag for game six in New York while, at the same time, making travel arrangements to their off season homes. Some players already knew that—win or lose—their days in Cincinnati were over. One of these was veteran outfielder Gus Bell.

David Russell Bell, Jr. was born on November 15, 1928, in Louisville, Kentucky. One of his neighbors growing up in Louisville was Dodger great Pee Wee Reese. Bell was signed by the Pirates' organization in 1947, but, in one of the worst trades ever made by Branch Rickey, was dealt to the Cincinnati Redlegs (as they were known in the McCarthy Era) for three nonentities in 1952. Gus, who could run, field, and hit with power, blossomed in Cincinnati and so did his family — he was the father of eight children. The biggest controversy Bell ever became involved in as a ballplayer was none of his doing. In 1957, last minute ballot-stuffing by the Cincinnati fans resulted in eight Reds being voted onto the starting National League All-Star squad. An incensed Ford Frick removed three of the Reds' players, substituting the New York Giants' Willie Mays for Bell. The next year the voting was taken away from the fans. By 1961 Bell was no longer All-Star material; the Reds, it was rumored, had placed him on the list of 136 players left unprotected, and thus eligible for the expansion draft.

The Yankees, world champions once again, arrived from Cincinnati by train at Pennsylvania Station on 34th Street and were greeted by a small cluster of fans; New Yorkers were used to the Bombers winning pennants by now. Dan Topping held a victory party for the team at the Savoy Hilton Hotel on October 10. Yogi's wife Carmen, dressed in a shimmering white silk gown with a fringed top and bottom a la the Roaring Twenties, was the "stylish stick out of the party."[5] By the time that the Yankees and their wives gathered at the Savoy, Gus Bell and hundreds of other players had learned their fate. Earlier that day, on the third floor conference room of Cincinnati's Netherland Hilton Hotel, National League president Warren Giles conducted the allocation of players to the new National League expansion teams. Houston general manager Paul Richards won the coin toss and chose the first player: Eddie Bressoud, a shortstop late of the San Francisco Giants. George Weiss followed by tapping another former Frisco player, catcher Hobie Landrith. Before taking on the job of Mets president, Weiss had been skeptical of expansion. He believed that the American League had moved too hastily in 1961, without proper preparation. "You can't build a team out of rejects," he said at the time.[6] At the Netherland, on October 10, Weiss spent $1,800,000 of Joan Payson's money on 22 players (Houston chose 23). Casey Stengel did not attend the draft conference, but he remained in constant communication with Weiss via telephone from New York.

The American League expansion draft the year before hadn't provided much in terms of quality to the new Washington and Los Angeles franchises. Warren Giles had vowed to do better, but it proved to be an empty boast. The eight National League clubs had made sure that all the players they wanted to keep were protected from the draft by August 30. Consequently, the National League was, in the end, no more generous than the American League had been. The biggest names in the pool for the Mets were the aforementioned Gus Bell and veteran Los Angeles Dodgers first baseman Gil Hodges, both clearly past their prime. Ex-Dodger infielder Don Zimmer was taken from the Chicago Cubs. Most of the players came with a $75,000 price tag. There were also four so-called "premium selections," which cost the Mets $125,000 each — Zimmer, outfielder Lee Walls (Los Angeles Dodgers), and pitchers Jay Hook (Cincinnati Reds) and Bob Miller (St. Louis Cardinals). Writing the next day in the *New York Journal American*, sports columnist Jimmy Cannon called them, quite appropriately, "familiar strangers."[7]

George Weiss had drafted some potentially good young players in outfielders Jim Hickman (St. Louis Cardinals) and Joe Christopher (Pittsburgh Pirates), but had failed to land a quality shortstop or a catcher with any hitting punch. New York did have an overall edge in power over the new Houston club. The players chosen by the Mets hit a combined 53 home runs in 1961 compared to the Colts' 22. However, Weiss didn't find much in terms of experienced pitching. The pitchers drafted by the Mets combined for a 13–16 record in 1961 (the Colts' pitchers 30–29). Right-hander Roger Craig, the biggest winner, was only 5–6 with the Dodgers the previous year. Not chosen by either expansion team was the most famous hurler on the list, Robin Roberts. The onetime ace was left unprotected by the Philadelphia Phillies after posting a 1–10 record in 1961. The Mets' scouts advised Weiss not to draft him. He was finished, they said. The Yankees decided to take a chance on Roberts and bought him from the Phillies on October 16 for $25,000 — far less than what the Mets would have paid had they chosen him in the expansion draft.

George Weiss, as mentioned earlier, didn't have much of a record in signing black talent. Of the 22 ballplayers he selected in the expansion draft, four were African Americans: pitchers Al Jackson and Sherman (Roadblock) Jones, infielder Sammy Drake, and catcher Clarence (Choo Choo) Coleman. Four were international players; that is, men born in a country other than the United States: Elio Chacón (Venezuela), Félix Mantilla (Puerto Rico), Joe Christopher (Virgin Islands), and Ray Daviault (Quebec, Canada). (The Mets would add another international player, Canadian–born pitcher Ken MacKenzie, the day after the draft.) Weiss greatly resented the accusation of prejudice for the deliberate fashion the Yankees went about integrating their team in the 1950s. The articles by Wendell Smith and others in the black press regarding Weiss' history at St. Petersburg, no doubt, did nothing for his disposition. But it must be said that in stocking the Mets' franchise, Weiss exhibited the same tendency as existed in the major leagues in the late 1950s and early 1960s: a preference for foreign born players over American blacks. To be sure, not many at the time would've made this distinction. In this era before affirmative action categories, Chacón, Mantilla, and Christopher were all classified as "Negroes" by *both* the mainstream media *and* the black press.

The new team's future home was expected to be the $19 million Flushing Meadows Stadium, originally intended for the New York entry in the now defunct Continental League. But in October 1961, Queens was a secondary consideration. What the Mets wanted more than anything else was to establish a connection between the new team and its potential fan base in Brooklyn and on Long Island. So, for both sentimental reasons and promotional potential, the most important player taken in the draft was Gil Hodges.

Gilbert Ray Hodges was born on April 4, 1924, in Princeton, Indiana, at the extreme southwestern tip of the state, bordering on the Ohio River. Hodges attended St. Joseph's College in Rensselaer, Indiana, where he played shortstop. When World War II broke out, he enlisted in the U.S. Army. Returning to the Dodgers after the war, Hodges was tried at third base and then catcher, where his path was blocked by Roy Campanella. Finding a home at last at first base, he became the finest fielder at that position in the National League. Hodges was nimble around the bag, but what most impressed observers was the size of his hands. Teammate Pee Wee Reese quipped that Gil's hands were so big he didn't need a baseball mitt. "He only wore one because it was fashionable."[8] As a hitter, Hodges was a perennial home run threat. On August 31, 1950, he hit four homers in one game, the first major leaguer to do so since Lou Gehrig. He was second to Gehrig all-time in grand slams, with 14. He currently had 361 lifetime round trippers, the same as Joe DiMaggio. Although Hodges had seen only limited duty with the Dodgers in Los Angeles the previous two years, Weiss and Stengel believed that his power would make him a good fit in the Mets' home field, the Polo Grounds.

Gil married a Brooklyn girl, Joan Lombardi, and raised a family in the borough. Living alone in a hotel in sprawling Los Angeles for the past four years, and playing in the cavernous LA Coliseum, he yearned for the intimacy of the Ebbets Field days—the balloon man, Hilda Chester picketing the hated Giants, and the "Symphony" tooting the "Bums" back to the bench. It was a family romance in so many ways: Jackie Robinson's high pitched squeal and Pee Wee Reese's Kentucky drawl as the team dressed in the tiny clubhouse, and the fans gathering around Joan at her box seat inquiring about Gil and the kids. Now, after four years in purgatory, he had returned. In the selling of the Mets' brand to the New York public, Gil Hodges was the *yin* to Casey Stengel's *yang*. Both were darlings of the New York press and much beloved by the public, but in radically different ways. Stengel was part managerial "genius" and part baseball clown, a master at self-promotion from the "dead ball era." Hodges, by contrast, was a Paul Bunyanesque character, a gentle man of super-human strength, touching modesty, and hard-rock integrity. Had *he* broken Ruth's home run record, the press would have been much kinder to him than they were to Maris. Roger was never comfortable with the public's hunger for heroes—and often reacted in ways that turned off both newspaper writers and fans. He exhibited neither the class of Gil Hodges nor the color of Casey Stengel—and paid the price for it.

The Mets couldn't be expected to perform on the level of the New York Yankees, but they could outdo them in public relations. Ralph Houk (nicknamed "the Major") was, in his own way, a shrewd self-promoter. But Houk, despite his sterling World War II record, had no real baseball pedigree; he wasn't a larger than life figure like Casey, a former Giants and Dodger player. Moreover, the Yankees' managing partner, Dan Topping, both jaded by his many championships and socially secure, saw little need for spectacle—the YES Network would eventually be the creation of a ring-hungry, provincial named George Steinbrenner. In the fall of 1961, the Mets, the new kids on the block, needed to attract the imagination of a skeptical public. So they consciously promoted a sense of nostalgia—even as they looked forward to future respectability on the field. For many New Yorkers, uprooted from their urban origins in Brooklyn and Manhattan, and having put down stakes in the new suburban communities of Nassau County on Long Island, Stengel and Hodges were reassuring figures. They and their kids may have *left* the old neighborhood, but Gil and Casey were coming *back!*

Not everyone wanted to leave the old neighborhood behind. In the fall of 1961, the residents of the West Village declared war on City Hall. At issue was the city planning commission's scheme to demolish a 14–block area encompassing 24 acres, bounded by West 11th, Hudson, Christopher, Washington, Morton, and West Streets. The neighborhood's demolition would clear the way for the proposed Lower Manhattan Expressway, the dream of the city's legendary master builder, Robert Moses. The Committee to Save the West Village, chaired by the architectural critic and author Jane Jacobs, led the effort to stop the scheme. On October 18, committee members leapt from their seats and shouted in protest when chairman James Felt (he of the Felt Forum) declared their neighborhood a "blighted area," suitable for urban renewal. Pandemonium ensued. Unable to restore order, Felt called in the police, who ended up dragging one man out by his feet.

Jane Jacobs and the West Villagers won the fight to preserve their neighborhood. For Gil Hodges, however, there would be no returning to his old playing grounds. On the last day of 1959, two men from opposite ends of Yonkers, New York, traveled separately to Flatbush to conduct a curious ceremony. Standing before the Ebbets Field entrance, Matt Burns, the resident representative of the Dodgers, handed over the keys of the ballpark to Seymour Goldsmith, vice president of the Kratter Corporation construction firm. Ebbets Field was razed on February 23, 1960, to make room for what was billed at the time as the largest apartment complex in New York City. With the Flushing Meadows Stadium still in the planning stages, this left two possible places for the Mets to play: Yankee Stadium or the Polo Grounds. The Mets, eager to establish a separate identity from the Yankees, didn't much care to play in the Bronx. That left the Polo Grounds, the abandoned home of the New York (now San Francisco) Giants. So, for one season at least, the Yankees and Mets would be playing on opposite sides of the Macombs Dam Bridge spanning the Harlem River.

Meanwhile, plans were going forward for what eventually would become the Mets' permanent home in the borough of Queens. The ground-breaking ceremony for the Flushing Meadows Stadium took place on October 26. Dignitaries present for the occasion included Ford Frick, Warren Giles, Branch Rickey, Bill Shea, and New York parks commissioner Robert Moses. Representing the Mets were Donald Grant, George Weiss, and Gil Hodges. Weiss posed for a photograph wielding a silver spade, flanked by Frick and Giles holding baseball bats. Hodges, meanwhile, signed autographs and greeted the curious fans. The stadium, which covered ten and a half acres just north of the World's Fair parade grounds, would seat 55,000. Another thirty-five acres would provide parking space for as many as 10,000 cars. The Mets had signed a 30-year lease with an option for ten additional years at $450,000 per annum. The Flushing Meadows Stadium was expected to be completed in time for the start of the 1963 baseball season.

Two years earlier, while still general manager of the Yankees, Weiss had bitterly opposed the construction of a new ball field in Queens. The Yankees, he liked to point out, paid $200,000 each year to the City of New York, and had received little help from either Moses or Mayor Wagner regarding their increasingly difficult parking problem. Meanwhile, Rickey and Shea's Continental League were to receive a spanking new stadium with plenty of space for cars. Since assuming the reins of the Mets, however, Weiss had undergone a change of heart. A state of the arts stadium would attract attention and perhaps distract potential fans from focusing too much on the foibles of what was expected to be a second-division team. But the stadium was in the future. Meanwhile, the Mets continued with their efforts to invent a sense of tradition for the brand new club. It was no coincidence that Gil Hodges, a visual link between the Brooklyn past and the Mets' future, was among those attending the ground-breaking ceremony.

The day's ground-breaking festivities continued with a luncheon that afternoon hosted by Mayor Wagner at the Commodore Hotel. Located at 111 East 42nd Street, the Commodore (named after the railroad magnate, Commodore Cornelius Vanderbilt) was part of a complex of hostelries and offices surrounding Grand Central Station. (We know it today as the Grand Hyatt Hotel.) Wagner used the occasion to honor the Mayor's Committee on Baseball, citing its "outstanding accomplishments in preserving New York as the sports capital of the world."[9] Feted by the Mayor was the committee's chairman, Bill Shea. Born in New York on June 21, 1907, William Alfred Shea was by profession a corporate lawyer, by reputation a power broker, and by universal acclaim the savior of National League baseball in the Big Apple. Shortly after the Dodgers and Giants departed for the West Coast, Wagner appointed Shea to investigate the possibility of bringing a major league franchise to the city. Rebuffed by the "Lords of Baseball," Shea, together with Branch Rickey, promulgated the idea of a third major league. The Continental League had a short shelf life, but the New York Metropolitan Baseball Club was eventually one of the two teams admitted into the National League in August of 1961.

Dan Topping, who had fought bitterly for years with Robert Moses for additional parking space at Yankee Stadium, wasn't at all pleased at the largess lavished on the Mets. But Topping could take some consolation from the post-season awards garnered by his world champion Yankees. The accolades came one after another in the first half of November. Whitey Ford won the Cy Young Award for 1961 (only one prize was awarded for both leagues at the time). Whitey had a record of 25–4 and a 3.21 ERA. He pitched 283 innings, notching 11 complete games and three shutouts. Asked to explain his success, the Yankee lefthander listed four reasons: "righteous living" (ha ha); an improved slider; the chance to pitch every fourth day; and the relief pitching of Luis Arroyo.[10] Arroyo was 15–5 with 29 saves on the year. He had 13 saves and five victories in games started by Ford, and copped the Fireman of the Year Award. Meanwhile, Roger Maris and Mickey Mantle finished neck and neck in the American League Most Valuable Player balloting. Maris won the MVP with just four more votes than Mantle (202–198)—because of (or in spite of) having broken Babe Ruth's legendary home run record. This was the second consecutive close election between the M&M boys. The previous year, Maris had won the award by just three votes over Mantle (225–222). Of the top ten MVP candidates in 1961, five were Yankees: Maris (1st), Mantle (2nd), Whitey Ford (5th), Luis Arroyo (6th), and Elston Howard (tenth). Howard finished second in batting in the American League with a sparkling .348 average.

The Mantle-Maris and Ford-Arroyo duos in the MVP balloting were in a way symbolic of the changes that had taken place in major league baseball since 1950—changes that many observers found problematical. Ford, Arroyo, and the rest of the Yankee pitching staff benefited from an unprecedented display of power hitting. In 1961, the Bombers had set a new team record with 221 home runs. Maris hit 61 home runs, Mantle 54, and Bill Skowron 28. Incredibly, the team's three catchers had all hit over 20 homers: Yogi Berra (22), Elston Howard (21), and Johnny Blanchard (21). There were various reasons offered for what some regarded to be an alarming rise in offense. The ball was still made of yarn, rubber and cork, but the material and manufacturing were of better quality than in 1920. In addition, some said, higher and coarser seams on the ball reduced its aerodynamic drag. The livelier ball carried five to ten percent further than it did 25 years earlier. Tests, it was said, proved that a 350-foot out in 1937 was now a 385-foot home run. Other factors gave a decisive edge to the batter. Umpires threw out balls much more frequently than before, so hitters had a better surface for seeing the pitch. Then there was the bat. The average bat in 1961 was 30 to 32 ounces, or six to ten ounces lighter than a quarter of a century earlier. Even ordinary hitters were now more inclined to "swing from the heels."[11] Teams had also brought their fences in to increase the probability of the long ball. Finally, there was the question of the strike zone. In 1950, its dimensions were officially changed vertically from the armpits to the letters, benefiting the batter at the expense of the pitcher. As a consequence of these changes, "small ball" — the bunt, steal, and hit and run — were becoming a relic of the past. The home run ruled.

Faced with the greater offensive threat presented by Maris, Mantle and company, pitchers had to work harder and harder to fool the hitters. They could no longer just throw the ball up and let them hit it — everyone it seemed was trying for home runs. They could also no longer safely rely on the bread and butter pitches—fastball, curve, and changeup. It's telling that Whitey Ford credited the addition of a slider in explaining his success on the mound in 1961. The pitchers weren't the only ones fretting about the proliferation of home runs. In fact, they had a staunch ally in Ford Frick. In the fall of 1961 the commissioner publicly called for amending rule 8.02 (a), which would make the spitball a legal pitch for the first time since 1920. "I would like to see the pitchers get this additional weapon," Frick declared. *The Sporting News* enthusiastically backed the commissioner. The Lords of Baseball, however, were divided on the "Big Panacea." American League president Joe Cronin backed the commissioner, but National League chief Warren Giles was opposed. Giles feared that the reintroduction of the spitter would result in more beanings.[12]

The Whitey Ford-Luis Arroyo duo in the MVP balloting points up yet another aspect of the dominance of offense in the era of Maris and Mantle. Managers were using more and more relief pitchers. In fact, with Arroyo, Larry Sherry, Elroy Face, Lindy McDaniel and others, the relief specialist had become institutionalized in the sport. Whitey Ford endured a great deal of teasing that winter about his reliance on Arroyo. The implication was that Ford's record wasn't quite heroic enough, tainted by his dependency on the bullpen. But it was Roger Maris who bore the brunt of criticism directed toward the modern game and the modern player. Old timers and sportswriters scoffed at Maris' home run feat, judging it to be the product of structural changes in the game, not skill. As mentioned earlier, Frick announced that Maris' record would carry an asterisk in the record book because it was set in the new 162-game schedule. It was a fair point — Maris hit 59 homers in the first 154 games. But beneath the surface there was the implication that whether set in 154 games or not, Maris' achievement was less than legitimate. The new rules gave him an advantage unavailable to players of an earlier era. Like Whitey, he was deemed less than heroic. Ford let the criticism slide off his back, but the more sensitive Maris chafed at these insinuations, causing much controversy between himself and Frick, the press, and old timers such as Mets coach Rogers Hornsby.

Almost forgotten in all this fuss over offense was the fact that the Yankees were an excellent defensive team. Ralph Houk took pride in the fact that his players rarely beat themselves. In 1961 the Yankees' .9801 fielding percentage led the American League. They committed the fewest team errors and turned the most double plays. Bobby Richardson, the Gold Glove winner at second in 1961, was not flashy but was an expert tagger who was adept at the reverse double play, ranging toward first for the ball and then throwing to second for the initial out. Clete Boyer, spectacular in the 1961 World Series versus the Reds, had the misfortune of playing third base in the era of Brooks Robinson. Roger Maris had won a Gold Glove in right field in 1960. In November 1962, however, the Yankee defense was put into question when it was learned that shortstop Tony Kubek had been called up for military service and would miss at least part of the 1962 season.

Kubek, a Polish Catholic, hailed from Milwaukee, Wisconsin. Casey Stengel had known his father (also named Anthony) from their days in the American Association. Like his mentor, John J. McGraw, Stengel loved players who could master more than one position. One of the most versatile of Yankees, Tony had played both infield and outfield for Casey and was the American League Rookie of the Year in 1957. Kubek had previously served six months of military duty with his Wisconsin National Guard unit in 1958. But in the summer of 1961, relations between the United States and the Soviet Union reached a crisis over Berlin. President Kennedy responded to Premier Khrushchev's threats by activating the reserves. Tony, 25, had married Margaret Timmel of Watertown, Wisconsin, just two weeks prior to the President's announcement. The bride and groom were now headed for Ft. Lewis, Washington. The Yankees, meanwhile, were thrown into a quandary. Without Kubek, their middle infield defense could be severely weakened. There was talk of moving Boyer to shortstop unless two promising rookies, Tom Tresh or Phil Linz, managed to fill the void.

For all of the Yankees' problems at shortstop, the Mets were in an even worse situation. George Weiss had been unable to acquire a quality shortstop in the recent draft and there was still no farm system to speak of. The club had entered into an arrangement with Triple-A Syracuse of the International League, but there was little to choose from there. Nevertheless, despite this and other worries, the Mets were determined to compete with the "Bronx Bombers" for the New York entertainment dollar. In doing so, they would appropriate one of New York's favorite icons.

"Lüchow's" had been a New York institution since August Lüchow, a German immigrant, opened the restaurant at 110 East 14th Street in 1882. Located across from the old Tammany Hall, and a block away from the old Academy of Music, it had once been part of the "old uptown," attracting both politicians and artists like the great tenor, Enrico Caruso. Lüchow's was demolished in the 1980s to make room for the expansion of the New York University campus. In 1961, however, the eatery still retained much of its original décor with its dark paneled walls and black iron chandeliers. The menu carried traditional favorites: boiled beef with horseradish sauce, roast pork, and sauerbraten (a favorite of Diamond Jim Brady's). The *umlaut* in the restaurant's name was removed as a patriotic gesture during World War I. The new owners restored the *umlaut* in the early 1950s in order to discourage diners looking for *chop suey* and *chow mein*. Beer, of course, is what Germans were most noted for producing. On November 13, 1961, Liebmann Brewers of Brooklyn, makers of Rheingold Beer, threw a party at Lüchow's to celebrate their new deal to sponsor Mets television and radio broadcasts. Present were Donald Grant, George Weiss, and Liebmann's CEO M.R. Weiss (no relation to the Mets' president). Madison Avenue, reportedly, was abuzz with rumors that Liebmann's had paid $1.2 million for the television rights and had agreed to purchase 100,000 Mets tickets to boot.

In clinching the deal with Liebmann Breweries (former sponsors of the Brooklyn Dodgers), the Mets also laid claim to another longtime New York City tradition: Miss Rheingold. Each August since 1940, hundreds of young women were invited to a breakfast at the Waldorf-Astoria Hotel, where they gathered to compete for the title. By the end of the morning, the list would be reduced to six contestants. Dealers and distributors subsequently received complete kits, featuring posters of the lucky six, pads of ballots, and ballot boxes in the shape of Rheingold cartons. Billed as "America's second largest election" (after the U.S. presidency), it attracted the attention of the entire New York metropolitan area between August and October. In the style of Boss Tweed and Tammany Hall, "people could vote early and often" for their favorite.[13] Men gawked at the well-scrubbed, wholesome, outdoor type women as they sipped their beers in local taverns, and young girls eyed them curiously in supermarkets. A photograph taken at Lüchow's on November

13, 1961, showed Donald Grant with an arm draped over the newly-crowned beauty, Kathy Kersh, with George Weiss, Philip Liebman, and the ubiquitous Gil Hodges looking on. She had made Rheingold the best selling beer in New York. Could she do as much for the Mets?

The Mets had yet to play a meaningful game, but the selling of the Mets' brand was already well under way. On November 16, the club announced that it had already sold 1,000 box seats, equally divided between individuals and corporate sponsors. This exceeded the 912 sold in 1952, the season following Bobby Thomson's famous "shot heard 'round the world" playoff home run. Prices for Mets tickets were set as follows: box seats, $3.50; reserved seats, $2.50, and general admission, $1.30. Some of the money already earned went to Ray Gotto, a cartoonist and frequent contributor to *The Sporting News*. Gotto received a $1,000 prize for winning the Mets' logo contest. Gotto's design depicted a scene from the New York skyline enclosed in a baseball. The sights (all in Dodger blue) included a church, the Williamsburg Savings Bank, the Woolworth Tower, the Empire State Building, and the United Nations. Superimposed on the Manhattan skyline were the letters *NY* and the word *Mets* (both in Giants orange). Inspecting the logo, a reporter asked Donald Grant what represented Queens. It was a good question, seeing that the Mets' permanent home would be the Flushing Meadows Stadium.

At this time, however, the Mets' publicity machine was aimed as much at the past, as it was at the future. Take the hiring of Cookie Lavagetto as a Mets coach. Enrico Attilio Lavagetto was born on December 9, 1912, in Oakland, California. The first day of school, his teacher informed him that the name Enrico in English was either Henry or Harry, and asked him to pick one or the other. The lad went home and discussed the situation with his parents. He chose Harry. The swarthy, black-haired Lavagetto began his career with the Oakland Oaks of the Pacific Coast League, where he earned another nickname (he was tagged "Cookie's boy," after the team owner). Cookie was a serviceable third baseman with the Pittsburgh Pirates and Branch Rickey's Brooklyn Dodgers until his career was interrupted by World War II. In the 1947 World Series, Lavagetto, now well past his prime, achieved baseball immortality. In game four, the Yankees' Bill Bevens was one out from pitching the first Series no-hitter when Cookie doubled home two runs to win the game for the Bums. The Mets counted on a sense of nostalgia evoked by Gil Hodges and Cookie Lavagetto—more so than on-field excellence—in luring former Brooklyn Dodger fans to the Polo Grounds in 1962.

George Weiss had hired Cookie with the idea of making him the manager in the event that Casey Stengel decided to pass on the job. Casey, of course, had signed on and was now the center of the Mets' publicity campaign. On November 23, 1961, 500,000 plus spectators witnessed Macy's traditional

Thanksgiving Day Parade. Festivities began at 9:15 A.M. at 77th Street, Central Park West, proceeded south to Columbus Circle, and continued down Broadway to Herald Square. It was touted as the biggest extravaganza in the 34 years of the event, with five massive balloons, 24 floats, and 12 bands. The Radio City Music Hall Rockettes, as usual, performed their dancing routines. Matinee idol Troy Donahue was the parade's Prince Charming. Actor Robert Morse — whose Broadway musical *How to Succeed in Business Without Really Trying* had opened in October to critical and popular acclaim — rode on the spaceship float. But, as far as adult viewers were concerned, the biggest attraction was the 71-year-old Casey Stengel. He lounged in a special Mets float surrounded by Gil Hodges, Billy Loes and Monte Irvin, all symbols of a glorious New York baseball past. At their feet sat Gil's son and daughter, Irene Hodges and Gillie Hodges, along with Monte's daughter, Patti Irvin. Obviously, the Mets' best emblem was not a team logo or the spanking new stadium in Queens but rather the larger than life figure of the Old Perfesssor.

With the Thanksgiving holiday over and the coming of the Christmas season, the biggest trading market for players was about to begin. George Weiss, bolstered by Joan Payson's cash, began to look for talent. On November 28, Lonesome George conducted his first major transaction, acquiring outfielder Frank Thomas from the Milwaukee Braves for $125,000 and a player to be named later. The six foot, three-inch Thomas was a dead pull hitter who had hit 35 home runs with the Pittsburgh Pirates in 1958. He was expected to take advantage of the short foul lines at the Polo Grounds. Stengel, as mentioned earlier, was fond of players who could play various positions. Thomas had played first base and third base, but was expected to be the team's opening day left fielder. On December 9, Weiss bought outfielder Richie Ashburn from the Chicago Cubs for $75,000. Ashburn (nicknamed "Whitey") was a former two-time National League batting champion with the Philadelphia Phillies. He had once been one of the top center fielders in the National League, but at 35 had much more limited range. On December 15, Weiss conducted his third major deal of the winter trading season, acquiring second baseman Charley Neal from the Los Angeles Dodgers for $100,000 and outfielder Lee Walls. Weiss had filled three holes in the starting line up. As to how well, only time would tell.

Mickey Mantle and Roger Maris were both blond, both were sluggers, and both wore Yankee pinstripes. But they were very different types of hitters. Mickey didn't fuss much at the plate, practicing his swing nonchalantly as he awaited the pitch. He was the "watching type," taking a lot of strikes— even strike three. He would step out after two strikes and occasionally ask the umpire to see the ball. As the pitch approached the plate, Mantle pivoted forward, his massive body tensed, swinging furiously through the ball. His tape measure shots into the upper stands were wondrous to behold. Mantle walked often and struck out often. In 1961, he registered 126 free trips while fanning 112 times. Maris, by contrast, was the nervous type at the plate, smoothing the dirt with his toes, checking to see that his stance was the proper width. He moved around with each delivery, often taking a cut at the first pitch. Maris was a wrist hitter, his bat moving in an oblique parabola, "like a buggy-whip." His homers were mostly line drives, which traveled with great speed into the lower right field stands.

The M&M Boys' Roger Maris and Mickey Mantles in typical lefty-righty pose. Maris, diffident and forthright, was often damned by faint or dubious praise. One sports editor said of Maris, "There just isn't anything deeply heroic about the man, and the American public loves heroes."

Maris struck out relatively little for a slugger. In 1961, he had 94 bases on balls, while fanning only 67 times.[14] Mantle and Maris, both pitchers' nightmares, were now also pitchmen, cashing in on their historic season.

What is today 335 Madison Avenue was in 1961 the site of the Biltmore Hotel. Built in 1913, it was, along with the Commodore Hotel, one of several hostelries that girded Grand Central Station. Among its marvels were the famous lobby clock and the Grand Central galleries, located on the second floor. Because of its strategic location, the Biltmore attracted conventioneers ranging from the usual union and political organizations to the more exotic Aid for Israel and Cuba exile groups. On December 12, 1961, the grand ballroom was the site of a press conference featuring Mantle and Maris. The Yankee stars were there to announce the launching of their new clothing line for men and boys. Marketed by UNI-Wear, Inc., the new line was expected to gross $25 million in 1962 and earn Mantle and Maris six figures in endorse-ment money. In recent years, *The New York Times* noted, the "trait of hero worship" had become a growing industry, with Madison Avenue spending $500 million a year on athlete endorsements. The new M&M deal with UNI-Wear was "biggest endorsement venture to date."[13]

For the baseball purist, Mickey's and Roger's venture into the world of Madison Avenue was another unwelcomed change in the game. *The Sporting News,* self-styled as "the bible of baseball" and guardian of its image, com-plained that major league baseball was "lacking in fun, comedy, and the col-orful figures that were once part of the game." There were fewer and fewer characters like Casey Stengel. Now it seemed as if "the brass" was discouraging any sort of colorful behavior. The escalating salaries—Mantle had just signed for $85,000—didn't help. Modern players, *The Sporting News* lamented, were "such businessmen that they do not go in for the light-hearted pranks and escapades of their lower-salaried predecessors." In *Esquire*, Robert Daley also condemned the preoccupation with outside business interests. "It destroys the fans' belief that the game is played for its own sake."[15] *The Sporting News,* it might be pointed out, didn't seem to mind so much when it was Casey who did the selling and not the "modern ballplayer."

In any case, despite the protestations of *The Sporting News*, the associa-tion of ballplayers like Maris and Mantle with Madison Avenue was a natural one. In the early 1960s, the American advertising industry was the target of endless scrutiny—much of it bad. Vance Packard's *The Hidden Persuaders*, an expose of the advertisement industry, had been a big seller, revealing many of the amoral secrets of the trade. Religious leaders lamented the ad men's lack of social obligation while academics claimed that "the Madison Avenue economic regime" was destroying individualism.[16] Americans were plagued by a lack of national purpose—a point made over and over again by John F. Kennedy's presidential campaign in 1960. Seen in that light, the use of athletes as pitchmen was both natural and necessary. Other than the Mercury astro-nauts, who in American society suggested individual achievement better than the M&M boys in their mutual quest to shatter Babe Ruth's fabled 60 home run record? Who was a better throwback to the frontier ethos than these two sons of the West? What could top that?

Perhaps the answer to this question was professional football. The game, noted Robert Daley, was "open, fast, and violent," and thus more seductive for the average fan living in "an age in which all men walk gingerly." Baseball was "too tame for the times." There was nothing tame or gingerly about the football game played in Green Bay, Wisconsin, the last day of 1961. The Green Bay Packers defeated the New York Giants, 37–0, to win the National Football League championship. The game's MVP was Packer halfback Paul Hornung, who set a playoff record by scoring 19 points, earning him the much-coveted Corvette sports car from *Sport Magazine*. Pro football's threat to the National Pastime was only just beginning. The money was primitive by today's standards—the championship game, the richest payoff in history, yielded $5,155.44 for each Packer.

Not everyone was yet convinced of pro football's ascendency to the title of National Pastime. After all, NFL commissioner Pete Rozelle had only recently moved the league headquarters from Philadelphia to New York; the Pro Football Hall of Fame in Canton did not yet exist; and the Super Bowl was still a little over five years away. Longtime baseball writer Dan Daniel blamed Branch Rickey for stirring up all this "anti baseball talk." Scoffed Daniel, "Until the gridiron pros are able to show two strong leagues getting along in amity and settling the national championship in a counterpart of baseball's World Series, all that talk about football passing baseball as America's National Pastime is tommyrot."[17]

That day had not yet come. But "tommyrot" or not, most of the elements that would soon allow pro football to replace baseball as the National Pastime were already in evidence. The short schedule (14 games in 1961) made for more meaningful games—for bettors and fans alike. The game was faster paced—or at least seemed to be when viewed on television. As football ascended, baseball's struggles continued. Pitchers' attempts to combat the surge in offense from the Marises and Mantles came at a price—longer games. In trying to fool hitters, they delivered more pitches per game. Twenty years earlier, a pitcher threw 90 to 100 pitches per nine innings. By 1962, the number had jumped up to 125 to 130 a game, a gain of 30 percent. The average game was now two and a half hours, or ten minutes more than it had been five years earlier. Moreover, baseball had made mistake after mistake in promoting the game. Bonus babies, unlike NFL draft choices, represented "false publicity."[18] While everyone expected Syracuse University halfback Ernie Davis to be a star in the NFL, too many baseball bonus babies fizzled out. Some called for a "sensible draft system" like pro football's to equalize talent.

There was, despite baseball's problems, tremendous cause for optimism. The return of Casey Stengel, "the most successful mastermind in Major League history"[19]—and its greatest salesman—was expected to turn turnstiles around the National League. The American League, meanwhile, would benefit from what many expected to be another record-shattering season by Roger Maris. These two men, Stengel and Maris—one a beloved symbol of baseball's hallowed past, the other, in many ways, a troubling embodiment of the modern-game, would carry out their destinies on opposite sides of the Macombs Dam Bridge in 1962.

2

"Safe at Home"

New York awoke late on Monday, January 1, 1962, to partly cloudy skies and a sprinkle of snowflakes. Times Square, scene of a boisterous celebration just hours before, was now ghostly quiet. The globe of lights that descended Times Tower as the clock struck 12, the thousands of merry-makers who welcomed the New Year, and the glaring television lights atop the Astor Hotel marquee, which recorded the scene, were all gone; the streets were scrubbed clean of the remains of fire crackers, party horns, and confetti. The party goers at the Latin Quarter, the Sheraton East Embassy Club, and the Waldorf Empire Room had long since retired. The Waldorf Astoria provided a "superior deluxe twin-bedded guest room, a New Year's Eve dinner including dancing, gifts for the ladies, a floor show starring Carol Channing, and breakfast in bed"—all for $50 a person.[1] In the Bronx, Brooklyn, Manhattan, Queens, and Staten Island, those who watched the New Year's Eve Party with Xavier Cugat and Abbe Lane from the Waldorf's Starlight Roof on TV-Channel 4, were snoring away peacefully. The bars opened at nine o'clock to yawning streets. By afternoon, however, the city was coming back to life. The bar flies had returned to their stools and the crowds had begun to gather at the Wollman Memorial in Central Park, and at the ice rink in Rockefeller Center. There were new skates from Santa to try on.

By Wednesday, January 3, 1962, George Weiss was back at the New York Mets' offices in the Canada House near the corner of Fifth Avenue and 54th Street. The New Year had begun with a transit workers' strike against the Fifth Avenue Coach Line. As stranded New Yorkers pounded the pavement below, 20 stories above them Weiss was engaged in the yearly ritual of mailing out player contracts. Thirty-four players received offers, Frank Thomas having already been signed. Lonesome George didn't expect to have any "serious difficulties" with holdouts. "After all," he said, "we're signing no pennant winners."[2] On January 11, along with some late Christmas cards and solici-

28

tations for the use of the Mets' logo, the incoming mail contained signed contracts from three Mets hurlers. They were right-handers Roger Craig and Jay Hook, and lefty Al Jackson. Although pleased with the signings, Weiss announced that he was still seeking an experienced pitcher, as well as a good-hitting catcher.

The quality of catching was a subject of much discussion in the early 1960s. The lowering of the strike zone a decade earlier and the manufacturing of mitts with additional lacing (making them, in effect, one-handed gloves) had helped popularize a new catching style. Backstops were abandoning the crouch and taking a position on one knee. Instead of using the old "palms down" approach, they were now more inclined to "box" the ball with one hand.[3] The result, according to knowledgeable observers, was an increase in passed balls. Besides defensive lapses, there also seemed to be a general lack of outstanding offensive catchers. Other than Yogi Berra, there were no future Hall Fame backstops in the horizon — and Yogi, by this time, had been supplanted by his longtime understudy, Elston Howard. Thirty years earlier, it was noted, there had been a plethora of outstanding receivers, such as Bill Dickey, Mickey Cochrane, Gabby Hartnett, Ernie Lombardi, and Al López — all future Hall of Famers — plus other top-flight players. Expansion naturally diffused the number of quality catchers. Making things worse was the fact that fewer and fewer prospects were attracted to the "tools of ignorance." The National League's most promising young catcher, Joe Torre of the Milwaukee Braves, was a converted third baseman who still lacked polish behind the plate.

Typical of the quality of major league catching in the early 1960s was George Weiss' first choice in the expansion draft, Hobie Landrith. Hobert Neal Landrith was born in Decatur, Illinois, on March 16, 1930. A squat five feet, eight-inches and 170 pounds, the handsome, articulate Landrith was smallish for a catcher. He was signed by the Cincinnati Reds organization and came up to the big club at the tender age of 20. After six years in Cincinnati, Hobie drifted to the Chicago Cubs, St. Louis Cardinals, and finally the San Francisco Giants. Twice he was traded for future 20-game winners. In 12 seasons in the majors he had played over 100 games just twice and had batted more than 300 times only once. His lifetime batting average was under .240. Landrith was famous, perhaps infamous, for his constant trips to the mound. In this age of increasing offense, Hobie believed in staying in constant communication with the pitchers. Communication apparently wasn't the forte of the other Mets catchers. Chris Cannizzaro (called "Canzinero" by Casey Stengel) was known as "Smiley" for his poker face. Clarence (Choo Choo) Coleman supposedly didn't learn that he had been taken by the Mets until a month after the expansion draft was over.

George Weiss had created the famous Yankee farm system of the 1930s and '40s, including the Newark Bears—a team so stacked with talent that it was considered superior to many major league clubs. The Mets' fledgling minor league organization was nowhere near as good. It boasted 128 players, 19 of which were affiliated with Triple-A Syracuse, New York. Among the Syracuse group was a 28-year-old, former Yankee farmhand named Rod Kanehl. But at this time, Weiss wasn't putting much faith in Kanehl, or anyone else in the farm system for that matter. Weiss' best hope was to squeeze a decent season or two out of the veterans purchased in the expansion draft, such as ex–Dodgers Don Zimmer and Charlie Neal.

Don Zimmer inked his contract on January 18, a day after turning 31. Born in Cincinnati, Zimmer was signed by the Branch Rickey Dodgers in 1949. A fiery five feet, nine inches and 160 pounds, he was a minor league sensation, seemingly destined to replace the Dodger captain Pee Wee Reese at shortstop. But life would not be kind to Don Zimmer. At St. Paul in 1953, he was leading the American Association in home runs and RBIs when an errant pitch came crashing into his skull. For 13 days he laid unconscious, undergoing two brain operations. He couldn't speak and lost most of his sight. Zimmer came back from that injury to claim Reese's mantle, but then more hard luck ensued. In June 1956, he was playing at Brooklyn when he was hit in the face by a pitch. His cheekbone was broken and his left eye damaged. For 12 weeks, he was not allowed to bend over, tie his shoelaces, pick up his kids, or drive a car—his doctors were afraid that the slightest motion would detach his retina completely. The ever resilient Zimmer was back at Ebbets Field in late September, working out, but his vision remained blurry. On Christmas Day, 1956, he received an unexpected "present": when he awoke, he could see clearly for the first time since the beaning.

In 1958, playing for the now Los Angeles Dodgers, he had his best season, hitting .262 with 17 homers and 60 RBIs. But with the sudden emergence of Maury Wills, Zim became expendable. After two seasons with the Cubs, the Mets drafted him as one of the so-called "premium players" for $125,000. It was more money than he would've fetched in an open market. But the Mets and their fellow expansion team, the Houston Colt .45s, didn't receive much in terms of charity from the existing teams. So Zimmer, aged and scarred but always scrappy, would have to make due for Casey Stengel at third base.

Like Don Zimmer, Charlie Neal at one time had been tabbed as the heir apparent to a Brooklyn Dodgers hero. Charles Lenard Neal was born at Longview, Texas, on January 30, 1931. Signed by the Dodgers in 1950, he came up to the big club in 1954. In 1957, the team's last year in Brooklyn, he replaced Pee Wee Reese at shortstop and hit 12 home runs. In Los Angeles, Dodgers manager Walter Alston moved Neal to his more natural position at second base. Charlie became adept at hitting homers over the left field screen at the Los Angeles Coliseum. The screen — built for the Dodgers by Del Webb's construction company — was only 251 feet from home plate, and an inviting target for right-handed hitters. Swinging with a swish of the bat at the last split second, the five-feet, ten-inch and 165-pound Neal swatted 22 homers in 1958. He was even better the following year, driving in 87 runs and winning a Gold Glove. With deceptive power, lightning speed, and sure hands, Neal was tabbed as the successor to Jackie Robinson.

Unfortunately, circumstances had gone steadily downhill for Charlie. Injuries and ugly racial encounters with fellow teammates had marred his last two years in the City of Angels. The Dodgers exposed Neal to the National League expansion draft; the club was afraid it had "too many Negroes," he charged. Now, like Zimmer, he was returning to New York. On January 22, he signed his 1962 contract. Casey Stengel professed to be a big fan of Neal's, calling him "the best second baseman the Dodgers have had since I managed them in the Thirties."[4] The Old Perfessor could be forgiven for skipping over Jackie Robinson. The Mets were grasping at all the straws they could find.

The day after Charlie Neal's signed contract arrived at 680 Fifth Avenue, Jack Roosevelt Robinson was elected to the Baseball Hall of Fame. Robinson had expressed doubts about making the Hall — and he was right to think so, for reasons that went beyond the question of race. First of all, the Hall of Fame electors were extremely stingy in their selections. Edd Rousch and Sam Rice, both .320 lifetime hitters, had failed to gain admission in the last election in 1960. In addition, players who had been unpopular with the media (Robinson among them) received rough treatment from the electors. The New York Giants' great first baseman, the gruff Bill Terry, was made to wait 16 years before gaining entry into the Hall. But even popularity with the press wasn't a sure fire way to get into Cooperstown. Joe DiMaggio, incredibly, had been passed over in his first year of eligibility. The electors, who met every two years, had not chosen a new member to the Hall since 1956. The balloting rules had been simplified after the 1960 election at the insistence of Commissioner Ford Frick. But there was still a large backlog of impressive candidates. The Baseball Hall of Fame election, for better or worse, had not become the media seeking, self-congratulatory production that it is today. The idea that it was *necessary* to induct candidates every year for the sake of publicity had yet to penetrate the consciousness of the caretakers of the sport. *New York Times* columnist Arthur Daley fretted about "blatant electioneering; Red Smith of the *New York Herald Tribune*, complained bitterly about the anointing of "sainthood at any cost mob."[5]

But Robinson did get in, garnering 124 of the 160 votes, four more than the 75 percent needed for election. (Bob Feller, Cleveland Indians pitcher and the greatest strikeout artist of his era, received 150 of the 160 votes cast, the most since Lou Gehrig was elected by acclamation). It may be said that Robinson was elected into Cooperstown both because of, and in spite of, his race. There were electors who declined to elect a black man to the Hall of Fame and purposely left him off the ballot. There were also those who thought other candidates more worthy; some excellent players had stood in line long enough, Jackie could wait. What could not wait, however, was the acknowledgement that a black man had endured trials that no white player would ever face, and that he had succeeded beyond anyone's expectations despite these trials.

Robinson had changed the game — and the nation — forever. Still, it was not easy for major league baseball, its fans, and even the Dodgers, to embrace Robinson. He was a college athlete at a time when few ballplayers, of any color, attended college. He was a U.S. Army captain at a time when the U.S. Army still fought in segregated units. He was a proud man in a sport used to condescending to unschooled and naïve youths. Jackie Robinson had more going against him than just being black. Unlike his fellow inductee, Bob Feller, he wasn't a shy, modest midwestern farm boy who headed east for fame and fortune in the big city. If not exactly farm boys, popular players like Mickey Mantle, Richie Ashburn, and Robin Roberts, all conformed to this geographical trajectory — as did Casey Stengel, and, less happily, Roy Hobbs in *The Natural*. Robinson clearly didn't fit neatly into major league baseball's "agrarian myth."

One who did fit this "agrarian myth" was the former Hoosier-turned-Brooklyn resident, Gil Hodges. On January 30, Gil came up from Brooklyn to the Mets' Fifth Avenue offices to ink his 1962 contract. Hodges had never gotten into a fight on the field (he was known as a peacemaker) and he wasn't about to squabble about his salary. He accepted $33,000, which was $2,000 less than he earned at Los Angeles the previous year. The ceremony was everything George Weiss could have wanted: a compliant star player submitting tamely to the rules of the game — that is, the reserve clause — with the New York media there to record the ritual. Gil hoped to play 130 to 140 games in 1962, once he was "straightened out mentally." Like many a player before him, he claimed that inactivity had robbed him of his timing, and thus his hitting stroke. It is also true that Hodges had become entranced by the left field screen at the LA Coliseum. He had hurt his hitting by trying to pull everything in sight. Now the Hoosier boy was back where he belonged, the symbol of both the Brooklyn past and the Mets' (hopefully) promising future.

A photo in the Long Island daily *Newsday* on January 31 captured the spirit perfectly. The handsome Hodges was seen smiling broadly and waving his contract, framed by an artist's rendition of the future Flushing Meadows

Stadium. The caption read: "You *can* go home again!"[6] And so it would be for the former Brooklyn residents in Mineola, Levittown, and Hempstead. Going to see Casey and Gil— even at the Polo Grounds— would be something like returning to the old neighborhood to visit a member of the family.

By the end of January, the Mets had signed three other sluggers: one for the coaching box, one for the outfield, and a third for the broadcast booth. The Old Perfessor, back in New York from Glendale, held a press conference on January 19, at which he announced the hiring of Rogers Hornsby as third base coach. Gus Bell, slated to play right field in Casey Stengel's proposed lineup for 1962, mailed in his signed contract a week later. At the end of the month, the Mets picked Ralph Kiner, the former Pittsburgh Pirates home run king, to join the recently hired Lindsey Nelson and Bob Murphy in the broadcast booth. The 42-year-old Nelson, known for his Tennessee drawl and loud checkered jackets, and Murphy, a 37-year-old Oklahoman with the smoothest of voices, would do 130 telecasts on WOR Channel 9, and all 162 games on ABC-Radio. None of these men had a long standing association with the City of New York. But then again, they didn't have to. It was Casey Stengel's and Gil Hodges' presence that was counted on to motivate fan interest. According to promotions director J.O. Adler, Jr., advanced ticket were selling "far beyond our fondest expectations."[7] Thus far, 1,200 season box seats had been sold. The Mets planned to open ticket offices in the waiting rooms at Grand Central and Pennsylvania Stations— two of the main gateways to the burgeoning suburbia of Nassau County, Long Island and Bergen County, New Jersey.

Meanwhile, work was beginning on refurbishing the Polo Grounds. There had been several stadiums on the Manhattan side of the Macombs Dam Bridge, the present one dating back 50 years. Unlike football stadiums, all of which measure 360 feet by 160, baseballparks vary in dimension. The Polo Grounds was one of the most distinct. It was a horseshoe-shaped structure with short foul lines and a cavernous center field that ended with one of baseball's greatest curiosities— the home and visiting teams' clubhouses. The Polo Grounds was famous for its "Chinese home runs." The left field foul pole was 279 feet from home plate; right field measured just 257 feet. Although Willie Mays was no longer patrolling its pastures, not many players were likely to hit home runs to dead center: it was 480 feet from home plate. The Polo Grounds would retain its dimensions; the Mets' $300,000 renovation was geared toward improving seating capacity and the building of a plush cocktail lounge for the exclusive use of season ticket holders— even though everyone expected the park to be abandoned in 1963. The New York Yankees had played here between 1912 and 1922, and the relationship between the two clubs would continue in 1962. George Weiss had struck a reciprocal arrangement for parking with the New York Yankees. Mets fans would be able to leave their cars at the Yankee Stadium lots and take the 15-cent subway ride to the Polo Grounds at 155th Street and 8th Avenue. The Mets would respond in kind. The suburban fan base had to be accommodated.

In the Yankees offices at 745 Fifth Avenue, Yankee general manager Roy Hamey was putting together the biggest payroll in club history — more than $700,000 in player salaries. Hamey already had the most important signature on paper — Mickey Mantle's. On December 13, the Yankees had held a press conference at the Crystal Room of the Savoy Hilton Hotel. Here, where Dan Topping had earlier announced the "retirement" of Casey Stengel, Mickey waved a contract that called for an estimated $85,000. This was up from the $72,500 he received in 1961. The amount was more than Babe Ruth's annual salary in the 1920s and thirties. It also put "the Mick" on the same level as Willie Mays of the San Francisco Giants, although Giants owner Horace Stoneham would soon elevate Mays' salary to $90,000. Mantle pronounced himself totally recovered from the thigh infection that had aborted his chase of the Babe's record in late September 1961 and had kept him out of much of the World Series against the Reds. He hoped to play five more good years— if his legs held up.

The Yankees chose a legendary Manhattan eatery to announce the signing of two other veteran stars. In September 1939, Bernard (Toots) Shor, a former bouncer, bought a parcel of land on the fringes of Rockefeller Center. For the next 20 years, "Toots Shor's," located across from Radio City Music Hall at 51 West 51st Street, was a favorite hangout for writers, actors, singers, athletes, and assorted star gazers. Joe DiMaggio ate at "TS" two or three times a week, and the Football Writers of America held their weekly luncheon there year round. The National Basketball Association was born there, and Branch Rickey announced the founding of his Continental Baseball League from the confines of its oak walls. In August 1959, the restaurant was razed, re-opening one block up at 33 52nd Street on December 28, 1961. Toots Shor a man of "elephantine proportions," held court around the circular bar, handing out a friendly insult and a slap on the back to his diverse clientele. According to the writer Tom Meany, Toots once introduced famed author Ernest Hemingway to Yogi Berra. After Hemingway had withdrawn, Berra asked Shor, "What's he do?" Toots responded, "He's a writer." "Oh, yeah," Yogi demanded, "What paper?"[8]

Yogi, now a published author himself, walked up to the second floor of Toots Shor's on January 16, 1962, for his contract signing ceremony. The Yankees gave him $52,000, an increase of $2,000 over the previous season. Asked about his biggest thrill of 1961, Yogi answered that it was conquering the treacherous left field shadows at Yankee Stadium. Also on hand for the festivities was Whitey Ford. The Cy Young-winning lefthander received a reported $50,000, an increase of $13,000 from the previous year. Whitey and Yogi were pictured in the papers the next day, looking at a baseball digest and delighting in their numerous World Series records. It was a good publicity stunt, but the book might have served them better had they taken it with them to their contract negotiations with Roy Hamey. As it was, in this era of the reserve clause, both Ford and Berra supplemented their income with off-season ventures. Yogi and former teammate Phil Rizzuto had a bowling alley emporium in Clifton, a town over from Yogi's home in Montclair, New Jersey. Ford, who had come in on the Long Island Railroad from Lake Success, Long Island, had his own bowling establishment in Smithtown, New York. That the post–World War II suburban craze for bowling was cutting into night game attendance at Yankee Stadium probably didn't cross their minds.

Four days after landing Berra and Ford, Hamey received Luis Arroyo's signed contract from Puerto Rico. Arroyo was born in Peñuelas, on the southwestern end of the island, on February 18, 1927. His father, Felipe, was a watchman on a farm in neighboring Tallaboa, where Luis and his three brothers grew up playing baseball. In the late 1940s, when Arroyo was breaking into organized ball in the United States, Puerto Rico was undergoing tremendous changes. Governor Luis Muñóz Marín launched "Operation Bootstrap," an experiment in rapid industrialization that turned the island into the economic miracle of the Caribbean. But modernization had its price: thousands of Puerto Rican peasants, like the farmers of Tallaboa, were displaced from the land. So they came to New York in droves. By 1962, there were nearly a million Puerto Ricans in New York City. The *Boricuas*, as they called themselves after the indigenous name of the island, worked hard, endured the harsh cold, and fought for respect — sometimes not in the best of ways. As Arroyo's contract was landing on Hamey's desk, Governor Nelson Rockefeller was receiving last minute pleas from former First Lady Eleanor Roosevelt and San Juan Mayor Felisa Rincón de Gautier asking him to commute the death sentence of Salvador Agrón, an 18-year-old Puerto Rican youth, nicknamed "The Capeman."

Although there were thousands of Puerto Ricans in New York by 1962, Luis Arroyo was the first to play for the Yankees. In 1950, George Weiss signed another Puerto Rico native, Vic Power, for the club. But Power — black, lithe, and quick to take offense — did not suit Weiss' idea of a Yankee. Arroyo — white, portly, and easygoing — did. Still, Luis arrived on the Yankees almost by accident. He was playing for the Havana Sugar Kings of the International League in July 1960, when the team, worried about the way the winds were blowing in Castro's Cuba, picked up stakes and moved to Jersey City. Weiss, needing help in the bullpen, sent head scout Bill Skiff across the Hudson River to look for talent. He found Luis Arroyo had a spectacular season in 1961: 15 victories against five defeats and 28 saves. He, along with the Pittsburgh Pirates' Elroy Face and the Los Angeles Dodgers' Larry Sherry, was one of the first relief stars of the television age. The Yankees rewarded him with a contract that called for an additional $10,000, almost a 100 percent raise from the previous year.

According to the 1960 census, the population of New York City stood at 7,650,000, a decline of three percent from 1950 — and enough to cost the city four congressional seats in the next U.S. Congress. Meanwhile, the New York metropolitan area — including the five boroughs and 12 adjoining suburbs on Long Island, New Jersey, and Connecticut — had grown by 12.2 percent. In 1955, Elston Howard's first year as a Yankee, local newspapers advertised sales of a split level house in Teaneck, New Jersey, for $17,800. Just a ten minute ride from New York City on Route 4 and the George Washington Bridge, it featured three bedrooms, two full baths, a full basement, a Kelvinator refrigerator, and an automatic gas range. The prospective buyer was assumed to be white and middle class. But in the mid and late fifties, Teaneck was also seeing a small, but significant black migration to the northeastern part of town. Although they numbered only 1,700 (about four percent of Teaneck's population), the rising numbers of blacks sparked bitter debates about integration of neighborhoods and schools. In October 1961, civic groups petitioned City Hall to enact an "open occupancy" policy.

Teaneck's most famous black resident was Elston Howard. In 1962 Ellie had a banner year, hitting .348 (second in the American League to Detroit's Norm Cash), stroking 21 homers and driving in 77 runs. Ellie, who had earned about $32,000 in 1961, was holding out for a $10,000 raise. Today, that doesn't seem like an outrageous demand for the heir to Bill Dickey and Yogi Berra and fifth-place finisher in the MVP balloting. But Roy Hamey announced that he and Howard were "far apart" in negotiations. It's not like the Yankees didn't have the money to spend; they had just given Ole Miss quarterback Jake Gibbs a $105,000 bonus. But the club was less generous with veteran players. (Bill Skowron had recently signed for $35,000, a mere $3,000 raise despite 28 homers and 89 RBIs in 1961.) Howard, however, was determined to get some of that "big money" that the Yankees were passing along. Like most black major leaguers, Ellie was a "race man," that is, active in civil rights. That January, he joined Jackie Robinson at the tenth annual southern regional conference of the NAACP at Jackson, Mississippi.[9] It was Howard as much as anyone who had pushed Dan Topping toward his "one roof" policy in Florida. Self-effacing though he was, Howard would no longer tolerate the humiliating rooming conditions in spring training. Nor would he accept anything less than what he deserved as one of the most valuable of Yankees.

Elston Howard's salary demands, in fact, were exceedingly mild compared to those of Roger Maris. Having snatched his second consecutive American League Most Valuable Player Award, and set the record books afire with his 61 home runs, Maris was looking to double his pay to $74,000 in 1962. Hamey, with Dan Topping's blessing, had just handed out $85,000 to Mickey Mantle. From the Yankees' point of view, Maris' two spectacular years did not merit the same consideration as the Mick's sterling decade of service. Underlying these salary demands, and the Yankees' refusal to accept them, was a general sense that Maris wasn't quite deserving of the adulation that was coming his way. At a luncheon at Toots Shor's on January 26, at which Maris received the Van Heusen Outstanding Achievement Award for 1961, Ford Frick showered Maris with faint praise, saying, "Roger and I argued last season ...under great strain he came along and broke *a* record" [italics mine]. Later, the commissioner insisted that he had meant to say, "Roger did not break an old record, he set a new record." Told of Frick's remarks, Maris acidly responded, "a season is a season ... but he is the commissioner and makes the rules."[10] For Frick and countless others, Maris represented much of what they saw as wrong with baseball in the early 1960s. Struggling with changing times, baseball had bowed to the inevitable and expanded to ten teams in 1961. But expansion, it was widely believed, had resulted in unwanted changes, such as Maris' breaking of the Babe's hallowed record.

The tension between baseball's past, and its future direction, also informed baseball's biggest event of the Hot Stove season. The Baseball Writers of America were the most prestigious and powerful organization of sports writers in the country. It was they who determined entry into the Hall of Fame. On January 28, 1962, the New York Chapter, the BBWA's elite corps, held its 39th annual dinner-show at the Waldorf Astoria Hotel. Conrad Hilton's renovation had seen a departure from more modernist forms and given the Waldorf a 19th century charm. Guests coming in through the Park Avenue entrance were dwarfed by the ten-foot wide, one-ton crystal chandelier. On this late January night in 1962, 1,400 invited guests gathered in the hotel's three-tiered ballroom, including representatives of the publishing, sports, entertainment, and political worlds. On the dais, the forces of tradition were well represented by Ford Frick, Warren Giles, and baseball's minister without portfolio, Casey Stengel. But the winds of change also blew through the dais that night. Bill Shea, the man who had done the most to bring National League baseball back to New York, was also seated at the head table, as was Jackie Robinson. *The Sporting News* publisher, J.G. Taylor Spink, "crusader and guardian of the game's morals," received the Bill Slocum Award for "long and meritorious service to baseball." Nothing, however, was mentioned regarding his radical proposal for reforming the game.

The dominant mood in the Waldorf's grand ballroom that night was that of nostalgia — much of it, ironically, provided by the *new* New York team. Gil Hodges received the Ben Epstein Good Guy Award, presented annually to the local ballplayer considered to be most cooperative with the press — although Gil had yet to put on a Mets uniform. Rogers Hornsby, recently named as the Mets' third base coach, received the Retroactive Award in recognition of his remarkable 1924 season, when he hit .424 for the St. Louis Cardinals. The Yankees, of course, won their share of accolades. Whitey Ford accepted the Babe Ruth Award for the outstanding performance in the 1961 World Series. Mickey Mantle and Roger Maris shared the Sid Mercer Player of the Year Award. But, again, the entertainment portion of the evening — a collection of songs and skits put together by the scribes under the title, "How to Succeed in Baseball Without Really Trying"— betrayed both a preference for the past and an anxiety about the changes overtaking the game. The scribes-turned-actors satirized, among other things, baseball's rising salaries and athletic endorsements — both, of course, associated with Roger Maris and his partner in crime, Mickey Mantle. The increasing prominence of the relief specialist was lampooned in a skit that poked fun at Whitey Ford and Luis Arroyo. The Roger Maris-Ford Frick argument over the alleged asterisk was irresistible material for satire, given that many, if not a majority of writers were not happy about a .269 hitter breaking Babe Ruth's hallowed record.

Roger Maris and his former manager, Casey Stengel, represented the two extremes — tradition vs. change — that haunted the National Pastime in the early 1960s. One skit had Casey Stengel (played by Ken Smith of the *New York Daily Mirror*) sitting with his feet propped up against a bank vault, crooning:

> Summertime, and the livin' is easy,
> Stocks are jumpin' and my bank's making dough,
> Oh, my wife is rich, and my suit is good lookin,'
> You know, Mr. Topping, where you can go.[11]

Casey, thank heavens, was back in the company of the writers, no thanks to the heartless ownership of the New York Yankees. On the other hand, the evening's theme, "How to Succeed in Baseball Without Really Trying," suggested the underlying discomfort of the writers with Roger Maris. The Broadway play's protagonist, the window cleaner-turned-executive J. Pierrepont Finch, had climbed to the top by adhering to his own manual for success, ignoring the "Company Way." Maris did much the same thing, succeeding in baseball without submitting to the myth-creating tendencies of the New York press corps. Indeed, Maris, often curt, at times surly, declined to be condescended to by the baseball scribes. He never acquired a nickname; the "Wild

Hawk of the Dakotas" bestowed by the *New York Herald Tribune* seemed forced. Although a small town boy from the west, no story line was ever weaved around Maris' name, as was the case with his fellow midwesterners, Mickey Mantle and Gil Hodges. His style didn't lend itself to mythologizing. Baseball's agrarian myth suited Mantle and Hodges better.

The Sal Terini Band played its final number, and the night mercifully ended for the publicity-shy Maris. A week later, Roy Hamey, Ralph Houk, and many of the writers who attended the BBWA dinner were on their way south for another season of myth-making. Meanwhile, the New York Yankees were opening an "advanced camp" for promising rookies and selected veterans at their new training base in Fort Lauderdale, Florida.

Fort Lauderdale's population had grown to more than 80,000 by 1962, an incredible 200 percent jump since 1950. Growth of this magnitude required major adjustments. Traffic had been considerably eased in recent times by the building of the New River Tunnel on U.S. 1. Ocean Boulevard had been widened and parking enlarged in the downtown area. Las Olas Boulevard and the 17th Street Causeway, two of the main arteries leading to the beaches, had also been widened. Fort Lauderdale had much to offer to its new residents in terms of leisure activities, but it was the seasonal population for which the town was most known. Eastern and Northwest Airlines made one trip a day each way at the height of the winter season. The coming of World War II had resulted in travel restrictions to the Caribbean. As a result, Fort Lauderdale had become the spring break destination of college students from the frigid East and Midwest. By the early 1960s, thousands of surf-loving, sun-worshiping, bongo-playing, beer-drinking young people descended on this Gold Coast resort in the weeks prior to Easter Sunday. Improvements in air travel — new jets had replaced the old propeller-pulled planes — helped to spur the yearly pilgrimage to Fort Lauderdale. The young people sometimes ran afoul of the police. But the City Fathers were generally welcoming of the young horde for the commercial potential they represented. As one local merchant astutely recognized, today's teenager was tomorrow's retiree.

In February 1962, the City Fathers braced for another northern invasion, this time in the form of the Bronx Bombers. For weeks, the locals had been anticipating the arrival of baseball's most famous team — and the profits that would come with it. Hotels and businesses with postage meters carried an inscription on their stamping machines: "The Yankees are coming to Fort Lauderdale in 1962!" Ironically, the Yankees wouldn't be staying in any of the downtown hotels. They were housed at an annex of the Yankee Clipper Hotel, on the west side of Route A1A. A year earlier, the Serano Hotel in St. Petersburg had rebuffed Dan Topping's "one roof" policy and refused to accommodate the team's black players. At the Yankee Clipper Motel, the Yankees

Elston Howard, star catcher and first black to play for the New York Yankees. Responding to pressure from the NAACP and black players like Howard, owner Dan Topping moved the Yankees' spring training camp to Fort Lauderdale in 1962. As a result of Topping's "one roof" policy, Yankee players roomed together in integrated facilities at the Yankee Clipper Hotel.

would have their own private wing and swimming pool. The club would eat and sleep together for the first since the late Al Lang lured the Yankees to the Sunshine State in 1927. Writing in the *New York Herald Tribune*, Harold Rosenthal hailed this "almost unbelievable giant step" in "off field equality."[12] However, as historic as Dan Topping's action had been, the move to Fort

Lauderdale wasn't a direct attack on Jim Crow, but rather an end around it. The Yankees were staying in a motel outside of town — equal, yes, but also separate from the other hotel guests.

Stanley Woodward of the *New York Herald Tribune* believed that the Serano Hotel would have given in to the "one roof policy," if Dan Topping had continued to apply moral pressure. C.H. Alberding's letter to Topping asserting the "status quo," as Bill Beck pointed out in the *St. Petersburg Times*, suggested otherwise.[13] In any case, a new chapter had opened in Yankee history. At Fort Lauderdale, both rabid fans and curious winter vacationers would see the club play in a new $1 million stadium. The park seated 8,000 fans with an equal amount of parking spaces — far more than could be accommodated at Yankee Stadium. Inside, the new park boasted a grandstand of concrete and steel with a cantilevered roof. There were no posts obscuring the view as there were back in the Bronx. The Yankees new spring training facility also featured something never before seen in any park: a corrugated 40 foot, charcoal-colored wall, located in dead center field just behind the wire fence, which provided a splendid background for hitters. The freshly manicured field boasted two 65-foot dugouts. All of this was the work of the Del E. Webb Corporation.

Del Webb was the silent partner in the Yankee ownership, but by no means an insignificant one. Born in Fresno, California, on May 17, 1899, Webb had been a run-of-the-mill minor league pitcher in the mid-twenties. Struck down by a bout of typhoid, he went to Phoenix, Arizona, to restore his health. The rest became like a Horatio Alger story. Arriving in Phoenix with a hammer and saw (so legend goes), Webb parlayed his carpentry skills into the largest construction company in Arizona. With the coming of World War II, the company began to compete successfully for U.S. Army contracts, establishing a national reputation. On January 26, 1945, Webb used his burgeoning wealth to join Dan Topping and Larry MacPhail in purchasing the New York Yankees for $2.8 million. Webb left the running of the club to MacPhail and Topping, remaining in Los Angeles, the center of his multi-million dollar construction business. Along the way, the tall, thin, bespectacled, and soft-spoken Webb became one of the most influential figures in post–World War II American culture. He amassed a $50 million empire, erecting motels and suburban shopping centers around the country. In 1946 and 1947 his construction company built the Flamingo Hotel for mobster Bugsy Siegel, helping to lay the foundation, literally, for modern Las Vegas. In January 1960, Webb opened Sun City, 12 miles northwest of Phoenix, the first major retirement complex in the United States and a model for the "active adult communities" to come.

In Florida, the Yankees' "advanced camp" for rookies and selected veterans was based on the Yankees' "instructional school" of the early 1950s. It was an idea attributed by some sources to the ex-minor league pitcher Del Webb.

About 2,000 fans were on hand early Monday morning, February 5, for the opening of the advanced camp training sessions at Del Webb's new stadium. The players emerged single file from the clubhouse to sustained applause. There was a pause, then minutes later, out came the familiar figure of number five, the "Yankee Clipper," Joe DiMaggio. The crowd broke into a loud roar. "Joe D" remained behind signing autographs and posing for pictures with adoring fans, as Ralph Houk and his coaches put the players through their paces. Veteran catcher Johnny Blanchard was the first Yankee in the batting cage, facing righty Bill Stafford. Blanchard was the first Yankee to hit a home run out of the new ballpark. Also in camp was former Cy Young Award winner Bob Turley. "Bullet Bob" sported a narrow four-inch scar, above and behind his right elbow, where doctors at Lenox Hill Hospital had removed bone chips and other debris the previous October. Besides Stafford and Turley, veteran pitchers included Rollie Sheldon, Tex Clevenger, Jim Coates, Hal Reniff, Robin Roberts, and Marshall Bridges, a left-handed reliever recently acquired from the Cincinnati Reds.

But it was the youngsters that became the focus of attention. The Yankee instructional school of the 1950s had produced the likes of Elston Howard, Tony Kubek, and Bobby Richardson. The 1962 group was considered to be one of the best "bumper crops" in years. There was, or seemed to be, a "stick-out" at every position: Charlie Keller the 3rd (son of the former Yankee outfielder) at first; Pedro González at second; Tom Tresh and Phil Linz at shortstop; and bonus baby Jake Gibbs at third. In the outfield there was Joe Pepitone, Dick Berardino, and Don Lock. Pitchers included lefty Al Downing, briefly with the Yanks in 1961, and righty Jim Bouton, hoping to make the grade from Double-A Amarillo. The New York Mets had tried to curry favor with old Brooklyn Dodger fans by signing Gil Hodges, Don Zimmer, Charlie Neal, Roger Craig, and most recently, reliever Clem Labine. The Yankees invited three Brooklyn natives to their advanced camp: pitcher Louis Romanucci and outfielders Ron Solomini and Joe Pepitone.

Joseph Anthony Pepitone was born in Brooklyn on October 9, 1940, and grew up just a few blocks from Ebbets Field. He was a Yankee fan in Brooklyn—a dangerous thing to be, but not as dangerous as an incident that occurred when he was 16 years old and a student at Manual High on 7th Avenue. One day, a fellow student approached him in the locker room, wielding a .38 revolver. The fellow, fooling around, pointed the gun at Joe. It went off accidentally, sending a bullet through Joe's chest. The slug missed his heart and spine by a mere half inch. Pepitone recovered quickly, his baseball career unharmed. In 1958 he was discovered by the Yankees playing for another New York institution, "Nathan's Famous Hot Dogs" on Coney Island. Joe married a St. Petersburg girl and invited himself to camp in 1960. He was tall (six-foot two-inches) thin, and raw, but the Yankees liked what they saw. In 1961 at Amarillo, he hit .316 with 21 home runs. By the time he arrived at Fort Lauderdale in February 1962, he was up to 170 pounds and eager to make a positive impression on the Yankee brass.

While Joe Pepitone and his fellow rookies labored under the watchful eye of the Yankee staff, Mickey Mantle and Roger Maris were in town filming *Safe at Home*, a low-budget Columbia Pictures production aimed at exploiting their recent fame as home run kings. Ralph Houk had a small supporting role; the rookies in camp were used as extras. The story was thin — a local boy boasts about his friendship with Mickey and Roger, is caught in a lie, and learns a valuable lesson. The movie has a happy ending, of course: the boy and his playmates get to meet the M&M Boys and their teammates. Mickey and Roger's parts could have been played by cardboard pinups given their stiffness, but the young fans for whom the movie was targeted could have not cared less about their thespian gifts. The boy in the film is lonely, his father preoccupied with his business and the woman in his life; the Yankees are a haven from the hurts and pains of the world. For Maris, that haven was a thousand miles away in Raytown, Missouri, far from the maddening crowds and the hurts and pains of fame. It would be quite a while before he was "safe at home."

The New York Yankees began training at St. Petersburg in 1927, when it was a town of 3,000 people. By 1962, it was the third largest municipality in Florida, with a population in excess of 180,000. Two technological innovations of the post–World War II era — air conditioning and jet travel — brought thousands more sun seekers each winter. One of the highlights of the winter season at St. Pete was the annual Sunshine Festival that began on February 4 and culminated with a parade on February 25. The "Sun God" and "Goddess," two college kids crowned the previous night at the annual Sun Ball, rode a 150-foot float through cheering crowds.

On February 17, a much more skilled performer took the stage at the Yankees' old home in St. Petersburg. Casey Stengel was in town (the team would not report until February 28) to plug his autobiography, *Casey at the Bat*. The book was a humorous mix of tales of yore and sagely homilies that underscored his reputation as a "baseball genuis." The Old Perfessor, who had been making public appearances from New Hampshire to California that winter, arrived at Maas Brothers Department Store at 10:30 A.M. For the next three hours, he autographed copies of his book and traded barbs with the patrons. One large man approached Stengel and bellowed, "I've got a lot to tell you." "I hope not too much," offered Casey mildly. The man, not to be denied, shot back, "You've got the ears to hear it."[14] Most others were more complimentary. Dressed in a blue suit and brown alligator shoes, the new Mets manager cut a dashing figure. "He's better looking than his pictures," one woman exclaimed. "And a lot younger, too," added another.

Stengel was back alright, but what about Roger Maris? The breaking of the Babe's hallowed record made Roger, as the *Atlanta Daily World* put it, "the marked man of 1962."[14] Issues off the diamond only exacerbated the situation for Maris. While Casey was surveying his old stomping grounds at St. Petersburg, back in Fort Lauderdale the Yankee slugger was sticking firmly to his demands. The club was reportedly offering $60,000 — much more than the $42,000 that Elston Howard eventually settled for on February 17. But with the advanced camp concluding and the real show looming on February 19, Maris was still holding out for $75,000. In the early 1960s, the press had watched benignly as owners built box seats extending halfway up the grandstands in major league ballparks in an effort to attract corporate fans. But while the Fourth Estate extolled the wonders of Candlestick Park and Dodger Stadium, it wasn't very sympathetic with Roger's demands. After all, having made $100,000 in endorsement related ventures that winter, why, they asked, quibble over a few thousands? Was it a matter of principle? "You could call it that," he replied tersely.[16] Money — or was it principle? — drove Walter O'Malley and Horace Stoneham to Los Angeles and San Francisco in 1958. In any case, with Maris or without Maris, the *real* spring training of 1962 was about to begin.

3

"What Are You Doin' in That Crummy Uniform?"

Charles Dillon Stengel wasn't used to being upstaged, least of all by a 40-year-old, Marine Corps pilot-turned-astronaut. But this is exactly what happened on February 20, 1962. At 9:47 A.M. at Cape Canaveral, Florida, after seemingly interminable delays, the final countdown ended, the giant Titan rockets ignited, and John Glenn was sent hurling into space, becoming the first American (and third human) to orbit the earth. At the other end of the Sunshine State, in St. Petersburg, the New York Mets clustered around a clubhouse radio to follow Glenn's progress. "He's over Africa, now," exclaimed the little catcher, Hobie Landrith, "He left just a minute ago." The Old Perfessor, however, was steadfastly unimpressed. "I don't care if he's coming down in left field in two minutes," Stengel snorted. "We have work to do."[1] That "work" actually began the day before, when the Mets' battery men (pitchers and catchers) and two position players, Ted Lepcio and Don Zimmer, who lived in St. Petersburg, made their debuts at Miller Huggins Field.

St. Petersburg wasn't the same town it had been when Casey Stengel was last there as Yankee manager in 1960. In February 1962, the Mets, who had replaced the Yankees as the tenants of Miller Huggins Field, and the St. Louis Cardinals, who trained at Al Lang Field, were engaged in a novel experiment in racial relations. The two clubs had abandoned the downtown hotels and instead were housing their players in motels at the outskirts of St. Petersburg. The Redbirds—both black and white—occupied a motel near the Sunshine Skyway. George Weiss, whom Wendell Smith and other black pundits feared would give in to the segregated housing policies of the past, instead rented a private wing for the team in the Colonial Inn Motel. The Mets would have their own dining and sleeping facilities. Like the Yankees at Fort Lauderdale, the new New York team at St. Petersburg would observe the "one roof policy."

Branch Rickey's Brooklyn Dodgers pioneered racial integration in spring training in 1948, converting a former naval station at Vero Beach into their private residential and training facility (called Dodgertown). But it took the determined efforts of the NAACP — and the positive actions of Yankees owner Dan Topping in response to these demands— which made the "one roof policy" the way of the future. In the spring of 1962, seven of the 14 major league teams training in Florida had integrated accommodations: the Dodgers, Yankees, Mets, Cardinals, White Sox, Braves, and Orioles (although the O's' lone black, Earl Robinson, chose to live apart from the team). Lagging behind were the Pirates, Senators, Tigers, Twins, Reds, and Phillies. The residential color line seemed to have been influenced by the accidence of geography and demography. The clubs that had integrated facilities were located in the larger Florida towns, where motels outside of the downtown area were more readily available. The motel owners, the new entrepreneurs in town were willing to set aside Jim Crow in order to capture the lucrative baseball business. On the other hand, the clubs that had failed to integrate by February 1962 were situated in smaller towns, where traditional Southern customs were more entrenched, and where there were no adequate motel facilities outside of town to compete with the established hotels. Still, racial equality, even under the "one roof policy," was not complete. Black players were not entirely welcome at these new residences. The Mets, for example, were forbidden to use the Colonial Inn swimming pool, and black players were discouraged from congregating in the motel lobby.

Not that the Mets had much time for play. These men were like the *ronins* in Akira Kurosawa's *Seven Samurai*: cast aside by their masters, burdened by broken dreams and passing years, and looking for one more chance at redemption. On Monday, February 19, the sun was shining brightly and a gentle breeze blowing through the Australian pines, as the players awoke at 7:30 A.M. in their private wing of the Colonial Inn. They dressed quickly and shuffled to breakfast, sitting in groups of two and three. Still mostly strangers to each other, they settled down to a breakfast of eggs, juice, and coffee, eying each with curiosity as they ate. At 9 A.M., a chartered bus pulled up in front of the hotel. The players walked through the lobby, past a sign on the front desk that read: "Stengelese is spoken here."[2] And so began the daily 30 minute trip to downtown St. Petersburg.

The clubhouse at Miller Huggins Field had been refurbished by Dan Topping for the Yankees just two years earlier. The aspiring Mets walked through the clubhouse entrance, their stocking feet touching the grey carpeted floor (Casey didn't allow them to wear cleats inside). Looking about the low-ceilinged structure, they took in the knotty-pined paneling and searched for their place among the 50 open wooden cubicles that had once belonged to

Berra, Mantle, Maris, Ford and company. Waiting for them at each cubicle was a new grey flannel uniform, the name "Mets" blazoned across the front in blue with orange fringe. At 9:45, the doors closed and the Old Perfessor addressed the players. He urged them to do their best, and promised them more money if they did. Still in their stocking feet, the players converged on the concrete apron located on the field side of the clubhouse, where they put on their spikes. Minutes later, with a wave of Casey's bat, the 23 men took the field for the first time as the New York Mets.

The small crowd of onlookers cheered and clapped politely as these "familiar strangers," as sportswriter Jimmy Cannon called them, ran onto the field. Roger Craig, eager to show the Dodgers that they had made a mistake in letting him go, bounded towards the mound to pitch batting practice. Waiting behind the plate in full catching gear was Hobie Landrith. The first batter, rookie pitcher Ed Donnelly, stepped in. The routine never varied: each player bunted three times, swung away six times, and ran on the seventh pitch. Ford Frick stopped by to watch the work out, and declared himself "tickled pink" in seeing the Mets. Team owner Joan Payson was also in attendance, a parasol protecting her from the Florida sun, as she observed the Whitney fortune at work. Surveying the field, she sighed, "We're finally here."[3]

At 11:45, the players broke for lunch, consuming a Spartan meal of vegetable soup, hard boiled eggs, carrots, celery and tomatoes. At 12:30 P.M., they were back on the field, grouping themselves around one of several Mets coaches— Rogers Hornsby, Cookie Lavagetto, Solly Hemus, and Red Ruffing —for further instruction. By 2:30 P.M., the workout had fizzled out. Back in the clubhouse, the players shrugged off their sweat-soaked uniforms. Trainer Gus Mauch, sporting a white nylon undershirt and matching white slacks, was waiting with his supply of antiseptic liniment and sun tan lotion, the bottles lined up in rows on the Formica table top. Mauch, who had left the Yankees to work for his old friend Casey Stengel, knew what to expect from the first days of practice. Rain brought soggy ground and pulled muscles, a hard dry surface brought shin splints and charley horses. His first patient was the Canadian pitcher, Ken McKenzie, who had a leg cramp.

Longtime observers perceived a different Casey Stengel that spring from the one who had managed the Yankees to ten pennants and seven World Series championships. In the Yankee years, Casey passed much of the time in the dugout talking to reporters, leaving the coaches to carry on with their duties. But now, as the Mets' field general, he seemed restless, wandering hither and yon in his familiar dogtrot gait. Jaw thrust forward, eyes sharply focused, the Old Perfessor took in everything, admonishing a player here, giving friendly advice there. At one point, he took a group of pitchers on a tour of the diamond, demonstrating base running techniques. It was essential, he emphasized, to hit the bag correctly and make the proper turn. At night, he pored over performance and scouting reports. Stengel had no illusions as to who was the real star of the team. "My face alone will populate the Polo Grounds," he boasted. But that didn't mean he wanted to be embarrassed. Alluding to John Glenn's recent space flight, he joked, "Well, I hope he found a new island out there. I'm gonna want to buy one if I finish in last place."[4]

In the last 50 years, there have been far fewer recognizable nicknames in major league baseball. Sure, there's an "A-Rod," for Alex Rodriguez but that's just a shortening of a player's name — serviceable, but not colorful or really descriptive. Derek Jeter, the face of the Yankee franchise for the last two decades, has no recognizable sobriquet. Once, before political correctness, when the mythologizing of players was the stuff of baseball — the sport abounded in nicknames. There were nicknames that referred to a player's place of origin ("Vinegar Bend" Mizell, Tex Clevenger, and Casey Stengel), ethnicity (Dutch Dotterer, "El Señor" for Al López, and Skoonj for Carl Furillo), and physical characteristics (Moose Skowron, Sad Sam Jones, and Yogi Berra). At one time, baseball abounded with "Reds" — Red Ruffing, Red Schoendienst, Red Wilson, Red Barber, and Mets coach Red Kress; and "Whiteys" — Whitey Ford, Whitey Kurowski, Whitey Lockman, and Whitey Herzog.

On February 25, the Mets signed another "Whitey," Richie Ashburn, for a reported $27,500. Ashburn was born in the small town of Tilden, Nebraska, on March 19, 1927. He started out as a catcher in the Philadelphia Phillies' chain, but was switched to the outfield to take advantage of his blazing speed. Whitey came up to the big club in 1948 and set a rookie record with a 23-game hitting streak. In 1950, he was one of the key members of the "Whiz Kids" who edged out the Brooklyn Dodgers for the pennant, before losing to the Yankees in the World Series (Eddie "Whitey" Ford was the winning pitcher in the final game). The five-foot, ten-inch and 170-pound Ashburn was a slap hitter, winning National League batting crowns in 1955 and 1958. He led the National League outfielders in assists three times, and tied or led in double plays three times. He began to slow down in 1959 and was traded by the Quakers to the Chicago Cubs. After two years in the Windy City, he was left exposed to the National League expansion draft. Ashburn was looking forward to playing in the Polo Grounds where in 1951, in a rare display of power, he hit three home runs in three games.

The day after Ashburn's signing, February 26, the Mets began their first full squad practice. At 7:30 A.M., the phones begin ringing in the 14 rooms in the private wing of the Colonial Inn, and so began the daily routine of morning and afternoon practice sessions. Arriving at the park, the players checked their valuables in the name-tagged boxes in the trainer's room, and then went to work. Six bats and two grey flannel uniforms were waiting in each cubicle. The "stars," Gil Hodges, Charlie Neal, Frank Thomas, Gus Bell, Don Zimmer and Richie Ashburn, occupied one side of the room. Some players, like Bell, were still working off their winter flab. Others concentrated on curbing their weaknesses. Hodges was swinging away in the batting cage under the close

Gil Hodges' huge hands helped make him the finest fielding first baseman in the National League. The Mets began their first formal practice on February 26, 1962, at Miller Huggins Field in St. Petersburg, Florida. Hodges was the Mets' most popular player.

scrutiny of Rogers Hornsby, concentrating on hitting the outside pitch. He finally emerged from the batting cage, his huge hands covered with blisters. As the players practiced on the field, a gaggle of fans, young and old, gathered to watch them. One of Hodges' female fans ventured a prediction: "Gil is going to lead this team to a pennant someday."[5]

At 2:30, the players returned to the clubhouse. They showered and dressed, grinded out their last cigarettes in the sand boxes provided for that purpose, and stepped outside. Joan Payson, in addition to player salaries, was shelling out a bundle in laundry bills and other sundry items. The players went through three sweat shirts and 200 towels a day. In one day, they consumed three gallons of purified water, 90 bottles of soda pop, and 500 ounces of soup. Curiously, the biggest expense of all was for disposable needles, which were utilized for flu shots, polio vaccines, and vitamin injections. The "Steroid Era" was far away in the spring of 1962, but the use of needles—150 by the second week of practice — suggested that no great paradigm shift was required when players began resorting to performance enhancing drugs. The players had long been accustomed to sticking needles into their bodies.

One of Casey's dictums was the rule, "You don't want players to hang around [the clubhouse after games] because they may start second-guessing themselves and each other."[6] Second-guessing wasn't the new Mets real problem that spring; it was trying to fend off the boredom. The $10 per diem stipend negotiated by the players' union did not provide much opportunity for the glamorous life. Some of the senior players had brought their wives and rented cottages along the beach, but most were staying at the Colonial Inn. Dinner was over by 7 P.M. Some players ventured out to see a movie or go to the dog track. Others stayed in their rooms and watched TV. Restless, some drifted in and out of the lobby, where a twist duo was entertaining, or ambled over to a corner where Rogers Hornsby held court. Black players, feeling unwelcome at the motel bar, made the trip by taxi to the black section of town. Although Stengel had no set curfew, most players were in bed by 10:30 P.M.

On February 26, the day that the Mets started full squad practice, Roger Maris finally came to terms with the New York Yankees. Maris accepted $70,000, which G.M. Roy Hamey hastened to say was *not* the 100 percent increase that Roger had wanted. But it was hefty enough — easily the highest raise, percentage wise, in the club's history. Maris joined the rest of the team on February 28 for the official start of spring training at the new Fort Lauderdale facility. Bobby Richardson was the first Yankee in the batting cage, followed by Maris. Roger was wearing a rubber sweat shirt under his uniform jersey. All of the award dinners that fall and winter had left him eight pounds over his playing weight of 204. On the first pitch, he laid down the customary bunt, and then hit three high flies to right field. A low line drive curved foul down the right field line. He hit no home runs.

Mickey Mantle stepped in. "The Switcher" was a trim 200 pounds and fully recovered from the upper thigh infection that had put an early end to his 1961 season and his quest for Ruth's record. As usual, he wore a heavy bandage and foam rubber padding to protect his vulnerable right knee. Batting right-handed, Mickey laid down a bunt, and then sent a rocket over the left field fence. Turning on the next pitch with all the strength of his massive body, he drove a shot over third base that nearly decapitated Clete Boyer. Mantle hit two more home runs to left and center before stepping out to talk to reporters. Asked for his season goals, he replied, "Well, just once I'd like to play every game of a schedule."[7] He also hoped to cut down on strikeouts, particularly from the left side of the plate. Returning to the batting cage, Mickey hit three more home runs, this time from the left side. In his next turn at batting practice, Maris again failed to hit the ball out of the new park.

While Maris and Mantle toiled in relative obscurity, back in New York another blond hero was dominating the newspaper headlines. On March 1, some 40 million people gathered in lower Manhattan for a ticker tape parade honoring Mercury astronaut John Glenn. At 12:05 P.M. the motorcade, accompanied by marching units and military bands, made the 20-minute trip up Broadway from the historic Bowling Green to City Hall Plaza — temporarily named "Astronaut's Way." The celebratory mood was spoiled when it was learned that an American Airlines flight had crashed into Jamaica Bay, killing all 95 on board. But John Glenn's heroic flight into space continued to dominate headlines. Writing in the *New York Herald Tribune*, Robert S. Bird hailed the Ohio-born Glenn as "a new image of American manhood ... a fully developed man ... of courage, intelligence, and character."[8]

Maris' lack of early home run prowess was the least of Ralph Houk's worries on the first day of spring 1962. In any other year, the Yankee infield would have been set. The corners were ably manned by Bill Skowron and Clete Boyer. The "Moose" had dipped to .267 in 1961, but still clouted 28 homers and 89 RBIs. Clete had hit only .224 but swatted 11 home runs and was a superb glove man. It was the Yankees' middle infield that presented problems for "the Major." Tony Kubek was still on active duty, pending a decision by President Kennedy to release the reserves. In the meantime, Houk would alternate Phil Linz and Tom Tresh at shortstop, hoping that one of the two could step in and do the job until Kubek returned from the army.

Thomas Michael Tresh had a solid baseball pedigree. His father, Mike Tresh, broke into the majors with the Chicago White Sox shortly before Tom's birth on September 20, 1938, in Detroit, Michigan. By age four, Tom had full run of the Chisox' dugout and clubhouse (his playmate was Judy Moses, daughter of Yankees coach Wally Moses). Mike Tresh taught his son to switch hit — but not to catch. In any case, young Tom was attracted to the shortstop position, having grown up watching Chicago's great Luke Appling. Signed by the Yankees out of Central Michigan University, he started slowly. In 1961, the six-foot, 190 pound Tresh blossomed into a sure-fire major league prospect, finishing with a .315 average at Triple-A Richmond.

Tresh's rival for the shortstop position was born Phillip Michael Linz in Baltimore, Maryland, on June 4, 1939. Signed by the Yankees in 1957, Phil Linz slowly made his way up the farm system ladder. In 1961 at Amarillo, he had his usual halting start, then, suddenly hit everything in sight, finishing with a .349 batting average to lead the Texas League. At six-foot, one-inch and 180, the lanky lad wasn't a power hitter. Phil was the kind of ballplayer that Casey loved in his old days with the Yankees—a jack of all trades who could fill in at both infield and outfield positions. He wasn't the smoothest of fielders, but he always seemed to get the job done. Linz was also fun to be around. Fellow rookie, pitcher Jim Bouton, who had roomed with him during various stops in their minor league days, said he was "a laugh a minute." Phil described himself as a "far out" kind of guy who liked "to listen to a little far out music at end of the day."[9]

Houk had less to worry about elsewhere in the lineup. At a time when major league baseball suffered from a scarcity of catching talent, the Yankees had an embarrassment of riches. Yogi Berra, who held the all-time home run record for catchers, was now, for all intents and purposes, the third stringer. The club did not suffer much as a result; in Elston Howard the Bombers had one of the best all around performers at that position in all of baseball. Johnny Blanchard, the "Supersub," had moved in as the second-string catcher. The outfield would again consist of Berra in left, Mantle in center, and Maris in right. Behind them were veterans Héctor López and Bob Cerv. Houk had been very impressed by rookie Joe Pepitone's quick bat and graceful play in the outfield during the advance camp sessions. Houk indicated that Blanchard, who starred in right field in the fifth game of the 1961 World Series, would also be on hand for picket duty.

Two years earlier, Johnny Blanchard had almost quit baseball altogether. Born in Minneapolis, Minnesota, on February 26, 1933, Blanchard had toiled in the minors for years before coming to the Bronx for good in 1960. In late July of that year, both Yogi Berra and Elston Howard were sidelined with injuries. It looked like Johnny would finally receive a chance to play. However, he soon learned that the club had decided to activate bullpen coach Jim Hegan and play him instead. An angry Blanchard stormed out of the clubhouse. The old man would never give him a chance, he moaned. He might as well pack it in. His temper tantrum was overheard by first base coach Ralph Houk. The Major, a former major league catcher who had managed him at Triple-A Denver, assured Johnny that he would receive his chance. When the Minnesotan came back to the Stadium from his New Jersey home on August 2, Houk, with a twinkle in his eye, told him to look at the lineup card. That day, Blanchard caught all 24 innings of a doubleheader against the Detroit Tigers, driving in the winning run in the 14th inning of the first game. He lost ten pounds that afternoon. A grateful Blanchard always believed that it had been Houk who had interceded with Casey Stengel on his behalf. Playing for Houk in 1961, he hit .305 with 21 home runs.

The core of the Yankee pitching staff had changed little from 1961. Whitey Ford (25–4) was the ace of the staff, followed by Ralph Terry (16–3), Bill Stafford (14–9), and Rollie Sheldon (11–5). Terry, despite his sterling record, was still trying to redeem himself in the postseason. He was the lone losing pitcher in the World Series against the Cincinnati Reds the previous October. Moreover, in the 1960 World Series against the Pittsburgh Pirates, he had infamously yielded Bill Mazeroski's dramatic ninth inning home run. Stafford hailed from the tiny upstate New York hamlet of Catskill. But he was a cool figure on the mound in the big city. Sheldon had been the star rookie of the 1961 camp, making the jump from Class-D ball.

In the bullpen, Houk planned to rest Luis Arroyo during much of spring training. Luis had pitched winter ball in Puerto Rico. Roy Hamey had acquired insurance in the bullpen in the form of Marshall Bridges, a 30-year-old veteran obtained from Cincinnati. Big Jim Coates, Bud Daley, and Hal Reniff returned for long relief/spot starter duty. Then there were the reclamation projects. The Yankees were hoping that "Bullet" Bob Turley, the Cy Young Award winner in 1958, would finally recover his form after off-season elbow surgery. Robin Roberts was hoping to show everyone that the Mets and Colts had made a mistake in passing him up in the National League expansion draft.

Meanwhile, at the Mets' spring training camp in St. Petersburg, Casey Stengel had a pretty good idea what his opening day lineup would be.

First Base	Gil Hodges
Second Base	Charlie Neal
Shortstop	
Third Base	Don Zimmer
Left Field	Frank Thomas
Center Field	Richie Ashburn
Right field	Gus Bell
Catcher	Hobie Landrith
Pitcher	Roger Craig

As with the Yankees, shortstop was the big question mark. George Weiss had failed to land a *bona fide* shortstop in the National League expansion draft at Cincinnati the previous October. The leading candidates that spring were the Puerto Rican, Félix Mantilla, and the Venezuelan, Elio Chacón. Neither had spent a full season at the position. Given that the rest of the diamond would be manned by aging veterans, the pitchers couldn't expect much in terms of defensive help. Behind Craig, Stengel was counting on the trio of Jay Hook, Bob Miller, and Craig Anderson, the first two $125,000 "premium players" in the expansion draft. The only lefthander of note was young Al Jackson, a former Pittsburgh farmhand. Perhaps Ken McKenzie, the Toronto native, or Ray Daviault, the French Canadian, or Sherman (Roadblock) Jones might surprise. If nothing else, the Mets had one of the smartest staffs in the National League. McKenzie had attended Yale University. Hook, an engineering major at Northwestern University, was doing graduate work on gas dynamics.

Stengel was the center of attention on March 6 for "Meet the Mets Day" at Miller Huggins Field. The team donned the white, pin striped home uniforms for the first time, as the cameras recorded a promotional film to be shown in New York later that month. Stepping gingerly over the miles of electric cables were the "Madison Avenue types in grey flannel overcoats," looking to recruit select ballplayers to pitch their products. Gil Hodges, Don Zimmer, and Gus Bell posed for a cigarette ad poster. They received $750 apiece for their testimonials. Clem Labine signed with a rival cigarette brand. The biggest pitchman of all, of course, was the Old Perfessor. The players were banished from the clubhouse for much of the morning and afternoon while Casey was inside filming a commercial for a headache and stomach ache remedy. In take after take, he clutched his stomach as if doubled up in pain. The pain would soon be real enough.

The Metropolitans opened their first spring exhibition season with two games against the other St. Petersburg club, the St. Louis Cardinals. The festivities at Miller Huggins Field on Saturday, March 10, had the feel of a high school football game. There was a 56-piece scarlet-coated brass band, and five girls sporting red pompoms and white boots, on hand to cheer the team on. The Cardinals, meanwhile, had a tailoring innovation of their own: the players' surnames were stitched on the backs of their uniforms. The Redbirds were following in the footsteps of Bill Veeck's Chicago White Sox, the first team to do so back in 1960. Ford Frick, who was present at the game, waxed poetic about "the culmination of a long and arduous expansion program."[10]

The game itself was not that long, 2:23, but certainly arduous—for the Mets, that is. The crowd of 6,872 watched Richie Ashburn loft a soft fly to Stan Musial in left field for the first out. It wouldn't get much better. The Cardinals routed the Mets, 8–0. Only two New Yorkers reached third base against the Redbirds' pitching. Sluggers Frank Thomas, Gus Bell, and Gil Hodges didn't have a single hit among them. Meanwhile, Mets pitchers Jay Hook, Clem Labine, and Craig Anderson were pounded for 12 hits.

The Mets came back on Sunday to win, 4–3. Choo Choo Coleman hit the first round tripper in the club's history to score two runs in the eighth. Rod Kanehl, still on the Syracuse roster, had tied the score with a single earlier in the same inning. Richie Ashburn's ninth inning double drove in Elio Chacón with the winning run.

The Mets moved on to Sarasota on March 12 and won their second game in a row, beating the Chicago White Sox, 8–4. Don Zimmer had four hits and two stolen bases, and made a diving stab at third. The following day, at Fort Myers, the Mets extended their winning streak to three games with a victory over the Pittsburgh Pirates. On March 14, George Weiss' first anniversary as president of the Metropolitan Baseball Club, the Mets' winning streak came to an end with a loss to the Dodgers. The Stengel men then proceeded to lose to the Reds, Braves, Phillies, Orioles, and Twins, extending their losing streak to six games.

Prior to the game with the Detroit Tigers on March 21, the City of St. Petersburg feted the Mets with a "Salute to Baseball Day." Casey and his players traveled in a motorcade from Miller Huggins Field to Al Lang Field. The Mets responded to this show of confidence with a 1–0 victory over the Bengals. The Old Perfessor reaction to this victory was short and to the point. "You can't lose them all," he said.[11] Stengel now braced for the long anticipated game on March 22 with the visiting New York Yankees.

The New York Yankees opened their spring training exhibition schedule at Fort Lauderdale on Saturday, March 10, 1962, against the Baltimore Orioles. Among the 7, 342 spectators who witnessed the pre-game festivities inaugurating the new stadium were American League president Joe Cronin and Florida Governor Ferris Bryant. The Orioles were managed by Billy Hitchcock, who had replaced the departed Paul Richards, now the G.M. of the other National League expansion club, the Houston Colt .45s. On August 2, 1960, Hitchcock had been a party to one of the strangest deals in baseball history. On that day, Cleveland Indians GM Frank Lane announced that he had traded manager Joe Gordon to Detroit, in exchange for the Tigers' manager, Jimmy Dykes. Hitchcock served as interim manager for one game against the Yankees at Yankee Stadium, before departing for Detroit to rejoin Gordon.

Hitchcock's lineup against the Yankees at Fort Lauderdale on March 10 included two future Hall of Fame managers (Whitey Herzog and Dick Williams); an all-Greek battery (Milt Pappas and Gus Triandos); and a pitcher (Joe Nuxhall) who had made his major league debut in 1944 at the tender age of 15. The Yankees beat Hitchcock's Orioles, 4–1, the highlight of the game being Mickey Mantle's 440-foot homer, which drove in the game-winning runs. The Yankees went down to Miami the next day and beat the Orioles again before 11,148 fans, one of the largest spring training crowds ever. Roger Maris exited early with a pulled muscle in his left side, the first Yankee casualty of spring training.

The Yankees weren't known for their success in the Grapefruit League, as the spring training exhibition season was called. In 1961, they had a 10–19 record in Florida, winning just three of 12 games at Al Lang Field, their home park at St. Petersburg. But 1962 was different. Having taken two in Miami from the Orioles, the Bombers went on to Pompano Beach and scored a victory over the new Washington Senators (the old Senators were now the Minnesota Twins). Robin Roberts pitched two innings against the Nats, giving up one run. Elston Howard hit two home runs (if only Roberts had received this kind of support from the Philadelphia Phillies).

The Yankees returned to Fort Lauderdale, winning three more games March 13 to 15. Roger Maris was still sitting out with a pulled muscle. Mickey Mantle, meanwhile, was pounding the ball with authority. His 400-foot shot on March 15 won the game over the World Series rival Cincinnati Reds. Robin Roberts' second appearance of the spring was scheduled for March 16 at Fort Myers against the Pittsburgh Pirates. Unfortunately, the game was washed out, as the Yankees ended up making a round trip of 280 miles for nothing. The next day was the St. Patrick's Day Parade in New York. A half million

New Yorkers came out in chilly, blustery weather to cheer on the marchers as they walked the 40-plus blocks from 44th Street to 86th Street. In Fort Lauderdale that morning, Yogi Berra was honored as "Irishman of the Day" at an Emerald Club breakfast. He showed up in the locker room later that day decked in a green coat, green vest, and green hat. "Erin Go Berra!"[12]

Roger Maris returned to the starting lineup on March 17 and contributed a two-run double in a victory over the Dodgers. Two days later he had a double, a triple and three RBIs as the Yankees ran their winning streak to nine games with a victory over Hank Aaron and the Milwaukee Braves. Off the field, Maris' uneasy relationship with the press continued. He was tired of answering questions about whether he could duplicate his feat of 61 home runs in 1962. The writers also continued to speculate as to whether he was really worth his $70,000 salary. Maris had a shouting match in the Yankee dugout with Oscar Fraley of the *United Press International.* Fraley had written a piece in which he claimed that Roger had a "swelled head" and was having a negative effect on team morale.[13] As a result of this row, Maris announced that he would no longer give any interviews to the press. By this time, he had become the favorite target of the boo birds, replacing their perennial target, Mickey Mantle.

On March 20, the Yankees were back in St. Petersburg for the first time since leaving for Fort Lauderdale to play the St. Louis Cardinals. They received a rough reception from the crowd of 6,117 fans—signs were held up calling them "traitors." The Redbirds, under their new manager Johnny Keane (he replaced Solly Hemus the previous July), handed the Bombers their first loss of the Grapefruit League season. Young Jim Bouton was victimized by a bad throw, losing 3–2. The next day the Yankees traveled to Clearwater for a meeting with the Philadelphia Phillies. Starting for the Bombers against his old Philly teammates would be Robin Roberts.

Robin Evan Roberts was born in Springfield, Illinois, on September 30, 1926. The Philadelphia Phillies signed him out of Michigan State in 1948. Two years later, he helped lead the Whiz Kids to the World Series against the mighty New York Yankees. For six years (1950–55), number 36 won twenty or more games. He pitched over 300 innings each of those seasons. His best was 1952 when he finished 28–7, and completed 30 of 37 games. Roberts, a solidly built six-foot, one-inch 190 pounder, was a speedy worker on the mound. He pounded the ball once or twice in his glove, smoothed his pant leg, tugged his cap, and looked for the sign. He was known for always being around the plate, challenging hitters with his fastball. In 1956 he set a major league record by giving up 46 gopher balls.

Americans have always been aware of their ethnic and racial diversity, but 50 years ago greater attention was placed on supposed differences among people of European origin. Roberts was of Welsh background, and a Welshmen was supposed to be stubborn. By the late 1950s, the workhorse was starting to wear out, but he refused to alter his style or adopt a new pitch. He was afraid it would affect his pitching rhythm.

In April 1960, Phils manager Eddie Sawyer quit after the opening game of the season and was replaced by Gene Mauch. The new skipper and the fading star did not see eye to eye. Mauch wanted Roberts to learn a new pitch, but the pitcher still resisted. After a 1–10 record in 1961, the Phillies exposed him to the expansion draft, but he found no takers. Philly owner Bob Carpenter sold him to the Yankees, giving him a new lease on life. At Clearwater on March 21, the Yankees got back on a winning track by downing the Philadelphia Phillies in a 13–10 slugfest. Robin Roberts started for the Bombers but was less than impressive, giving up five hits and four runs to his ex-club. Afterward, the Phillies honored their ex-teammate with a cocktail party at the Causeway Inn. In a ceremony officiated by owner Bob Carpenter, Roberts' uniform number "36" was officially retired. Ralph Houk was among those attending the dinner.

The 9–1 Yankees headed to St. Petersburg once again, this time for their first encounter with their new New York rivals, Casey Stengel's Mets.

"In all my years of baseball I've never been so excited about one game," so said Casey Stengel before the game on March 22 between his old team, the Yankees, and his new team. Casey's recent autobiography left little doubt about the extent of his resentment against Dan Topping. He yearned for redemption against his former club. The Yankees themselves received their old manager fondly, if a little bit awkwardly. Spying the Old Perfessor, Ralph Houk "bolted from the bench as if flung by a catapult" to greet him. Mickey Mantle sidled up shyly to say hello. Stengel, cheered on by the St. Pete crowd, wandered from group to group of Yankee players. "Just hit grounders today," he implored of Mickey and Roger Maris. On seeing Héctor López, Stengel cried out: "Hello, amigo. Got three of them fellers on my team, which is why I now speak your language." Stengel saved some of his best barbs for Yogi Berra. "Mr. B.," he teased, had "slimmed down running to the dog track." Yogi, who had special fondness for the dogs, protested his innocence. He hadn't gone to the dog track all spring. Suddenly, Frank Thomas bounded on Yogi's back. "Who's this Big Donkey that's got me," yelled Berra. Yogi decided to give back some needling. Approaching Don Zimmer, he said, "Hello, Zim. What are you doin' in that crummy uniform?"[14] This, of course, was coming from a man last seen in a green St. Patrick's Day outfit. The player in the "crummy uniform" enjoyed the last laugh. Zimmer went 2–4 with two RBIs, and Richie Ashburn's pinch-hit drove in the winning run in the ninth, as the Mets beat the Yankees, 4–3, in their first meeting ever.

There was one unpleasant moment that afternoon. A *UPI* cameraman asked Roger Maris to pose with Mets coach Rogers Hornsby. Maris refused. Hornsby, a .358 lifetime hitter who held the all-time single season batting average of .424, had been highly critical of Maris during his chase of the Babe's home run mark. Hornsby was quoted as saying that "a no account hitter" like Roger had no business breaking the record. The press heaped all the scorn it could muster on Maris for refusing to pose with Hornsby. He was a "problem child," they said, "not a real man like John Glenn." The venerable *Herald Tribune* columnist Red Smith called Maris' actions "strictly bush." Smith surmised that Roger had "not yet learned to live with fame." He hoped that the Yankee right fielder would learn from this experience and "grow up." Ralph Houk, while diplomatically avoiding criticism of Hornsby, defended his star player. The Major made it emphatically clear that Maris' actions were not a cause of dissension on the Yankee club. Mickey Mantle was less subtle in defending his teammate's gesture toward Hornsby. Said Mickey, "I don't blame Roger one damn bit."[15]

Meanwhile, the victory over their future neighbors seemed to have inspired the Mets. They won two games in a row to match their longest winning streak of the spring. Bill Shea and Joan Payson were in attendance at West Palm Beach on March 24, as the Mets squared their spring record at 7–7 with a victory over the Kansas City Athletics. The Mets streak, however, was cut short as a result of high-scoring losses to the Minnesota Twins and Baltimore Orioles. In the contest with Minnesota, Hobie Landrith became the first Met to be thrown out of a game. The loss to the O's was especially painful, an 18–8 debacle. Jay Hook gave up eight runs and nine hits in the sixth inning alone. The mechanical engineering student from Northwestern left the mound in tears. "I wanted him to get nine innings' worth of work; he got it all in one inning," deadpanned the Old Perfessor.[16]

The Yankees and Mets met again, this time at Fort Lauderdale on March 27. Donald Grant and Joan Payson came down from Hobe Sound to see the Metropolitans get tripped up by the Yankees, 3–2. Ralph Houk penciled in all of his starters into the lineup — evidently, he didn't want to loss to Casey again. At least Casey's Mets didn't embarrass themselves. For seven innings the Yankees' Bill Stafford and the Mets' Roger Craig were locked in a 2–2 pitchers' duel. Al Jackson took over for Craig in the eighth and walked leadoff batter Johnny Blanchard. The Mets were done in by a freak play. Elston Howard hit a seeming double play ball down to Félix Mantilla at shortstop. The ball, however, took an inexplicable bounce over Mantilla's head as Blanchard lumbered to third. The Supersub came in to score the winning run on a 400-foot sacrifice fly by Bill Skowron.

The Mets followed the loss to the Yankees the next day, March 28, with a dramatic 4–3 victory over the Los Angeles Dodgers at Miller Huggins Field. The Stengel men were trailing the Dodgers, 3–1, with Sandy Koufax apparently about to pitch his first complete game of the spring. The mighty Koufax had struck out a record 269 batters the previous year. But now he weakened under the Florida sun, putting Mets on first and second with two outs. Stengel surveyed the Mets' bench for a sacrificial lamb and set his eyes on Rod Kanehl.

Roderick Edwin Kanehl was born in Wichita, Kansas, on April Fools' Day, 1934 and grew up in Springfield, Missouri. He was discovered by Tom Greenwade, the same Yankee scout who had signed Mickey Mantle and Ralph Terry. Rod was not as fortunate as they, spending eight long years in the Yankee chain. His most memorable moment as a Yankee came in the rookie instructional school in 1955, when he dove over the fence for a fly ball. Kanehl finally reached the big club's Triple-A affiliate at Richmond in 1960, but was sent back to Double-A. Inching up on 30, with a wife and four children to support, he was about to quit baseball when fortune finally shone. Rod was drafted by Syracuse of the International League in the winter of 1961; when George Weiss negotiated a working agreement with the club, he became Mets property. Casey apparently remembered Kanehl from his over-the-fence catch at the Yankee instructional school. Rod was one of four Syracuse players invited to camp at St. Petersburg for the Mets' inaugural season.

"You want to win it for me?" asked Casey about facing Koufax. Rod was recovering from the extra-curricular activities of the night before and wasn't expecting to play. Now, suddenly he was up against Koufax, knees shaking, vision blurry. The first pitch whizzed by; he never saw it. From the dugout he could hear the Old Perfessor's raspy growl, "Butcher boy! Butcher boy!"[17] It was Casey's way of telling him to just meet the ball. On the next pitch, "Hot Rod" did just that, delivering a double to right field that tied the game at 3–3. Moments later he came around to score the winning run on a single by Joe Christopher. The game on March 28 against Koufax was the beginning of the legend of Rod Kanhel.

On March 31, for the first time ever, a Mets exhibition game was broadcast on WOR-TV. Stengel started Gil Hodges for the benefit of the New York fans. But Gil, suffering from a leg injury, departed after one inning. It was the newcomer, Rod Kanehl, who shone for the new team. He had three hits in a 2–1 victory over the Philadelphia Phillies. With the roster cuts looming, the versatile Kanehl (he played all infield and outfield positions serviceably, if not well) had put himself in the running for a roster spot with a .400 spring batting average.

The Mets' fortunes began to turn for the better after their victory over the Yankees at St. Petersburg, as they won eight and lost eight to finish their first Grapefruit League season at 11–18. One of the keys to their surge was pitching. The staff, which had combined for 15 wins and three complete games in 1961, had put in a credible performance. Sherman (Roadblock) Jones, Al Jackson, Ray Daviault, Bob Morehead, and Herb Moford were not names to scare anyone, but they had done a creditable job. On the other hand, Jay Hook and $125,000 man Bob Miller were profound disappointments. Roger Craig, the Dodgers' castoff, had emerged as the ace of the Mets' staff and would be the opening day pitcher.

Yet, there were still problems aplenty to be addressed. The infield, with Félix Mantilla winning the starting job over Elio Chacón at shortstop, was not adept at the double play. The outfield of Frank Thomas, Richie Ashburn, and Gus Bell let too many fly balls fall in — a testament to the aging process. Rookie Jim Hickman was a good defensive player, but no one was sure yet whether he could master major league pitching. Meanwhile, the receiving corps remained weak in the offensive department, with Hobie Landrith slated to be the opening day catcher.

On April 7, Stengel and his Mets broke camp. They would debut against the St. Louis Cardinals in St. Louis on April 10.

On March 21, President Kennedy announced that with the formation of two new U.S. Army divisions projected for service in August and September 1962, the 156,000 reservists would be released from active duty at the first possible date. Pending Tony Kubek's return, Ralph Houk had come to a final decision regarding the shortstop position. Tom Tresh received the nod over Phil Linz. "The Ragamuffin," as Linz was called, had actually hit for a higher average than Tresh — .348 to .302 — but Tresh was a switch-hitter and had more power. The two were judged about equal defensively. Both, in any case, had made the team. So had Joe Pepitone, who had been impressive subbing for Mickey Mantle in center field.

The Yankees finished with one of their best Grapefruit League seasons in years, 17–9, including an 11–3 record at Fort Lauderdale. But as spring training came to an end on April 7, Houk faced some unexpected problems with the starting rotation. A viral infection was threatening to affect Whitey Ford's opening day start on April 10. Bill Stafford, who had enjoyed a sparkling spring with a 1.54 ERA in 41 innings of work, was the logical replacement. Houk remained unsure about his fourth starter. Rollie Sheldon, a pleasant surprise as a rookie in 1961, was mired in the sophomore slump. If he continued to falter, Bud Daley or Jim Coates would replace him. Luis Arroyo, recovering from a bout of bronchitis, now had help with the addition of Marshall Bridges. Young Jim Bouton, who had impressed the coaches with his poise and assortment of pitches, was the lone rookie pitcher to make the team. Finally, there were the veterans Bob Turley and Robin Roberts. Neither had been particularly effective that spring. Turley had pitched eight innings, giving up 14 hits. Roberts had surrendered seven runs and 13 hits in nine innings of work; the New York writers gave him only a 50–50 chance of surviving the subsequent cut on May 15. In any event, both men were going north with the club and the season opener at Yankee Stadium.

With the coming of April came the annual predictions. In an informal poll, the New York metropolitan area sportswriters chose the Yankees to repeat as American League champions in 1962. As for the Mets, two writers picked them to finish seventh, four to finish eighth, and four to finish ninth. One writer had the Mets as high as sixth place. The Mets were deemed likely to beat out the Philadelphia Phillies and perhaps the Chicago Cubs in the National League standings. Tenth place was universally accorded to the other expansion club, the Houston Colt .45s. Houston's Paul Richards had never been a match for the Old Perfessor when both were in the American League.

The fact that eight Mets players had failed to hit .200 in spring training might have given the scribes pause. But, after ten pennants and seven world championships, who was going to wager against Casey Stengel with George Weiss supplying new players? One of the true believers was the Mets' centerfielder Richie Ashburn. Gesturing toward Ol' Casey, Whitey turned to a reporter from the *Philadelphia Inquirer*, and said: "Who knows how much that fellow right there will mean to this club?"[17] How many games would the Mets win in 1962 was one of the two major questions vigorously debated by the media and sports fans that spring. The other involved how many homers Roger Maris would hit. The answer on both counts would begin to be revealed later that spring as the Yankees and Mets began their seasons on opposite sides of the Macombs Dam Bridge.

4

"We Hope to Build This Team Bigger Than the Yankees"

On Monday morning, April 9, metropolitan-area readers opened to an advertisement in the city papers. The ad featured one mastermind, two icons, and one mascot, posing together in the lower box seats of the Polo Grounds. Flanking the master mind, George Weiss, were the two icons: Casey Stengel and Kathy Kersh, also known as Miss Rheingold '62. Sitting at Miss Rheingold's feet was the mascot, a dog named Homer. Holding Homer's leash was a dyspeptic-looking Weiss. The ad's caption read: "We're saving a seat for you!" As with their choice of nickname, logo, general manager, field manager, players, and corporate sponsor, the New York Metropolitan Baseball Club invited a return to yesteryear, even as it looked forward to future success. The same dual theme was reflected in the *Mets 1962 Yearbook*. The front cover showed a baby in diapers walking on unsteady legs, wearing a Mets cap; the back cover featured the ravishing Kathy Kersh and the blurb, "My beer is Rheingold, the dry beer."[1] Like Miss Rheingold, who was recast with a fresh face every year, the Mets strived to be young and old, new and traditional, at the same time.

The living, breathing Mets arrived at New York's Idlewild Airport at 7:53 Sunday evening from Portsmouth, Virginia, where their last exhibition game (against the Baltimore Orioles) was rained out. They walked quickly and virtually unnoticed through the arrival corridor. Casey Stengel stopped to sign a few quick autographs and then boarded the chartered bus waiting for the team at the airport. Casey was dropped off at the Essex House, overlooking Central Park. Gil Hodges would, of course, go back to Brooklyn. The rest of the players were bound for the Hotel Manhattan at 76th Street and Broadway. On Monday morning, April 9, the Mets held a workout at the Polo Grounds under grey skies and drizzle. The players took their first look at the "Howard

Clothes" ads in left and right field. Every time a Met hit one of these signs during the season, he would earn one point toward the gift of a $7,000 motor boat. Unfortunately, not everyone would be around to compete for the prize. Needing a utility infielder, Casey "had to fire a fellar for a while."[2] It was outfielder Joe Christopher, who went to Syracuse on 24-hour recall. The remaining Mets were soon aboard a National Airlines plane, flying 875 miles to the west for their opening game against the St. Louis Cardinals.

As Casey Stengel and the Mets were conducting their first workout at the Polo Grounds, Mayor Robert F. Wagner was receiving the New York Yankees at a celebration on the steps of City Hall in Lower Manhattan. A slight crowd of approximately 2,000 spectators watched as the Bombers' 26th pennant was raised over City Hall — the first time the Yankees had been so honored. Dan Topping and Del Webb spoke briefly, and afterward, Wagner introduced the players. The few boos in the crowd were reserved for Roger Maris. Later at a luncheon at Toots Shor's, the Yankees presented Mayor Wagner with a check for $100,000. The money would be used to blacktop a baseball field in Macombs Dam Park. The Yankees would use the space for parking on game days (it would be turned over to the neighborhood kids during road games).

That same day, 500 miles away, the Cleveland Pipers of the fledgling American Basketball Association won the ABL championship with a 106–102 victory over the Kansas City Steers. The star of the game was the Pipers' guard, Dick Barnett. The Pipers' owner was a 31-year-old Cleveland shipbuilder named George Steinbrenner.

The weather in the middle of the country was no better than it was on the East Coast. Rain was in the forecast. On the morning of April 10, the Mets had a late breakfast, and, with outside conditions still discouraging, hung around the hotel lobby reading the papers and trading jokes. There was much cackling over an incident the previous day, in which 17 Mets players had been stuck in the hotel elevator. Hobie Landrith, the five-foot, eight-inch catcher, had his nose pressed against the chest of the six-foot, four-inch pitcher Roger Craig the entire time it took to rescue them. "Hobie Landrith is a player who has to have a roommate," quipped Craig, "because if his room was up on the 22nd floor, he would need a roommate to press that high on the elevator [button]."[3]

At 4:45 P.M. the players and coaches finally left for Busch Stadium. The one-armed man who haunted the ballpark entrance was there to heap abuse on the Metropolitans. Busch Stadium, long known as Sportsman's Park, seated 30,500 customers. There wasn't much parking available, so fans took the street car, or parked further away and finished the trip on buses. Busch Stadium, as might be expected, was the only park in the National League that sold draft beer. It was available in cupfuls for 25 cents. Hot dogs (grilled, not boiled) cost 30 cents. The scoreboard still followed the old custom of posting inning by inning line scores of out-of-town games. These quaint habits, however, would soon be a thing of the past. Plans were underway to replace the 81-year-old structure with a new facility seating 55,000. Like the Flushing Meadows Stadium, it was expected to be ready by 1964. In the meantime, the old, cramped clubhouse would have to do. At 6:15 the players were lounging in their underwear, going over signs, when the announcement came that the game had been called because of rain.

The St. Louis Cardinals, managed by Johnny Keane, had finished in fourth place in the National League in 1961 with a record of 80–74. The team had some solid performers in third baseman Ken Boyer, first baseman Bill White (both Gold Glove winners at their respective positions), second baseman Julián Javier, and center fielder Curt Flood. The Redbirds strengthened their offensive attack during the winter by acquiring outfielder Minnie Miñoso from the Chicago White Sox. The ageless Cuban, better known to Latin American fans as *Orestes Miñoso*, would play right field. In left field was the 41-year-old legend, Stan (the Man) Musial. The starting mound corps featured Larry Jackson, Bob Gibson, Curt Simmons, and Ray Sadecki. In the bullpen was one of the best firemen in the business, right-hander Lindy McDaniel. The Cardinals were well regarded; some pre-season polls had them challenging the Dodgers for the pennant. In truth, they were a good team, but several players away from being truly serious contenders for an National League title. (Future catcher Tim McCarver was toiling at the old Ponce de Leon Park for the Triple-A Atlanta Crackers). For Casey Stengel's Mets, however, the Cardinals proved to be an overwhelming challenge.

On Wednesday, April 11, 1962, the season — and Mets history — finally got under away. Casey picked Roger Craig to start against St. Louis ace Larry Jackson. The Redbirds raked Craig and his successors for 16 hits, winning 11–4. Gil Hodges and Charlie Neal homered for the Stengel men (Gil's was the 362nd of his career, passing Joe DiMaggio for 11th place on the all-time list). Gus Bell made several fine throws from the outfield, but there was also some less than sterling defensive play. The Cardinals stole three bases on Hobie Landrith. On one occasion, Landrith called for a pitchout — and Curt Flood stole second anyway. Stan Musial went three-for-three with two singles, a double and two RBIs. The game was still a close 6–4 in the sixth inning, but an error by Neal opened the floodgates for a four-run rally that clinched it for the home team. The tired Mets left St. Louis on a midnight flight to New York, reaching the Hotel Manhattan at five A.M. They wouldn't be in bed for long.

For the Yankees, Ralph Houk's routine varied very little on game days. On Tuesday, April 10, 1962, he rose at 7:00 A.M. in the ten-room house that he rented on 18 acres in Saddle Brook, New Jersey. Living with him were his wife Bette and sons Dick and Bobby (his daughter, Donna, had married the year before). The Major ate a big breakfast and scanned the morning papers. It had rained overnight, but the weather forecast called for fair, mostly sunny skies, with the temperature in the 60's. By 9:30 A.M., he was dressed and on the road to the Bronx for the 40th opening day at Yankee Stadium — "The House that Ruth built."

For Americans weaned on Roseanne Rosannadanna, Bruce Springsteen, and *The Sopranos*, New Jersey can be seen as seedy, working class, and dangerous — a place from which to escape. Beyond the Meadowlands and the refineries along the New Jersey Turnpike, the picture told a different story. The population of Bergen County, where Saddle River lies, had grown by 40 percent to 750,000 in the ten years since the 1950 census. With people came traffic. Plans were underway for the building of a massive interchange, linking the Garden State Parkway with Interstate Route 80. As Ralph Houk approached the confluence of Routes 4 and 17 he could see stores at Paramus Mall and the Garden State Plaza. Since opening in 1957 on what had been celery fields, the Paramus shopping complex had grown to 125 specialty stores earning $150 million a year, and had become a shopping Mecca for a respectable middle class clientele from New Jersey, neighboring Rockland County, and even New York City. In short, Bergen County was fast becoming one of the richest counties in the United States. It was a place that the Yankee manager and players, along with hundreds of thousands of others, escaped to — not from.

Ralph Houk turned east on Route 4 and headed toward Fort Lee and the George Washington Bridge. The GWB would soon be double-decked, ensuring an even larger influx of population to Bergen County. Paying the 50-cent toll, he crossed over and swung north, joining the growing stream of traffic on the Cross Bronx Expressway. Above him, on both sides of the road, were the ruins of what had once been family-owned businesses and working class and lower middle class neighborhoods. Ahead on the Major Deegan Expressway was the gleaming white pile of Yankee Stadium. Looking across the Harlem River from the Macombs Dam Bridge, the Major could see the outlines of "Coogans's Bluff" and the Polo Grounds, the home of the Yankees' new hometown rivals, the Mets.

The manager's office at Yankee Stadium had been completely refurbished by Dan Topping after Casey Stengel's departure in October 1960. Gone from the walls were Casey's celebrity photos. The office now had a vaguely military look fit for a World War II hero like Ralph Houk. The walls had been painted a tasteful green and wooden paneling added. A modern new desk replaced the battered old roll top that had served Yankee managers since the Stadium

officially opened on April 18, 1923. An aluminum spittoon was placed strate-
gically underneath. Houk sat down in the new green leather swivel chair and
began the day's preparations. He made some phone calls, sorted through mail,
and went over the roster of the Yankees' opening day opponents, the Baltimore
Orioles. While the Old Perfessor was renowned for his prodigious memory,
his mind a compendium of players, situations, and tendencies, the Major had
a different *modus operandi*. He had been recording every pitch thrown by the
opposition since his days as manager at Triple-A Denver. Having dispensed
with the paperwork, Houk met with both the New York area and out-of-town
sportswriters. The Baltimore press might let some information slip that would
be useful later on.

The Baltimore Orioles, nicknamed the "Baby Birds," had challenged the
Yankees for the pennant in 1960, until faltering in a fateful showdown at the
Bronx in mid-September. After finishing a disappointing fourth in 1961, they
revamped their lineup under new manager Billy Hitchcock, who, like Houk,
was an ex–Army major. Joining first baseman Jim Gentile and third baseman
Brooks Robinson in the infield were veteran second baseman Johnny Temple
and shortstop Jerry Adair. Adair had replaced Ron Hansen, who, like Tony
Kubek, was in military service. Gentile had a spectacular year in 1961, hitting
.302 with 46 homers and 141 RBIs (tying him for the league lead with Roger
Maris). Robinson won the Gold Glove at third. Flanking center fielder Jackie
Brandt were two newcomers: right fielder Earl Robinson and an imposing
six-foot, four-inch and 215-pound rookie left fielder, John "Boog" Powell.
An Associated Press poll chose the redheaded Powell as the most promising
new player in the American League. Behind the plate was Gus Triandos, co-
holder with Yogi Berra of the American League record for most home runs
by a catcher in a single season, with 30. Opening day starter for the Orioles was
lefty Billy Hoeft. Hitchcock hoped the southpaw would neutralize the Yankee
left-handed power, while forcing Mickey Mantle to hit right handed into
the cavernous left field power alley. Hitchcock would have preferred to start
another lefty, Steve Barber. But, like Kubek and Hansen, Barber was in the
army.

The opening day crowd started to squeeze through the turnstiles beginning at 11 A.M. The George Suffert Band was on hand to entertain the fans.
At 1:40 P.M., Ralph Houk led the traditional parade to center field and raised
the 1961 pennant flag over the monuments. It had been quite a journey for
Houk: from Lawrence, Kansas, where he was born on April 19, 1919, to hero-
ism in World War II at the Battle of the Bulge ("I had the good fortune to
stay alive," was all that he said).[4] And, from there, to third-string catcher,
minor league skipper, first base coach, and finally manager of the World
Champion Yankees in 1961.

The Major and the players returned to the center of the diamond for additional ceremonies. Roger Maris and Luis Arroyo received their Most Valuable Player and Fireman of the Year awards, respectively. Among the 22,978 spectators watching the awards ceremony were Sal and Rose Marie Durante. Sal, who had caught Roger Maris' 61st home run the previous October, had season tickets courtesy of Maris. There were also a larger number of children in attendance than usual; New York City teachers were on strike. Martha Wright, star of Broadway's *Sound of Music*, sang the National Anthem. Claire Ruth, the Babe's widow, threw out the ceremonial first ball to Elston Howard. The public address announcer, Bob Sheppard, introduced the starting lineups. Tom Tresh would make his debut at shortstop. Héctor López would play left field in place of Yogi Berra. The last sweet notes of the National Anthem were replaced by plate umpire Joe Paparella's harsh bark of "play ball." Ralph Houk settled back against the steel dugout beam nearest the bat rack. The wad of chewing tobacco firmly pressed in his cheek, he assembled his notes and settled in to watch the game through pale blue eyes.

Billy Hitchock's strategy of starting a lefty to neutralize the Yankee power backfired that afternoon. Billy Hoeft was clinging to a 3–2 lead going into the bottom of the fifth, when Bobby Richardson and Tom Tresh hit consecutive singles to start the inning. Roger Maris, with the count 1-and-2, buggy-whipped a Hoeft delivery ten rows deep into the lower right field stands, putting the Yankees ahead. Bill Skowron and Mickey Mantle also took advantage of the "hitter's wind" blowing out from home plate, hitting homers in a 7–6 victory over Baltimore. Skowron's was an inside-the-park home run to the center field wall, 461 feet away.

Whitey Ford started for the Bombers and went six shaky innings, giving up four runs on eight hits before being replaced by winning pitcher Ralph Terry. "Big Ralph" needed help from little Luis Arroyo in the ninth. For Ralph Houk and the Yankees, it was just another day at the office. As the *Herald-Tribune*'s Jerry Izenberg put it, it was "like watching a movie on the late show." You had seen it all before.[5] It took all of two hours and 28 minutes to play. The Yankees departed for a short five-game road trip that would take them to Detroit, Baltimore, and Cleveland. New York now belonged to the Mets.

On Thursday morning, April 12, 1962, the City of New York held its second ticker tape parade in six weeks. This time it was not an astronaut, a general, or a president that was honored. Nor was it the world champion New York Yankees. In fact, the Yankees had never been given an official ride through the Canyon of Heroes. On August 19, 1949, Del Webb, Joe DiMaggio and other members of the Yankee organization rode in a motorcade from the Bowling Green to City Hall, but they were not the center of attention. The crowd of 300,000 was there to honor the longtime Philadelphia Athletics owner-manager, Connie Mack.

No, the honorees on April 12, 1962, were a baseball team that no one in New York had ever seen play, and which to date, owned a pristine record of 0–1. It didn't matter. Casey Stengel was back in town. Starting at 12:05 P.M., a crowd of 40,000 looked on as the 15 convertibles carrying Casey and his New York Mets nosed their way up Broadway. The Old Perfessor sat in the first car alongside Bill Shea. The players, three to a car, dressed in their home pinstriped uniforms, threw out plastic baseballs bearing Stengel's signature. Four big brass bands provided musical accompaniment. Twenty-five minutes later, Mayor Robert Wagner greeted them on the steps of City Hall, calling out the name of each player: "Mr. Bell ... Mr. Craig ... Mr. Hodges ... Mr. Neal ... Mr. Thomas. Afterward, surrounded by reporters, Casey grandly announced: "We hope to build this team bigger than the Yankees."[6]

New York City baseball, as New Yorkers had known it for generations, ended at 4:35 P.M. on a sunny afternoon at the Polo Grounds on September 29, 1957. Frank Thomas, then playing first base for the Pittsburgh Pirates, took a throw from shortstop Dick Groat to retire the New York Giants' Dusty Rhodes for the last out of the game. The ball had yet to reach Thomas' glove when thousands of fans, ignoring public address announcer Jim Gorey's pleas for order, scaled the railings and streamed onto the field. Within seconds, Thomas was running for dear life in the direction of the Polo Grounds clubhouse in dead center field along with his Giant teammates and Pirate players and coaches, as delirious fans stalked after them. From the relative safety of the clubhouse, they watched as the fans pulled up, tore out, and grabbed souvenirs. It would have broken John McGraw's heart.

Frank Thomas was expected to be one of the Mets' prime power hitters. Thomas was born June 11, 1929, in Pittsburgh, Pennsylvania. A Roman Catholic, he considered the priesthood, but chose baseball instead, signing with the Pirates in 1947. The Pirates played him in the outfield, but he also put time in at first and third base. The six-foot, three-inch 205-pound Thomas was the Pirates' most dependable power hitter of the 1950s after the retirement of Ralph Kiner. He set a rookie record by hitting 30 home runs in 1953. He also hit one in the last game at the Polo Grounds in 1957. Thomas hit a career-high 35 home runs in 1958 and might have had more if he hadn't injured his thumb in August of that year. The injury persisted, and Frank began to drift from team to team in the late fifties and early sixties: the Cincinnati Reds, the Chicago Cubs, the Milwaukee Braves, and finally the Mets. The big-eared, crew cut Thomas was known for his boisterous and obstinate character. His nickname, appropriately enough, was the "Big Donkey." One of his favorite pastimes was betting other players $100 that he could

The Mets' home opener took place at the Polo Grounds, against the Pittsburgh Pirates, Friday, April 13, 1962. (Notice the clubhouses in center field.) The Mets lost, of course, their second defeat of the season following an opening day loss at St. Louis on April 11. Said Casey, "We hope to build this team bigger than the Yankees." They would drop 118 more.

catch their hardest throw barehanded at a hundred feet. One of the players he collected from was Willie Mays.

The Polo Grounds had undergone a thorough refurbishing since Frank Thomas and Willie Mays raced to the clubhouse steps on September 29, 1957. The 8th Avenue entrance was awash in the new team's blue and orange colors. Inside, bright green paint covered the expanded box seats section. New telephone booths, washrooms, and ticket booths had been installed. The club had spent $50,000 on a new scoreboard, topped by an ad for Rheingold Beer. The clock above the bleachers in center field was replaced, as was the stadium lighting system, which had been cannibalized by the Giants for their spring training camp in Phoenix, Arizona. A fresh recording of the Star Spangled Banner was introduced. The center field flag now featured 50 stars—Alaska and Hawaii having entered the Union since major league baseball was last played at Coogan's Bluff. In all, the Mets spent $300,000 of Joan Payson's money fixing the Polo Grounds for the home opener on Friday, April 13, 1962. It seemed, in a way, like money poorly spent. The Mets expected to be playing in the new Flushing Meadows Stadium in 1963. In the meantime, tradition had to be served — or, perhaps more accurately, invented.

The centerfield clock showed 1:30 P.M. when Mayor Robert Wagner, flanked by his wife and Blanche McGraw, the widow of John J. McGraw, threw out the ceremonial first pitch. Despite the enthusiasm shown by the crowd the day before in lower Manhattan, the game wasn't a sellout. Only 12,447 fans braved the elements on a drizzly and cold April afternoon. Among those in attendance were the Rheingold Girl, Kathy Kersh, and the immortal Ralph Branca, who had served the pitch to Bobby Thomson — the "shot heard 'round the world"— back in October 1951.

Jim Murphy of Deal, New Jersey, drove the 60 miles from the Jersey Shore to the Polo Grounds to see the Mets. He had witnessed Thomson's famous home run, but since 1957 had been resigned to traveling to Philadelphia to see National League games. Some old fans couldn't quite get the handle on the new team. "I hope the Giants—I mean, the Mets—do real good," said one old Polo Grounds visitor. A fat man with a cigar shouted, "C'mon, you bums, youse." Indeed, it seemed as if much of the crowd on this Friday the 13th was composed of fans who had taken the "D" Train from Brooklyn to see the game. Mets or Dodgers, a natural rivalry was being born. "Nuts to the Yankees. They win all the time," exclaimed Brooklynite John Sterno.[7] Nassau County executive Eugene Nickerson, who had been a Dodger fan, now swore his allegiance to the Mets. The crowd called for Gil Hodges, the most popular Dodger of all, but Gil was unable to play on opening day, slowed by a muscle pull behind his right knee.

While the Mets were getting ready for their trip down the Canyon of Heroes, the chartered jet carrying the Pittsburgh Pirates was coasting to a stop at Idlewild Airport in Queens. Manager Danny Murtaugh and his charges collected their gear and headed up the Van Wyck Expressway to upper Manhattan and the Polo Grounds for what they hoped would be a practice session. When they arrived, they found the place in shambles. The visitors' clubhouse had no functional lockers or showers. The floors were being sanded. The stairs leading from the clubhouse to the playing field were in disrepair. Work tools were everywhere. The Pirates turned around and went back to their hotel. By some miracle, the repair work was completed by the time that Sherman (Roadblock) Jones took the mound on Friday for the Mets' home opener against the Pirates.

Jones' starting assignment had been somewhat problematic. The right-hander had been one of the bright spots in Florida. But a few days earlier, the head of a lit match accidently flew into his left eye. His vision was blurred and he had had to wear a white eye patch as a precaution. Jones, apparently recovered, threw a fastball that Pirates leadoff batter Bill Virdon took for a call strike to start the first Mets home game. Roadblock pitched decently enough — and collected the Mets' first hit at the Polo Grounds, a single in the third. But the non-stop drizzle and soggy turf proved to be his undoing. In the second inning, Charlie Neal made a great stop on a ball hit by Smokey Burgess. But Jim Marshall, Gil Hodges' replacement at first base, was slowed by the mud and unable to reach the bag on time. Burgess subsequently scored on an opposite field double by Don Hoak. Then Bill Mazeroski lifted a fly to right-center field. Richie Ashburn looked like he was about to make the catch, then backed off at the last minute. Right-fielder Gus Bell sloshed through the waterlogged outfield, but too late to make a stab. The ball splashed down for a triple, scoring Hoak. The Mets were behind 2–0 and never caught up. At 4:45 in the afternoon (the stadium lights had been on since the first inning) the first Mets home game was in the record books. The final score was Pittsburgh 4, New York, 3.

On Saturday, April 14, a crowd of 9,231 showed up at the Polo Grounds to witness what they hoped would be the Mets' first home win of the season. Once again, it was Ebbets Field at the Polo Grounds. Gil Hodges earned the biggest cheers, along with Cookie Lavagetto, Don Zimmer and the other ex–Dodgers. Perhaps the crowd cheered just to keep from freezing. The weather was horrible — in the forties with snow flurries throughout. The sky was so dark that the lights were turned on once again from the beginning of the game. But George Weiss was loath to call it quits. The Mets-Pirates game was being telecast nationally on NBC-TV and Weiss didn't want to forfeit the $25,000 telecast fee. The on-field results were less profitable. Lefty Al Jackson, an ex–Pirate, was victimized by a four-run Pittsburgh fourth, and lost 6–2.

The Mets and Pirates returned to a cold, soggy Polo Grounds on April 15 for a Sunday doubleheader. The results of the first game were the same as the previous day. The Corsairs roughed up Roger Craig for a 7–2 victory. The Mets were ahead after two and a half innings of the second game when it was called by the umpires at 6:36 P.M. The weather was actually better than the day before, but since the Stengel men weren't on national TV on Sunday, there was no extra incentive. The Mets remained 0–3.

While the Mets were losing their home opener to the Pittsburgh Pirates at the Polo Grounds, the Yankees were at Tiger Stadium in Detroit on April 13 for the first of two games with the Tigers. Called Briggs Stadium as late as 1960, the Bengals' home field was located two blocks east of the John Lodge Expressway. Although conveniently situated near a major highway artery, Tiger Stadium (capacity 52,904) offered limited parking facilities to drivers. Those lucky few who did find spaces had to make do in small lots and even backyards. It was easier to park further downtown, riding a bus the rest of the way. The more adventuresome made the stroll down Michigan Avenue to the ballpark. Once inside, conditions improved considerably; unlike Yankee Stadium, where poles obstructed the view of the playing area, there were no particularly bad seats at Tiger Stadium. Ushers welcomed tips but didn't demand them as they did in the Bronx. A five-man band waltzed through the stands, playing requests — a throwback to an earlier age. The Tiger fans themselves were knowledgeable about the game, but, as Roger Maris found out, not always well-behaved.

The Bengals, under first-year manager Bob Scheffing, battled the Yankees for most of the 1961 season before yielding ground in September. They had a core of All-Star players. First baseman Norm Cash (.361, 41 homers, 132 RBIs) won the American League batting crown. Leftfielder Rocky Colavito hit .290 with 45 home runs and 140 RBIs. Right fielder Al Kaline was the best all-round player on the club, if not in the league. He posted a .324 batting average (striking out just 42 times in 586 at bats) and won a Gold Glove. The Tigers also boasted an outstanding pitching staff, led by the "Yankee Killer," Frank Lary (23–7). Behind him were Jim Bunning, Don Mossi, and Hank Aguirre.

On April 13, Ralph Houk and his players endured flurries, drizzling rain, and an icy gale in a 5–3 loss to Detroit. The winning pitcher was Lary, who ran his lifetime record against New York to 28–10. The Yankee Killer had to leave the game after he pulled up lame running out a triple in the seventh. The Tigers number two starter, Jim Bunning, a future Hall of Famer, came on to finish off the Yankees.

For Roger Maris, the Yanks' first lost of the season was not only miserable but dangerous. He narrowly avoided a serious injury when a Tiger Stadium fan threw a bottle that brushed his right sleeve. Enraged, Maris picked up the bottle and retired to the dugout. Once there, he exchanged some heated words with umpire Bob Stewart before finally returning to the game. As he ran toward his position in right field, Maris saluted the fans with an obscene gesture. After the game, he was still fuming. "I'm paid to play not to get killed," he snapped.[8] Maris remained unapologetic about his arm-raising gesture to the Tiger Stadium fans. In fact, he wasn't the only Yankee attacked that day. Yogi Berra reported that he had been pelted by shards of glass in left field and Elston Howard complained of being hit by what felt like marbles. But it was the thin-skinned Maris who lost his temper and incurred the wrath of the crowd.

After beating the Tigers the next day, 11–5, the Yankees had two days off before they returned to the diamond at Baltimore from April 17 to 19. Memorial Stadium, the home of the Orioles, was located in a pleasant neighborhood about three miles from the city center. On most occasions, this would mean a 20-minute drive past block after block of Baltimore–style row houses. But with the Yankees in town, drivers were advised to give themselves an extra 15 minutes. Memorial Stadium had a seating capacity of 49, 375. Unlike Yankee Stadium, parking was plentiful — and also cheap. The two large lots next to the ballpark charged just 50 cents a car. Inside the park, the culinary delight was, of course, Maryland crab cake (35 cents). For Roger Maris, who had just endured a trying time in Detroit, Baltimore represented something of a haven from the storm. His ex-teammate on the A's and neighbor from the Kansas City suburbs, Whitey Herzog, played for the Orioles and offered him hospitality whenever the Yankees came into town.

Ralph Houk hated those off-days on the road. The players lost their edge, having nothing to do but watch movies or loll around hotel lobbies. As it turned out, the Major worried for no reason. The Yankees shook off the rust and took two of three games from the Orioles at Memorial Stadium. Their record for the young season stood at 4–2. Ralph Terry already had three victories, including a ten-strikeout, six-hit performance against the O's on April 19. But the Yankee pitching remained an issue for Houk. Whitey Ford had two no-decisions; Bill Stafford, who had a brilliant spring, was winless so far in the regular season. The Major hesitated to use either Bob Turley or Robin Roberts. As for the Yankee hitting, it also ran hot and cold. Mickey Mantle had enjoyed a fast start. Clete Boyer was hitting surprisingly well and Johnny Blanchard was living up to his Super Sub billing. But Roger Maris had done little since his opening game home run. Still, they were the Yankees.

The Stengel men may have gone down to defeat in the borough of Manhattan, but in neighboring Nassau County, they were hailed as conquering heroes. Garden City, New York, was one of the first planned communities in America, the creation of department store pioneer A.T. Stewart in the 1870s. Although his real estate venture in the Hempstead Plains wasn't an immediate success, by the early 1960s, Garden City, with its extravagantly wide streets and large lots, was very much the tony community he had envisioned. As everywhere, of course, change was in the air. Like the celery fields of Paramus, New Jersey, Roosevelt Field was now a sprawling shopping mall anchored by Macy's and other metropolitan chains. The county was negotiating with the Department of Housing, Education, and Welfare, hoping to turn 235 acres of what was Mitchell Field into the campus of Nassau Community College. Despite these changes, Garden City still held to its old glamour, and nothing symbolized it more than the 61-year-old Garden City Hotel.

On Monday evening, April 16, as the Yankees were arriving in Baltimore, Casey Stengel was at the Garden City Hotel for "Adopt the Mets!" night. Joining him for the festivities were Gil Hodges, Don Zimmer, Gus Bell, Frank Thomas, Hobie Landrith, Rod Kanhel, and other Mets players. As Joan Payson, Edna Stengel, and the players' wives looked on, county executive Eugene Nickerson and 700 other guests, paying $10 a plate, greeted New York's newest sports club. Nickerson presided over a carnivalesque adoption ceremony. A dummy, representing the "Brooklyn Bum," was "buried" in a cardboard box. It would be shipped west to Dodgers owner Walter O'Malley. Following the "burial," Terry Rhodes, a three-year-old from Huntington, was brought on stage dressed in an oversized Mets uniform. The past, however, wasn't entirely abandoned — not while the Old Perfessor was still around. Called to speak, Casey rose to the podium. He began by saying, "Beautiful ladies and gentlemen," before rambling on for 15 minutes. His diction may not have been very good, but he did have a shrewd sense of property values on Long Island. "I'm going to build ten houses in Nassau County" he vowed, "if my wife, who bosses the Essex House, will leave me do this."[9]

Having been a smash hit on Long Island, the Mets returned to the Polo Grounds on Tuesday, April 17. Their opponents were their fellow expansion team, the Houston Colt .45s. The Houston club was expected to be easy pickings. Despite their nickname, the Colts, managed by Harry Craft, had very little power in their lineup. On April 17, however, it was the long ball that sent the Mets to their fifth straight defeat — and first extra-inning loss. After Gus Bell had tied the game of 2–2 with a homer in the ninth, a three-run shot by Houston's light-hitting shortstop Don Buddin in the 11th inning boosted the Colts to a 5–2 victory over the Mets.

The Mets ended their homestand with two games against their opening day opponents, the St. Louis Cardinals. The results were again dismal. On April 18, the Redbirds beat up on the Polo Grounders for 18 hits in a 15–5 victory. Starter Sherman Jones pitched more like EZ Pass than Roadblock, yielding six runs on eight hits in the four innings he worked. Frank Thomas and first baseman Ed Bouchee both homered for the locals, but, by the time they did so, the score was already 8–0. The next day the Cards did it again, whipping Casey's team, 9–4. Thomas hit two upper deck shots while Bouchee, playing again in place of the injured Gil Hodges, clouted his second homer in as many days. But it was too little, too late. Stan Musial, meanwhile, went on a hitting rampage, tying Babe Ruth on the all-time list for total bases.

On April 20, an exasperated Casey Stengel put the Mets through their paces at the Polo Grounds. For several hours the Mets practiced running the bases (the club had chalked up at least five base running boners against Houston). One of the culprits was Gil Hodges, caught in a rundown after circling first base on a single. Don Zimmer, perhaps too emboldened by the recent ceremony at Garden City, tried to steal home and was thrown out easily. The hitting, in fact, had not been much better. The veterans acquired by George Weiss were putting up appalling statistics, including Richie Ashburn (.200), Gus Bell (.190), Gil Hodges (.167), and Don Zimmer (.103). Frank Thomas had hit four home runs, but Ed Bouchee's round tripper against St. Louis on April 18 was the first with men on base. Bouchee and Jim Marshall had pushed Hodges momentarily off first base, despite the letters coming to Casey imploring him to play Gil. The Old Perfessor was considering replacing either Zimmer or shortstop Félix Mantilla with Elio Chacón. That, change however, would remain to be seen. The workout over, the Mets crossed the George Washington Bridge into New Jersey and headed for Newark Airport. Casey Stengel and his men were off to Pittsburgh, still in quest of their first victory.

The Yankees returned to the Bronx from Baltimore for a short homestand April 21 to 25 against the Cleveland Indians and Chicago White Sox. Cleveland was managed by the 35-year-old Mel McGaha, starting his first year at the helm. McGaha had a New York connection, having played one season in the nascent National Basketball Association. He was a guard for the 1948–49 New York Knickerbockers. McGaha had his work cut out for him in 1962. The Indians' last victory at Yankee Stadium had come on May 12, 1960. On Friday, April 21, the Yankees ran the Tribe's losing streak in the Bronx to 19 straight, with a 3–1 win. Whitey Ford finally won his first game of the season, with help, of course, from Luis Arroyo. However, McGaha's Indians ended their jinx the next day, with a Sunday doubleheader sweep over the Yankees. New York's early season record dropped to 5–4. Young Jim Bouton made his major league debut in game one, pitching three scoreless innings in a losing cause. In the second game Arroyo was roughed up for six runs on seven hits. The M&M Boys managed one bunt single in 17 at bats during the doubleheader. Roger Maris found the Yankee Stadium fans to be no more charitable than those in Detroit. They showed their displeasure by pelting him with a barrage of Easter eggs, oranges, bananas, and hot dogs.

Maris was understandably angered by the abuse. Mickey Mantle, while escaping the barrage, was in his own way equally as frustrated as Maris. More often than not, the bat was taken out of his hands. American League pitchers had given him 17 free passes in the first nine games. At that rate, he would have fewer than 400 at-bats for the season. The frequency with which Mantle walked pointed up a major difference in playing style between the two major league circuits. American League pitchers were much less likely to challenge big hitters than their counterparts in the senior circuit, as Robin Roberts had done during his heyday with the Philadelphia Phillies. In 1961, Mickey had 514 at-bats and walked 126 times. By contrast, in the National League that year, Hank Aaron had batted 603 times and walked 56 times. If Mantle had the opportunities afforded Aaron or even Willie Mays (585 at bats, 81 walks), it is likely that he — not Maris— would have obliterated Babe Ruth's home run record.

Meanwhile, in the Bronx, the Yankees' miseries continued. The Chicago White Sox, managed by the "Gay Caballero," Al López, were one of the teams expected to challenge the Yankees for the American League pennant. They came into town April 24 and handed the Yankees their third consecutive loss.

The Bombers' record sunk to 5–5. They climbed back over the .500 mark the next day, but with unhappy results for the Ford-Arroyo combination. Whitey chalked up another no-decision, giving up six runs and 11 hits in six innings. Meanwhile, Houk announced that "Little Looie" would be sidelined indefinitely with a strained ligament in his left elbow. The Chicago series also spelled the end for one of the newest Yankees.

Robin Roberts knew that when Ralph Houk called him into his office he was either receiving his first start of the season or was being given his unconditional release. It was the latter. Roberts, with a career record of 234–199, was easily the winnest pitcher on the club. He would have been a multiple Cy Young Award winner had the prize existed during his incredible run between 1950 and 1955. But Ralph Houk had been unable to find work for Roberts, given the quick recovery of Bob Turley from elbow surgery and the fine performance of Jim Bouton. Roberts was given his release well ahead of the roster cutdown date of May 10, said the Major, in order to give him a chance of catching on with another team.

A tearful Roberts walked back across the green carpet to his locker, shrugging out of his uniform and packing his gear under the sympathetic eye of reporters and now former teammates. Bob Turley, who had competed with him for a spot all spring, was the first to shake his hand. Another competitor, rookie Jim Bouton, expressed regret at Robin's leaving. "Even though I knew we were fighting for the same job ... I wanted him to show those batters they couldn't knock him around," said Bouton. He added, "He was a good man."[10] Bouton's use of the past tense was all too appropriate. An unconditional release was the baseball equivalent of a death in the family. Roberts returned to his Meadowbrook, Pennsylvania home, in the Philadelphia suburbs to await a phone call from some club. The pitching poor Mets, however, weren't picking up the phone. "I have spoken with Casey Stengel," said George Weiss, "and he is definitely not interested in Roberts."

Roberts' now former teammates, the 6–5 Yankees, packed up their gear and headed south to the nation's capital to play the Washington Senators. Unlike Casey Stengel's Mets—who one pundit thought would finish as high as sixth—the Nats, an expansion club managed by Mickey Vernon, were everybody's favorite to finish last in their league. Vernon's team played the role of patsies to the hilt, dropping all four games to the Yankees at the new District of Columbia Stadium from April 27 to 29. Thanks to the Senators, the Bombers completed April with a 10–5 record. Ralph Terry ran his record to 4–1. Whitey earned his second victory and Bill Stafford his first. The biggest beneficiary of Washington pitching was Roger Maris. The Yankee slugger came into the series with just one home run and a .152 batting average. He hit three homers and three doubles against the hapless Nats and raised his batting average to .262. Joe Pepitone replaced Maris in right field in the eighth inning of the second game on April 29. With Ralph Houk's blessing, Roger departed early, taking an eight o'clock flight to Kansas City. He hoped to spend some quiet time with his family before rejoining his teammates at Chicago on May 1.

Casey Stengel, a native of Kansas City as the name implies, found fame and fortune in New York City. Gil Hodges, also a Midwesterner, achieved both public acclaim and private happiness in the borough of Brooklyn. For Roger Maris, home was Raytown, Missouri, a suburb of Kansas City, "a damn friendly place" where the mantle of fame and celebrity hung loosely on his shoulders. Here he and his wife Pat were raising their four children. Within a one-mile radius were the homes of some of his former teammates on the Kansas City Athletics, Whitey Herzog, Bill Tuttle, and the man he had been traded for in December 1959, Norm Siebern. His current roommate, reserve outfielder Bob Cerv, also lived nearby. In the off-season, the men would bowl, hunt, golf, and socialize together. Mary Lou Herzog, Lucille Tuttle, Pat Maris, and Liz Siebern bowled every Tuesday. Cosentino Brothers Market became a gathering place for shopping and small talk. For those of us craving the pace and diversity of the New York metropolitan area, it might be difficult to fathom the attraction of small town life; it was the kind of life that drove Thurman Munson, another contrary Midwesterner, to seek a pilot's license so that he could fly home between games. Speaking for Maris and his other player friends, Herzog said, "Don't forget that we are all Midwesterners at heart."[11]

Yet another Midwesterner, Tony Kubek, was yearning to be home. "The rumors say we're getting out in June," said a hopeful Kubek to a *New York Journal American* reporter.[12] While Tony was on maneuvers at Fort Lewis, Washington, sleeping in pup tents and eating K–rations, young Tom Tresh was more than holding his own at the shortstop position. But the real revelation in April was yet another Midwesterner, Clete Boyer. For Yankee fans coming of age in the 1960s, there remains an enduring memory of the Yankee third baseman. In our mind's eye, we can still see him, hurling himself leftward through the air, his shoulder scarcely scraping the ground, before rising on one knee to nip a runner at first.

Cletis Leroy Boyer was born on a farm at Cassville, Missouri (population 350), in the extreme southwestern corner of the state on February 9, 1937. He and his seven brothers all played in the Ban Johnson amateur league that had also spawned Ralph Houk and Ralph Terry. Two of his siblings, Cloyd and Ken (currently starring with the St. Louis Cardinals), preceded him to the major leagues.

Clete was signed as a bonus baby by the Kansas City Athletics in 1955 and traded to the Yankees in one of George Weiss' typical blockbuster deals with that club in 1957. Casey Stengel was intrigued by the younger Boyer's fielding at third base, but didn't have much patience with him at the plate. In the 1960 World Series, Casey humiliated Clete by calling him back for a pinch-hitter before his first appearance at the plate. Boyer's big break with the Yankees had actually occurred during Stengel's absence from the team. In late May of 1960, Casey was felled by a virus infection that sent him to Lenox Hill Hospital for a week. First base coach Ralph Houk took over the team and inserted Clete at third base. With the retirement of Gil McDougald, Boyer became the Yankees' regular third sacker in 1961. He immediately gained notice for his fielding prowess, which would have earned him many a Gold Glove if he hadn't played in the same league as Brooks Robinson. In 1962, tutored by Wally Moses, Clete's hitting began to improve, with results that were astounding. His .429 average in April was second best in the American League and his five round trippers led the Yankees. Whitey Ford teased him by saying, "Hey Clete, why not write a letter to (Ted) Williams and tell him all about how it's done."[13] Of French descent, Boyer's handsome Latin looks would've made him a natural sex symbol in New York's metropolitan area. But he said, "I'm a farm boy ...I don't want the big house in Jersey or Long Island."[14] He, his wife Marilyn Sue, and their daughters, Valerie and Stephanie, lived in the New Jersey suburb of River Edge during the baseball season. But he preferred the open country. His offseason home was Webb City, Missouri, located near Mickey Mantle's motel in Joplin. Due in great part to Boyer's efforts, the Yankees finished the month of April with a 10–5 record, which was good enough for first place in the American League standings, a half game ahead of the second-place White Sox.

The Mets completed the last third of April with road trips to Pittsburgh and Cincinnati, before returning home for the last series of the month against the Philadelphia Phillies. Forbes Field, the home of the Pirates, was located in the Oakland section of Pittsburgh, about three miles east of the downtown area. The ballfield, which seated 35,169, was nestled amidst the trees of Schenley Park and the complex of buildings that made up the University of Pittsburgh. Unlike the Polo Grounds, there were no ads on its ivy-covered outfield walls. A pole obstructed the view down the right field line, and spectators had to beware of the pigeons hiding in the girders on the roof. The specialty of the house was a drink concoction known as lemon blend. Pizza and fish sandwiches were also served. Ushers were capable and, as in Yankee Stadium, expected tips. As in the Bronx, stadium parking was limited and expensive (as much as $5 a car). The fans were advised to take the trolley to home games. And, like the Polo Grounds, Forbes Field's days were numbered. The Pirates were expected to move into a new downtown facility by the mid–1960s.[15]

The Bucs, or Corsairs as they were also known, had slipped to sixth place in 1961 after the fabulous World Championship run the previous year. The hitting had remained robust — Roberto Clemente led the league with a .351 batting average and first baseman Dick Stuart slugged 35 home runs. It was the pitching that had hurt Pittsburgh's chances of repeating. Cy Young Award winner Vernon Law went from 20–9 to 2–3. Bob Friend had slipped from 18–12 to 11–19, Vinegar Bend Mizell from 13–5 to 7–10, and the "Baron of the Bullpen," Elroy Face, from 12–8 to 6–12. In addition, the bench, which had supplied timely hitting in the pennant-winning season, had all but disappeared. Manager Danny Murtaugh (known affectionately as "the Irishman") had slimmed down during the winter of 1961–62. After all, sixth-place managers don't receive too many dinner invitations.

Thus far in the 1962 season, however, results were turning up perfectly for the Pirates. While the Mets were looking for their first win, the Murtaugh men had yet to taste defeat, sporting a perfect 8–0 record. They needed three more victories to break the National League record for consecutive wins at the beginning of a season. The Mets brought them one game closer, dropping an 8–4 decision to the Bucs on April 21. The Polo Grounders collected 13 hits in the loss. Hobie Landrith was hit by the bat of Bob Skinner in the seventh inning and was taken to Presbyterian Hospital, where doctors needed eight stitches to close the wound on his head.

The next day, Easter Sunday, a crowd of bonneted, corsaged, and wind-blown fans saw the Pirates beat the Mets, 4–3. In winning, the Bucs extended their record to 10–0, drawing abreast of the 1955 Brooklyn Dodgers. In losing their tenth in a row, the Mets established a record of their own, tying the 1918 Dodgers and 1919 Boston Braves for most losses at the start of a season. To turn the knife even more, it was Bill Mazeroski who beat the Polo Grounders with a triple in the eighth inning. Thinking back on Maz's dramatic ninth inning homer in the seventh game of the 1960 World Series — which undoubtedly led to his firing by Dan Topping — Stengel groused, "He's been a devil for me."[16]

Finally, on Ladies Night, April 23, the New York Mets won their first game of the season, defeating the Pirates, 9–1. Jay Hook went the distance, pitching a five-hitter and driving in two runs to help his cause. In winning, the Mets prevented the Pirates from setting a new record for victories at the start of a season, and kept themselves from setting a new consecutive loss record.

Casey's hold on the media was amazing to behold. Reporters were gathered at the Mets' clubhouse door before Hook had delivered the final pitch of the game. Once inside the dressing room, the team celebrated as if it were the last game of the World Series — not the first victory of its young career.

Stengel obliged reporters by posing for picture after picture; as he said earlier, it was his face that people came to the ballpark to see. A young Pittsburgh fan, however, put the Mets' situation in perspective. After securing his autograph, he looked up at the old man and said: "Good luck, Case. You're gonna need it."[17]

The Mets' first road trip in their history ended with two games at Cincinnati against the Reds on April 24 and 25. Crosley Field, with a capacity of 30,274, was the smallest ballpark in the National League. Located within walking distance of Union Station and with a new expressway running just a few blocks away, it attracted a large out-of-state, mostly southern crowd. The parking lots had room for 6,000 cars. Cincinnati, known as the Rhineland, still had a large German aura to it in 1962, something which was reflected at the concessions stands. Customers were treated to varieties of German sausages, bratwurst and mettwurst, which could be downed with 16-ounce lemonade. In 1962, Old Crosley was posed tenuously between past and present. The ballpark still had its curious upper incline in the outfield. But a screen had been installed in left field, eliminating the cries of "it's over the laundry" that accompanied home run balls in the past. Like the Polo Grounds, Busch Stadium, and Forbes Field, its days were numbered.

The Reds had been a surprising pennant winner in 1961, losing the World Series in five games to the Yankees that October. Led by manager Fred Hutchinson (known as "the Bear"), they boasted a young and formidable club. Right fielder Frank Robinson drove in 137 runs and was voted the league's Most Valuable Player. Center fielder Vada Pinson batted .343 and was considered second only to Willie Mays at the position. At the corners, first baseman Gordie Coleman and third baseman Gene Freese had both hit 26 home runs. The pitching staff of Joey Jay, Jim O'Toole, and Bob Purkey combined for nearly 60 victories. The bullpen was anchored by "the Professor," Jim Brosnan (his diary of the 1961 season, *Pennant Race*, had just come out in print).

The National League was so balanced that the Reds weren't favored to repeat as pennant winners. The Reds' chances, in fact, had suffered a severe blow when Freese broke his leg sliding into second in an early spring training game. Weakened though they were, the Cincinnati Reds had little trouble with the visiting New York Mets, beating them twice in a row. Craig Anderson and Bob Miller were the losing pitchers.

The Mets ended the month of April at the Polo Grounds. On April 27, they lost to the Philadelphia Phillies, 11–9, their 12th defeat of the young season. Two passed balls, a wild pitch, and at least two mental errors that did not find their way into the official statistics, contributed to the defeat. Don Zimmer, 0-for-31, had tried everything to get out of the slump—changing bats, changing stances. With two out in the ninth Zim came up with the tying run at the plate. He promptly struck out.

The next day the Mets beat the Phils, 8–6, with a five homer barrage, two by Charlie Neal. In spite of the victory, there was the usual share of mishaps. In the second inning, Philly starter Jim Owens hit a slow roller between first base and the mound. Bob Miller bobbled it, chased it down, bobbled it again, and finally nudged the ball five feet with his glove to Gil Hodges for the out, as the crowd cheered.

The Tony Awards dinner and ceremony was held on Sunday, April 29, at the Waldorf Astoria Hotel, with over 1,000 guests in attendance. *How to Succeed in Business Without Really Trying* was recognized as best musical, and its star, Robert Morse, who had shared the spotlight with Casey Stengel in the Thanksgiving Day parade the previous November, was cited as best actor in a musical. Earlier that day, at Coogan's Bluff, the Mets were trying — and modestly succeeding — in a Sunday doubleheader against the Phillies. The Polo Grounders won the first game, their second consecutive victory, 8–0, over the Phils. Al Jackson threw the first shutout in Mets history, helped along by a seven-run fourth inning. Frank Thomas and Jim Hickman both hit home runs. But the Stengel men soon returned to form, dropping the second game, 10–2.

The Mets' woes weren't confined to the baseball diamond. A couple of weeks earlier, an advertisement had run in the New York dailies showing the Old Perfessor demonstrating his bunting technique, with Miss Rheingold, Kathy Kersh, looking on while holding a baseball. At their feet were several cans of Rheingold beer framed by the Mets' logo. Ford Frick announced that Stengel had been fined $500 for "violation of baseball rules which prohibit men in uniform from posing for alcoholic beverage ads."[18] Still, the commissioner might have shown a little compassion. With a 3–13 record, who could blame Casey for wanting a beer to drown his sorrows?

For those that wanted to believe, there was a silver lining: the Mets had won two out of their last three games in April. Was it the beginning of a surge by the Polo Grounders? Was it the confirmation of the Old Perfessor's reputation as a baseball genius? As the first full month of play would show, the answer, unfortunately, was no. After stirring hopes in the hearts of New Yorkers for the first three weeks of May, the Stengel men would fall into an abyss from which they never recovered. In its own way, the month of May would prove to be just as painful for the Yankees as it was for the Mets.

5

"The Real Magic Number"

Fifty years ago, a subway series between the Yankees and Mets was more of a whimsical slogan than a viable idea. America was firmly attached to the automobile and the blacktop. Few fans coming from New Jersey ever ventured beyond Yankee Stadium's 161st Street and River Avenue address to Bronx County and the art deco apartment houses that lined the Grand Concourse. The Bronx had its wonders, but not for fans who witnessed mostly the desolation caused by Robert Moses' building of the Cross Bronx Expressway. Recognizing the driving preferences of their clientele, Yankee owners Dan Topping and Del Webb had three weeks earlier deposited $100,000 in the New York City Hall coffers. In exchange for their "gift," the city would blacktop the public baseball diamond in Macombs Dam Park, creating additional parking for Yankee home games. It was much less than Mayor Wagner had done for the Mets with the Flushing Meadows Stadium project. The locals, however, were outraged by this action and rose up in protest. Although the area would be empty when the Yanks were on the road, the protesters refused to be swayed. Representatives of 20 neighborhood organizations, including 75 children and their parents, planned to picket the Stadium in the first week of May.

As for the Mets, for the moment at least they had one foot planted in the Jet Age, but the other one out. At 4:00 P.M., Friday, May 4, 1962, Lou Niss was at Pennsylvania Railroad Station puffing nervously on a cigarette as he waited for the New York Mets' baggage trucks to arrive from the Polo Grounds. Niss, 58, was a former editor of the *Brooklyn Eagle*. Two years earlier, he had been hired as publicity director for the New York entry in Branch Rickey and Bill Shea's ill-fated Continental League. When Joan Whitney Payson bought its National League successor, the Metropolitan Baseball Club, Niss stayed on at the 680 Fifth Avenue offices. In October 1961, George Weiss hired former Yankee assistant Tom Meany to handle publicity. Niss became the Mets' traveling secretary, which explained his presence at Penn Station that Friday afternoon.

The Stengel men's recent surge had seen a healthy rise in their batting averages. Hobie Landrith, Jim Marshall, Ed Bouchee, Charlie Neal, Gil Hodges, and Félix Mantilla were all hitting over .300. But elsewhere, trouble abounded. Shortstop Elio Chacón (.182) and right fielder Gus Bell (.154) were in dreadful slumps. Mantilla had taken over at third base for Don Zimmer, who had a microscopic .068 batting average (3-for-44). Defensively, the team was young and uncertain on the left side of the infield, old and plodding in the outfield, and weak in catching. Jim Hickman had replaced Richie Ashburn in center, with Whitey no longer displaying the range he once had during his heyday at Philadelphia. The pitching staff, meanwhile, had surrendered 11.5 hits, 2.5 walks, and 1.3 homers per game. Roger Craig, Al Jackson, Jay Hook, and company pitched to a collective ERA of 6.30, while registering just two complete games. Exasperated, the Old Perfessor dispensed advice ranging from the practical to the nonsensical. He told Yale graduate Ken McKenzie: "Pretend you're pitching against Harvard."[1] If only it were so! The Mets *did* have a better record than the last-place Washington Senators in the American League. Unfortunately for Casey, he was no longer managing in the American League.

The state of the team, however, did nothing to damper the enthusiasm with which New Yorkers and the baseball world in general greeted Stengel's return. As Les Biederman of the *Pittsburgh Press* put it, the "real magic number" wasn't Roger Maris' 61 homers but rather Casey's uniform number of "37."[2] On May 1, three days prior to the departure for Philadelphia, Stengel was honored as "Salesman of the Year" by a group of Madison Avenue executives. Casey accepted the award, but took issue with the "Madmen's" choice. The real winners, he insisted, should've been the snake-oil salesman known as the National League owners. "They only made four mistakes," said the Old Perfessor, meaning only four of his players were worth the $75,000 draft price.[3] Charlie Neal, presumably, was one of the four. There was a rumor that George Weiss was trying to trade Neal to the San Francisco Giants for first baseman Willie McCovey.

Unfortunately, Casey Stengel's magic with the public didn't translate to the baseball diamond. He left Madison Avenue for Coogan's Bluff, where his Mets dropped an 8–2 decision that night to the Cincinnati Reds. The rest of the Cincinnati series was rained out. So on Friday, May 4, the Mets assembled at Pennsylvania Station, decked out in their new blazers with the Mets' logo sewed in over the left side pocket. After what seemed like an eternity, the trucks lumbered in from the Polo Grounds carrying 98 pieces of baggage, 50 suitcases, five equipment trunks, and 43 duffel bags. Lou Niss breathed a sigh of relief. Off to Philly they went.

The Yankees were in first place, just a half game ahead of Chicago, as they prepared to square off with the White Sox at Comiskey Park on the first of May. The Old Comiskey was no one's idea of a long ball hitter's ballpark. Yet, in one of those anomalies of baseball, Roger Maris had hit 13 of his 61 home runs on the White Sox's home field, his largest number at any visiting park. Mindful of Maris' pull-swinging tendencies, Chisox manager Al López devised a strategy formerly reserved in the American League for Ted Williams: placing three fielders on the right side of the infield and challenging Maris to hit the ball to left.

The "Go Go White Sox" had relied on speed and defense to win the American League pennant in 1959 (the Yankees finished third that year). After the World Series loss to the Dodgers, Chicago owner Bill Veeck decided to convert the Chisox into a power-hitting club. The results were minimal. Veeck had sold his interest in the club to Arthur Allyn, Jr., in 1962, and the new regime had begun shedding its aging stars.

Only four starters remained from the 1959 pennant-winning team: Nellie Fox, Luis Aparicio, Al Smith, and Jim Landis. Newcomers Floyd Robinson (.441) and Joe Cunningham (.351) were hitting at a fearsome clip. Robinson, with 22 RBIs, and Landis, with five home runs, were both among the league leaders. Neither Maris nor Mantle had cracked the top list in either category. The White Sox's young hurlers, Juan Pizarro and Joel Horlen, showed promise. Also around was 23-year veteran Early Wynn, who was creeping up on 300 career wins.

Casey Stengel was fired by the Yankees at least in part due to the unorthodox use of his pitching staff in the 1960 World Series. Conventional wisdom dictated that Stengel should've pitched Whitey Ford in the opening game of the series against the Pirates, rather than relying on the considerably less talented Art Ditmar. But another counterfactual argument could be made with regard to the 1960 World Series: if the Old Perfessor had turned to young Bill Stafford instead of Bob Turley in the seventh and final game at Forbes Field, Bill Mazeroski's dramatic home run might not have ever happened. Stafford was just four days past his 21st birthday when he made his major league debut on August 17, 1960. He would go on to post a 3–1 record with a sparkling 2.25 ERA. Stafford's debut was such a pleasant surprise that Casey mulled over the idea of starting him in the seventh game against the Pirates, before settling on Turley, the former Cy Young Award winner who had struggled since his banner 1958 season.

William Charles Stafford was born in the tiny hamlet of Catskill, New York (population 500), and grew up in nearby Athens. But he refused to be intimidated by life in the big city. In 1961, the six-foot, two inch, 190-pound Stafford settled in as the number three starter behind Whitey Ford and Ralph Terry, posting a 14–9 record. He finished second in the American League in

ERA (2.68) to the Senators' Dick Donovan and then pitched the third game of the World Series against the Reds. Stafford was known for his coolness on the mound, a trait he inherited from his father, a semi-pro pitcher in Athens. "My dad," Stafford remembered, "always told me that you've got to ...look and act like you're the best pitcher in the world."[4] And so he did. Stafford walked briskly to and from the mound, arms straight at his sides, shoulders square. His teammates teased him about his walk — a cross between a strut and a waddle — but there was no question of their respect for his poise and command of his pitches.

After a terrific 1962 spring training, Bill Stafford got off to a slow start. His fortunes were about to change in the Windy City. On May 1, Stafford had little difficulty with the revamped White Sox lineup. He had a no-hitter going after five innings, but pulled a muscle swinging at a pitch from Juan Pizarro in the damp, cold weather, and had to leave the game. Rollie Sheldon took over and continued to no-hit the "Pale Hose" until Nellie Fox finally broke the spell with a bloop single in the ninth. The Yankees cruised to a 6–1 victory and Stafford evened his record at 2–2.

The New Yorkers split their last two games at Comiskey, remaining a game and a half in front of second-place Chicago as they jetted back to New York to host the Washington Senators on May 5 and 6. Due to rain outs and the open dates that dotted the early schedule, Ralph Houk had been able to get by with just three starters— Ford, Terry, and Stafford. As the Yankees entered their first full month of play, however, a fourth starter was needed. Houk decided to see what his young pitchers could do. Sophomore Rollie Sheldon, who had been terrible that spring after going 11–5 in 1961, would pitch Saturday, May 5. The rookie, Jim Bouton, a resident of Ridgewood, New Jersey, would take the mound in the second game of the doubleheader on Sunday, following Ralph Terry. The Major informed Bouton of his first major league start while still in Chicago. That way, Houk teased, he would have time to invite all of his friends and relatives from New Jersey. Bouton fired back: "Maybe you're using me to build up the gate."[5]

Running a baseball club has always entailed more than just player salaries. The New York Mets spent approximately $200,000 on travel expenses in their maiden season. Of this total, $30,000 went for meals (the players' union, led by Robin Roberts and Harvey Kuenn, had negotiated a $10-a-day allotment two years earlier at the winter meetings in Miami Beach). Hotel accommodations cost another $30,000. The biggest outlay of all was for transportation expenses ($130,000). Most of the time, jet travel was the norm. On May 4, however, the journey from Penn Station in New York to Penn Station in Philadelphia was something like the good old days before California baseball. The Mets' train rolled out of its cement cavern and into the New Jersey meadowlands, arriving in Philly at 5:30 P.M., barely an hour after leaving New York. Their duffel bags were sent to the Warwick Hotel; the rest of the equipment went on to Connie Mack Stadium in time for the 8:00 P.M. game.

That night, the Mets lost to the Phillies, 6–5. The only bright light was Don Zimmer. Back in the lineup at third base, Zip Zimmer doubled against winner Dallas Green, breaking his 0-for-34 hitting drought. The Mets then continued their losing ways. On Saturday, May 5 they were beaten by righty Cal McLish. An Oklahoman who claimed Choctaw heritage, McLish was known as much for his elaborate moniker as for his pitching: Calvin Coolidge Julius Caesar Tuskahoma McLish. The multi-named McLish out-dueled Al Jackson, 2–1.

The Stengel men finally ended up on the winning side on Sunday, pounding out a 7–5 extra-inning victory. Two of the most popular Mets combined for the victory: with the bases loaded and one out in the top of the 12th, Gil Hodges singled in Rod Kanehl with what proved to be the winning run.

As the Mets were beating the Phils, George Weiss was finalizing a series of deals. He traded Zimmer to Cincinnati for third baseman Cliff Cook and pitcher Bob Miller. The Mets now had two Bob Millers on their pitching staff: Robert Gerald, the righty, and Robert Lane, the lefty. Jim Marshall, who had knocked in a run in the victory over the Phillies, was sent to Pittsburgh for veteran lefty Vinegar Bend Mizell.

The Mets' road show continued westward. Casey Stengel and company made the United Airlines DC-7 flight from Philadelphia to Chicago with oil leaking from the number two engine. Not that it mattered much to Frank Thomas. While his teammates were reading, dozing, or playing cards, the Big Donkey put on an apron and proceeded to serve dinner to the 43 passengers on board. Stewardess Pat Skinner was quite impressed, calling Thomas "a very nice man who knows exactly what he's doing." His teammates weren't nearly so impressed, but nothing deterred Thomas from his self-imposed duties. Up the rows of the airplane he went, asking sweetly, "Milk, coffee, or soda?"[6] George Weiss, who was also on the flight, had more pressing decisions to make. Whom should he cut to get to the 25-player limit: Rod Kanehl or John Demerit?

There would be no night games against the Chicago Cubs. Wrigley Field, the home of the Bruins, the only major league club with no lights. The ballpark, however, had been subject to a $600,000 renovation before the start of the 1960 season. New seats were installed and the entrances redesigned. From the players' point of view, the most telling change was the new, more spacious locker room — one of the small victories scored by the players' union in the battle against the owners. Remaining untouched by the renovation was Wrigley's brick-faced outfield wall, with its signature ivy. Also unaffected by the changes was the undershirt crowd atop of the four-story buildings over-looking the outfield. Most people weren't so strategically placed — the park was about ten miles from the Loop. Fans left their cars six to eight blocks away and took public transportation to Wrigley. Once inside, the moving belt speed walks took them from street level to the grandstand and upper deck.

In addition to not having lights, the Cubs didn't have a manager either. Owner Phil Wrigley, who two years earlier swapped Cubs manager Charlie Grimm with TV-radio announcer Lou Boudreau, had initiated another move worthy of Bill Veeck. The Bruins were presently led by a rotating "college of coaches," who took turns running the team. The "faculty" consisted of Elvin Tappe, Charlie Metro, and Lou Klein, the current "head coach." This raised the question: if the Cubs won the pennant, which coach would be named Manager of the Year? So far, the question was strictly hypothetical. The Cubs had lost three more games than the Mets (Chicago had won two more) and were just a half game ahead of the New Yorkers in the standings. The Cubs had a solid core of sluggers: first baseman Ernie Banks and outfielders George Altman and Billy Williams. Youngsters like third baseman Ron Santo, second baseman Ken Hubbs, and outfielder Lou Brock showed great promise. But the team was poor in the field, slow on the bases, and short of front line pitch-ing. If the Mets were to turn their season around, and escape from last place to ninth, Wrigley Field was the place to begin.

Casey Stengel chose Jay Hook to pitch the opening game against the Cubs on May 8. James Wesley Hook was born November 18, 1936, at Waukegan, Illinois, a city on the western end of Lake Michigan, about 40 miles north of Chicago. A scholar-athlete in the true sense, Hook was a grad-uate of Westlake High School in Chicago and Northwestern University. He was currently working on a masters' degree in engineering and was on the NASA mailing list. Hook broke into the majors with the Cincinnati Reds in 1957, his first victory coming at the expense of the Chicago Cubs. The six-foot, two-inch, 180-pound Hook had his best season in 1960, when he posted an 11–18 record with a second-division club. Injuries kept him from figuring prominently in the Reds' pennant-winning drive in 1961. His only victory was at the expense of the Cubs.

Jay Hook's winning streak against his hometown team continued. Pitch-ing on a cold, chilly day in Chicago, he beat the Bruins, 3–1. Hook gave up only four hits in running his record to 2–1. A leaping catch by Gus Bell in right, and two diving stops by Gil Hodges at first helped Hook to a complete game victory. It was the Mets' second win in a row. The trip, however, proved to be an expensive one for the Polo Grounders. Only 1,369 fans braved the elements to attend the game at Wrigley Field on May 8. As a result of the poor turnout, and two subsequent cancellations due to inclement weather, the

Mets' visiting club check came to a measly $400. The club spent that much in one day on meals alone. Canceling games due to bad weather was nothing new in baseball. But the National League's expansion to ten teams in 1962 had resulted in an earlier start to the season and a greater likelihood of postponements. But then again, as David Condon pointed out in the *Chicago Tribune*, the Mets were "only nominally in the baseball business." They were really in "the television industry." Casey Stengel, according to Condon, had "enabled the fledgling organization to sell its television rights for a ransom relatively the size of a Congressional appropriation."[7]

Casey Stengel was a huge draw, no doubt, the very symbol of baseball's colorful past, a welcome antidote to the diffident Roger Maris. But if Maris was a "marked man" in 1962, so was Stengel. During his 12 years as Yankee manager, the Old Perfessor had burnished the reputation of being something of a baseball genius. For many pundits as well as fans, the Mets' fortunes depended upon the septuagenarian's formidable baseball IQ. He was expected to literally pull tricks out of his hat, turning a ragtag bunch of castoffs and rookies into a respectable club. So far, the results were modest. With their victory at Chicago, the Mets were now .007 percentage points out of the cellar, having handed that distinction to the hapless Cubs. No one was more pleased by this turn of events than the Old Perfessor himself. "Fix your ties fellows," growled Casey, "we're going back in 9th place."[8]

Well, not everyone was going back to New York. Roadblock Jones, the opening day pitcher at the Polo Grounds on April 13, and French Canadian reliever Ray Daviault were shipped to Syracuse. There was also a new arrival on the scene. On May 9, George Weiss swung a deal with the Baltimore Orioles, acquiring first baseman Marv Throneberry for a player to be named later.

With Casey and the Mets traveling in the Midwest, the Yankees again had New York to themselves. They celebrated their return to the Bronx on May 5 with a 7–6 victory over the Washington Senators. Yogi Berra and Joe Pepitone both homered in a five-run eighth, sending the Nats spiraling to their 15th loss in 18 games. The Yankees had now won eight of their last nine games, strengthening their hold on first place in the American League. Bob Turley made his first appearance of the season, hurling a scoreless eighth to get the win. Pepitone's home run was almost nullified by another Yankee rookie. Phil Linz who was on first base at the time, forgot to touch second as he rounded the bag. He realized his mistake and recovered just in time to avert embarrassment. Later, the Ragamuffin quipped, "[I] just felt I had to do something to get my name in the papers again."[9]

On May 6, the Yankees split a Sunday doubleheader with the Senators, dropping the first game, 4–2, and winning 8–0 in the second. Ralph Terry was the loser in game one, despite a tremendous drive by Mantle that landed in the 32nd row of the right-centerfield bleachers. In game two, Jim Bouton won his first major league game, tossing the first Yankee shutout of the season. Bouton gave up seven hits and seven walks among his 136 pitches. However, he didn't allow a runner past second base until the ninth. Three double plays and three fine catches by Héctor López helped keep him out of a jam. Roger Maris and Mickey Mantle both homered in the first inning to get things started. Mantle homered again in

Jim Bouton was the only rookie on the Yankees' pitching staff in 1962. On May 6, 1962, Bouton won his first major league game, shutting out the Washington Senators, 8–0. He threw 136 pitches, giving up seven hits and seven walks in going the distance. The game took 2:34 to play. Afterward, in the clubhouse, Mickey Mantle laid a trail of white towels ending at Bouton's locker.

the seventh inning, giving him three round trippers on the day.

Jim Bouton's seven-hit, seven-walk shutout performance took 2:34 to play. Afterward, Bouton received the red, or rather white carpet treatment. Seeing the rookie being interviewed on television outside of the clubhouse, Mickey Mantle ordered John Blanchard to watch the door. "Keep him out," he barked. Mickey then proceeded to lay a path of white towels running from the clubhouse door to Bouton's locker. "Wait a minute!" hissed Whitey Ford. He snatched Luis Arroyo's Fireman of the Year trophy and set it down on the towel nearest Bouton's dressing area. When the rookie finally entered the clubhouse, there was Mantle standing by his locker, beaming widely. It was, Bouton later recalled, the most thrilling moment of his baseball career.[10]

After an exhibition game at West Point against Army on Monday, May 7, the Yankees returned to the Bronx for two games against the Boston Red Sox. Due to rain, they played only one. On Wednesday, May 9, the Bombers beat Boston, 4–1. The Red Sox's Bill Monbouquette held the Yankees hitless for six innings. In the seventh, a three-run double by Elston Howard settled the contest, sending Monbo to the showers. Whitey Ford won his third game against one loss. The game, which took just 1:41 to play, was the shortest of the season thus far. It could've ended in just 1:35, but with two outs, Tom Tresh, Joe Pepitone, and Ford got their signals crossed, and let an infield pop by Jim Pagliaroni fall in for a single. The league-leading Yankees now left for the Midwest and a four-game encounter with the Cleveland Indians.

"WE LOVE THE METS!
ROD KANEHL"

So read the first banner put up at a Mets game at the Polo Grounds in the spring of 1962. Kanehl and the rest of the ninth-place Mets came back to Coogan's Bluff May 11 to 13 for a four-game series against the Milwaukee Braves. Things started poorly for the Stengel men on May 11, Marv Throneberry's debut as a Met. An 8–5 loss to the Braves put an end to New York's modest two-game winning streak. Suddenly, the Mets caught fire. On Saturday, May 12, they beat Milwaukee twice for their first doubleheader win ever. In the first contest, the Mets were trailing, 2–1, going into the ninth against the Braves' ace, Warren Spahn. With two out and Rod Kanehl on first, Hobie Landrith hit the second serving from Spahn into the upper deck for a 3–2 victory. Game two was tied at 7–7 in the bottom of the ninth when Gil Hodges stepped up to the plate. Gil parked a Hank Fischer pitch into the upper deck in right field, as the 19,748 fans roared their approval. Craig Anderson, who relieved in each game, ended up winning both ends of the doubleheader. The Mets then fell back to earth, losing the last game of the series, 3–2, despite a six-hit complete game from Jay Hook (2–2). With that loss, the Mets had gone full circle. They were once again in last place.

Last-place teams are rarely popular. So the Mets pulled all the stops to lure skeptical fans to the Polo Grounds. They invented tradition, with their hybrid uniforms, logo, corporate sponsor, and charismatic manager. But the club also wanted to remind potential fans of greater days in Queens. The *Mets Official 1962 Yearbook* celebrated Casey Stengel, Gil Hodges, and Miss Rheingold, but it also included an aerial view of their future home in Flushing Meadows. The copy read: "Vehicular traffic will travel over a new $110,000 complex of widened parkways with quick, easy access to forty-five acres of parking lots."[11] It was enough to make Dan Topping and Del Webb gag. The

Mets' new home in Queens was, in fact, slowly taking shape. The sandy, swampy construction area at the old Willets Point Park was strewn with pipes, beams, shell piles, and concrete litter. Amid the apparent chaos, the dimensions of the Flushing Meadows Stadium were slowly coming into view. When completed, the new ballpark would be bound on the north by Northern Boulevard, on the south by Roosevelt Avenue, and to the east by 136th Street. The Grand Central Parkway passed the field at an angle, running southwest and northeast. In a year, the Mets would bid good bye to the Polo Grounds. Meanwhile, the Chicago Cubs, managed by their current head coach, Lou Klein, were coming into town to defend their ninth-place position in the standings against the tenth-place Mets.

In the opening game of the series on May 15, Hobie Landrith, who had homered to beat Warren Spahn, played the hero once again. It wasn't a home run that did it this time. Hobie took four pitches for a bases loaded walk that bumped the Polo Grounders back in ninth place. Roger Craig, the star-crossed "ace," earned the win in relief. The Mets did it again on May 16, another 6–5 extra-inning victory over the Bruins. This time, the winning run was produced by a bases loaded single from the bat of Félix Mantilla in the 11th inning. Earlier, Gil Hodges had tied the game in the eighth with a 455-foot inside the park home run—courtesy of the Cubs' shoddy defense. Left fielder Lou Brock made two swipes at the ball before fielding it and then overthrew the cutoff man. Second baseman Ken Hubbs committed the final blunder when his relay throw sailed away from home plate, allowing Hodges to score. Asked later what he was thinking when third base coach Solly Hemus waved him home, Gil replied, "Think? By then I couldn't even see."[12]

The Mets were making a genius of Casey Stengel. Winners of six of their last eight games, the Polo Grounders were in a buoyant mood as they began a fateful 12-game western swing that would take them to Milwaukee, Houston, Los Angeles, and San Francisco.

With a capacity of 73,811, Cleveland's Municipal Stadium was the largest ballpark in the American League. Fronting Lake Erie, it was located about one half mile from Public Square, the hub of Cleveland's downtown. The Stadium could accommodate about 8,000 cars, but with the post–World War II dominance of the automobile, it was not quite enough. Many fans parked downtown and took shuttle buses the rest of the way. Once inside, patrons were treated to live musical entertainment; a three-piece band performed at all home games. The concession stands offered pizza and fish sandwiches. Even more pleasant were the pregame dinner parties held by companies and fraternity groups in the grassy area beyond the outfield. In May 1962, the Indians' fans had something else to feast over. Their team was in the thick of the early pennant race, having pushed past the White Sox into second place, one and a half games behind the league-leading Yankees. They would face the visiting league leaders in a four-game series May 11 to 13.

Like the Chicago White Sox, the Cleveland Indians had taken on a new look between 1959 and 1961. Their mercurial former G.M., Frank Lane, known as "Trader Lane," had unloaded a host of untried players, including Roger Maris and Norm Cash, as well as established stars like Minnie Minoso and Rocky Colavito. Lane's swap of the popular Colavito, the American League's home run champ in 1959, for that year's batting champion, Harvey Kuenn, was considered a capital crime by many Cleveland fans.

In 1962, the revamped team, managed by first-year skipper Mel McGaha, was mostly middle distance hitters, such as shortstop Woodie Held, catcher John Romano, and first baseman Tito Francona. The frontline pitching had great potential with Jim Perry, Barry Latman, Gary Bell and veteran Dick Donovan, the ERA leader in 1961 with the lowly Senators. Another potential star, Jim (Mudcat) Grant, was currently on furlough from military service at Fort Belvoir, Virginia. The Tribe, behind the pitching of Grant and Donovan, and the hitting of Held, Francona and the lightly-regarded Jerry Kindall, dealt the Bombers three losses in four games. The Yankees arrived on Lake Erie in first place; they departed a half game behind the now front-running Cleveland Indians.

The combination of jet travel and expansion had altered the pattern and pace of the major league season. As late as 1960, the New York Yankees alternated trips along the eastern seaboard to Boston, Baltimore, and Washington, with westward journeys to Cleveland, Detroit, Chicago, and Kansas City. Instead of continuing west from Cleveland, Ralph Houk's men flew east to Boston to play the Red Sox. On May 15 at Fenway Park, the Red Sox handed the Yankees their third consecutive loss, a 14–4 pounding. Sophomore sensation Carl Yastremzski, Ted Williams' heir apparent in left field, collected four hits, including a home run and three RBIs. The Yankees recovered to win the remaining two games of the series and returned to New York tied for first with Cleveland at identical 18–11 records. There was one piece of bad news, however: Roger Maris pulled a thigh muscle and was out indefinitely. More bad news was on the way.

The idiosyncratic scheduling created by expansion and coast to coast travel was tiring for everyone involved, from Casey Stengel, to the players, to the harried Lou Niss. It was especially rankling for veteran players. In the days when both the Dodgers and Giants still played in New York City, Gil Hodges, a Brooklyn resident, slept in his own bed nearly 100 out of 154 games.

But bad as it was, Jim Hickman would not trade it for life in the minor leagues. James Lucius Hickman was born on May 10, 1937, in Henning, Tennessee, a suburb of Memphis. The six-foot, four-inch 200-pound Hickman was signed by the St. Louis Cardinals out of Ripley High School in 1956. Then his travels began. In the next six years he toiled at Albany, Georgia; Winston-Salem, North Carolina; Billings, Montana; Tulsa, Oklahoma; and Portland, Oregon. "Travel? You'll take anything after the minors," Hickman exclaimed.[13] Picked up from the Cardinals in the National League expansion draft the previous October, he had never hit .300 in the minors, and his previous year's average (.250) didn't warrant much respect. He was, however, a good fielder and thrower — no mean commodity on a club with aging picket men like Richie Ashburn and Gus Bell. By the beginning of May, Hickman had dislodged Ashburn from his center field position. He also surprised Casey Stengel with his power hitting, and was currently second on the club in home runs. Hickman's leadoff homer in the first inning of the second game of a doubleheader at the Polo Grounds on May 12, against the Braves' Carlton Willey, had powered the Mets to their first doubleheader sweep.

On May 18, Jim Hickman and the Mets began a four-game series against the Braves at Milwaukee. Located four miles from the downtown area, the Braves' home field, County Stadium, had a capacity of 44,276. Unlike Yankee Stadium or the Polo Grounds, it was an automobile commuter's dream. There were 11,000 parking spaces; it cost just 25 cents to park. Once inside, patrons were treated to the "best grandstand eating in baseball: "bratwurst, hot corned beef, cheeseburgers, and two kinds of hotdogs, with, of course, enough beer to wash it all down. Milwaukee was known for beer and plenty of it was available at the stadium. Braves owner Lou Perini had installed a picnic area between third base and left field, called, in these politically incorrect days, the "Braves Reservation."

Still, for all its amenities, the Braves were no longer drawing the huge crowds. The Braves had enjoyed enormous success — both artistic and financial — since moving from Boston to Milwaukee in 1954. They had taken the World Series from the Yankees in 1957 and were leading 3–1 in the 1958 October Classic. They then dropped three games in a row, losing the series to the Bombers, the last world championship victory for Casey Stengel. The Braves came close again in 1959, losing a one-game playoff to the Dodgers. They finished second again in 1960, but fell to fourth in 1961. The club, managed by Birdie Tebbets, was still formidable with sluggers such as Hank Aaron, Eddie Mathews, and Joe Adcock, and a supporting cast that include two top flight catchers, the veteran Del Crandall and young Joe Torre. A *Sports Illustrated* article described young Torre as "a good-looking, thick-chested twenty-year-old Latin ... a burly matinee idol."[14] The pitching staff was led by Warren Spahn, who was nobody's idea of a matinee idol, just the winninest lefty in baseball history.

Warren Spahn took revenge on the Mets for his loss at the Polo Grounds on May 12 by taming the visitors, 5–2. Joe Torre replaced Del Crandall behind the plate and caught Spahn's 313th career win. Spahnnie gave up just three hits, two of which were homers by Gil Hodges and Frank Thomas. The Polo Grounders came back to win the next day, 6–5, as Frank Thomas hit his tenth home run. To the delight of Casey Stengel, the Mets repeated their perform-ance of May 12, by sweeping the Braves once again on May 20. Thomas hit home run number 11 in game two. The club was now in eighth place, one and a half games ahead of Houston, and two and a half over Chicago in the National League standings.

When the Mets left Milwaukee, one player stayed behind. Gus Bell was dealt to the Braves as part of the completion of the Frank Thomas deal the previous winter. Gus had fond memories of the Polo Grounds, where years earlier, as a member of the Cincinnati Reds, he had broken up the Sal Maglie's consecutive innings scoreless streak for the Giants. He had hoped to duplicate the old glory, but it was not to be. A .149 batting average with one homer and six RBIs—and the emergence of Jim Hickman—had spelled his fate. While Bell was getting acquainted with his new club, his ex–Mets teammates were on the way to Houston, Texas, in what would be the turning point of their season.

How many home runs would Roger Maris hit in 1962? That was one of the major questions that dominated discussion in the Hot Stove League that winter. So far, the much anticipated repeat of the home run 1961 derby between Roger Maris and Mickey Mantle had failed to materialize. Detroit's Al Kaline and Los Angeles' Leon Wagner were currently the league leaders with ten homers each. Mantle, however, was enjoying one of his best starts. Going into the weekend series in the Bronx with the Minnesota Twins, he was hitting .326 with seven home runs, the best on the club. He had scored 25 runs on 28 hits. He was happy, relaxed, and healthy. Nearly two years ear-lier, at the conclusion of a Memorial Day doubleheader at the Stadium, he had been mauled by fans as he exited the field. Overheated boys—and fully grown men—clawed at his glove and pulled at his cap, nearly gouging his eye. But since his feat of 61 home runs, it was Roger Maris who excited this kind of love-hate attention. He was the "marked man." The Mick was set free from the overblown expectations of fans and the press alike. People suddenly marveled at his sense of humor. He was like a schoolboy on the last day of school before summer vacation. But at 10:23 P.M. on Friday, May 18, 1962, Mickey's wonderful spring came to an end. His powerful, but fragile body failed him once again.

With two outs in the bottom of the ninth inning, and the Yankees trailing the Twins, 4–3, Mantle hit a sharp grounder to deep short. He bolted out of the batter's box and ran full tilt toward first. Looking out of the corner of his eye, he noticed that shortstop Zoilo Versalles was having trouble handling the ball. With the Yankees fighting for the league lead against Cleveland, everyone was giving full effort; he put on an extra burst of speed in an effort to beat the throw. Suddenly, five steps away from the bag, Mickey's right leg buckled — sending him tumbling to the infield, his left knee absorbing the shock. He writhed in pain, as Ralph Houk and anxious Yankee teammates hovered over him. He refused a stretcher, limping off the field in the arms of his teammates. The putout at first ended the game and sent the Yankees tumbling into third place behind the Indians and Twins. But that was the least of the club's worries at the moment.

On Saturday night, May 19, President John F. Kennedy was the principal speaker at a Democratic Party fund-raising rally at Madison Square Garden, coinciding with his 45th birthday celebration. Gathered at the Eighth Avenue venue were some of the most renowned stars of the entertainment world: Jack Benny, Harry Belafonte, Henry Fonda, Ella Fitzgerald, Maria Callas, Jerome Robbins, Bobby Darin, Jimmy Durante, and the comedy team of Mike Nichols and Elaine May. As heavy rains pounded the New York pavement, the President sat in a box on the 50th Street side of the old Garden, puffing on a cigar, enjoying the show. The highlight of the evening was provided by Marilyn Monroe. Arriving late, dressed in a glittering white gown that hinted at her obvious assets, the bombshell shimmied to the microphone and purred the song, "Happy Birthday," to the President. Later, beginning his address, Kennedy remarked, "I can now retire from politics after having had Happy Birthday sung to me in such a sweet and wholesome way."[15]

As Marilyn Monroe sang for the President on the east side of Manhattan, another brittle blond was resting comfortably in his room at Lenox Hill Hospital. Mickey Mantle, according to team physician Dr. Sidney Gaynor, had suffered a "reasonably severe" tear of the adductor muscle in his upper right thigh. X-rays of his knee — the trick knee first injured in a freak play during the 1951 World Series — thankfully showed only a bruise. Dr. Gaynor estimated that Mantle would be lost to the Yankees for a period of two to four weeks. Ralph Houk made the necessary adjustments. Roger Maris would play center field against left-handed pitching. Rookie Joe Pepitone would take over center against righties, with Maris returning to his normal position in right-field. With this makeshift lineup, the Bombers went on to win two of the three remaining games of the series with the Twins, regaining their first-place tie with the Cleveland Indians.

As a result of scheduling that defied common sense — even in an age of cheap fuel — the Yankees flew to Los Angeles on May 21 for a single game against the Angels. As Ralph Houk and company were jetting across the continent, a recent teammate had found employment once again. Robin Roberts, released by the Yankees on April 26, signed with the Baltimore Orioles for $30,000 — less than half of what George Weiss paid for most of his expansion draftees. Nearly a month earlier, Jimmy Cannon of the *Journal American* had virtually written Roberts' obituary, calling him a "proudly obstinate man" who refused to recognize the inevitable.[16] The Welsh stubbornness was about to be rewarded at last. Robin pitched two perfect innings in a 10–7 loss to Cleveland. With the win, the Indians took over first place once again, a half game in front of the sky-bound Yankees.

On May 20, as the Yankees were cursing their bad luck over the injury to Mickey Mantle, Casey Stengel and his Amazin' Mets were celebrating their good fortune. They had left Milwaukee in eighth place in the National League standings, having won five of their last six games. This is where the majority of media observers and their fellow major league ballplayers expected them to finish. But suddenly, in the midst of all this optimism, the Mets hit a wall. The first omen of what was to be a disastrous season manifested itself as the team left Milwaukee for Houston to play a two-game series against the Colt .45s. The flight from the Midwest was delayed two hours. Once in the air, the plane was detoured to Dallas due to heavy fog over Houston. The team finally arrived at their destination at 8 A.M. on May 21.

That night, the exhausted New Yorkers dropped a 3–2 decision to the Colt .45s. That ended the Stengel men's three-game winning streak, dropping them to ninth behind the Colts. The game of May 22 brought more of the same. Jay Hook was one out from finishing the eighth inning in a 1–1 game. But singles by Billy Goodman and Román Mejías, and a triple by Norm Larker sealed the Mets' fate. At least the Stengel men were still out of the cellar, with four fewer losses than the Chicago Cubs, as they headed for their first trip to the West Coast.

If Roger Maris was a "marked man" with Mickey Mantle batting behind him, life would be even worse without Mantle in the lineup. Pitchers gave Maris very little to hit. In the lone game against the Angels at Los Angeles on May 22, he was walked five times, four times intentionally for a major league record. Mantle wasn't the only key Yankee player to go down with an injury. The Bombers put Luis Arroyo on the 30-day disabled list with an inflammation of the tendons over the left elbow. If the loss of the team's best batter and bullpen stopper wasn't enough, the Angels' game would produce yet another casualty. On May 22, four Yankee pitchers— Whitey Ford, Jim Coates, Bud Daley, and Bob Turley —combined for a one-hitter in a 2–1 victory over the Angels in 12 innings. Whitey left after the seventh inning with pain in the back of the left shoulder, the result of an unbalanced throw in the fourth.

Ralph Houk and company retraced their journey, flying east to New York to open a series against the Kansas City Athletics on May 23. The lowly A's provided a much needed tonic for a bruised and tired club. The Yankees won a 13–7 slugfest on May 23, a game that Mickey Mantle watched from his room at Lenox Hill Hospital. Rookie Joe Pepitone hit two home runs in an eight-run eighth inning. Rookie Phil Linz, subbing for Clete Boyer, hit the first round tripper of his career. On May 24, Pepitone homered again in a 9–4 rout of Kansas City. The Bombers had five wins in six games since Mantle's injury, regaining their lead (by one game) over Cleveland in the standings. But the injuries continued to pile up. Boyer, hit on the left wrist by a pitch, was out indefinitely.

The Mets' next stop on their western road trip was Los Angeles. Walter O'Malley, unable to reach an agreement with the City of New York for a new stadium, had moved the Dodgers from Brooklyn in 1958. After four years of purgatory playing in the Los Angeles Coliseum, O'Malley finally had his dream park in Chavez Ravine. The $18 million Dodger Stadium was already being touted as the Taj Mahal of major league ballparks. The four-tiered structure, made of reinforced concrete, accommodated 56,000 people. The parking lot had room for 25,000 cars. Four terraced parking levels easily transported fans from the parking decks to their seats. The most expensive seats, located at the dugout and Stadium Club levels, cost $5.50. The restaurant atop the grandstand provided a panoramic view of City Hall and beyond it, the San Gabriel Mountains.

The Dodgers' recent home, the Los Angeles Coliseum, was a lopsided structure, part major league park and part minor league field. Its most bizarre feature was the 254-foot screen in left and a veritable Death Valley in right. Dodger Stadium, by contrast, was laid out in symmetrical fashion: 330 feet down the lines, 380 feet in the power alleys, and 410 feet to dead center field.

The Dodgers of Brooklyn fame were now mostly a memory. Duke Snider, the only slugger of yore still with the team, was now strictly a part time performer. The club had finished second in 1961, four games behind the Cincinnati Reds, with a squad composed of mostly younger players. Shortstop Maury Wills and centerfielder Willie Davis provided speed on the bases. The six-foot, seven-inch, 250-pound right fielder, Frank Howard, and Brooklyn native Tommy Davis provided the power. But, more than anything else, it was the formidable pitching staff—consisting of Don Drysdale, Sandy Koufax, Johnny Podres, Ron Perranoski, and Larry Sherry—which led many experts to pick the Dodgers for the National League pennant in 1962.

The biggest gripe among major league players in 1962 was the crazy-quilt schedule. The scheduling of games after getaway dates was especially resented—and the Mets had more of them than any other team. As the Yankees were flying eastward from Los Angeles to New York on May 23, the Stengel men were headed westward for a 5:45 A.M. arrival at Los Angeles Airport.

The Yankees, at least, faced a second-division Kansas City team. The Mets were less fortunate. That night at Chavez Ravine, Roger Craig lost, 3–1, to ex-teammate Don Drysdale. The next day, May 24, the Mets lost, 4–2, and dropped to tenth place. There was nothing close about the last game of the series at Dodger Stadium. The home team crushed the Polo Grounders, 17–8. It was the highest score compiled by the Dodgers since leaving Ebbets Field in 1957.

After absorbing two more defeats by the Dodgers, the Mets headed north to San Francisco to face Willie Mays and the Giants in their first visit to Candlestick Park. They dropped all three games to the Giants May 26 to 27. The first game of a doubleheader on May 27 proved to be the most memorable game of the Mets-Giants series. In the seventh inning, with Mays on first, Roger Craig hit Orlando Cepeda with a pitch. An angry Cepeda started toward the mound, and then thought better of it. Play resumed. Craig then tried to pick off Mays at second. As the Giants' centerfielder was sliding back into the bag, he nicked Mets shortstop Elio Chacón with his spikes. Chacón, enraged, took a swing at Mays. Willie, making like a professional wrestler, picked Elio up bodily and flung him to the ground. Meanwhile, Cepeda, inspired by these events, decided to go after Craig, swinging wildly as he was being tackled by Giants manager Al Dark. When order was finally restored, Elio was kicked out of the game. The rest of the Mets had to stay to the bitter end.

The debacle finally complete the Mets arrived at New York at 6 A.M. on May 28 — with an eight-game losing streak and dead last placement in the National League. For Casey Stengel, the road trip had started as a demonstration of his "managerial genius." It had ended in disaster.

Having said goodbye to the Kansas City Athletics, the Yankees ended their short homestand by hosting the Detroit Tigers May 25 to 27. They lost the series opener, 5–4 as Bill Stafford was undone by the least likely of Bengal bangers. Chico Fernández and Dick McAuliffe cuffed him for home runs. The crowd of 32, 267 saw the Yanks drop back into a first-place tie with Cleveland. The next day, May 26, the Bombers lost again, dropping a 2–1 decision to Hank Aguirre. It was a pyrrhic victory for the Tigers. On the last play of the game, Al Kaline, the Tigers' splendid right fielder, broke his collar making a diving catch of a sinking line drive by Elston Howard. Al skidded on his right shoulder and did a somersault, incurring a longitudinal fracture of the right collar bone. He walked off the field under his own power, but then fainted in the clubhouse from the intense pain. He was taken to Lenox Hill, where he was x-rayed, and a diagnosis made by the Yankee team physician, Dr. Sidney Gaynor. Kaline, one of the league leaders in home runs, would be out at least two months. Detroit, three games behind the league-leading Yankees and Indians, would never recover from the blow.

Al Kaline's unfortunate injury was the subject of conversation during the next day's doubleheader between the Yankees and Tigers. As if whistling through a graveyard, Roger Maris wondered out loud if Al's splendid right throwing arm would ever be the same. "It shows," said Maris, "you have to be lucky to survive in this game." The atmosphere at the Stadium wasn't entirely grim, however. Before the doubleheader, Jim Coates, Bud Daley, and Marshall Bridges placed bets on the size of the crowd. Bridges said 50,000. Coates said less than 50,000 less, and Daley said 50,000 plus. It was not a good bet for Bridges. Out at the batting cage, Whitey Ford yelled out to rookie Jim Bouton, "Hey Jim. Why do you waste your time trying to hit? You're in our way. You should be back in the clubhouse doing crossword puzzles or something."[17] No one said anything about writing a diary.

"There's no reason for the crowds at Yankee Stadium to rush downtown for their fun after the game," said new Bronx borough president Joseph F. Periconi.[18] After all, there were the Bronx Zoo, the Botanical Gardens, and the newest attraction, Freedomland. Shaped like the continental United States, Freedomland was a 205-acre amusement park located in the Baychester section, at the juncture of the New England and the Henry Hutchinson parkways. Today, this area is dominated by Co-op City, but in 1961, 1.7 million visitors had thrilled to the rides, like the cable car trip, and listened to jazz concerts in the 500-seat outside arena. While Freedomland geared up for what figured to be even bigger crowds in 1962, the Yankees left town on May 27 to finish the month in the Midwest.

Kansas City didn't prove to be as inviting as usual. On May 29, Jim Bouton lost his first major league game, 2–1 to the A's. Moving on to the Twin Cities, Yankees played one of those infamous day-night doubleheaders that were the bane of the modern ballplayer. The day began for the Yankees at 11 A.M. local time, and concluded with the second game at 8 P.M. A combined crowd of 75,355 fans watched the New Yorkers split the marathon with the Twins. Afterward, the Yankees took a flight to Los Angeles for the beginning of their June schedule. As they were flying westward to Los Angeles on May 31, Robin Roberts was making his first start for the Baltimore Orioles against the Cleveland Indians. Robin gave up just three hits in five innings. But in the sixth, Tito Francona's two-run triple propelled the Tribe to a 4–3 victory, giving the Indians sole possession of first place. The Yankees, wounded warriors that they were, ended the month one game out, still without the services of their best player and clubhouse leader, Mickey Mantle.

On the last two days of May, the New York Mets welcomed the Los Angeles Dodgers to the Polo Grounds, their first appearance at Coogan's Bluff since September 8, 1957. From early morning, May 30, the Macombs Dam Bridge and other spans and streets leading to the Polo Grounds were groaning with the weight of cars trying to capture the few parking spaces available. The sub-way trains, meanwhile, opened their doors, expelling the eager fans like orange crates at a farmers' market. The fans, many of them making the trek from Brooklyn, began gathering at the stadium entrance on Eighth Avenue at 7 A.M. The gates were mercifully opened at 9:10 A.M., easing the crush of human-ity and vehicular traffic on the jammed streets outside the Polo Grounds. For latecomers, there wasn't much prospect of getting inside. The bleacher seats were sold out an hour and a half before game time.

According to Julie Adler, the Mets' promotions director, the Mets had been preparing for this moment since the previous November. But the actual turnout went beyond anyone's greatest expectations. The 56,637 fans filled every nook and cranny of the old horseshoe, with standees planting them-selves five and six deep behind the grandstand. The fans clogged the ramps beyond the bleachers in right field. Tradition was being reinvented that after-noon; the spirit of the old Dodgers was everywhere. Ralph Branca, the victim of Bobby Thomson's famous home run, threw batting practice. Ralph Kiner came down from the broadcast booth to introduce all of the players, stretched out between home and third. Dodgers manager Walt Alston was booed, as was Leo Durocher, the former Giants manager of the 1950s, now coaching under Alston. The biggest cheers were reserved for the last player to be intro-duced: the longtime Dodgers center fielder, Duke Snider.

The Dodgers' visit to the Polo Grounds, the *New York Herald Tribune*'s Jerry Izenberg's predicted, would be "equal parts sentiment and money and a large dose of impending misery."[19] And, so it was. The festivities over, the Dodgers ran the Mets' losing streak to 11 games. On Wednesday, May 30, the Dodgers swept a doubleheader. They took the single game on Memorial Day, 6–3. Maury Wills, the base stealer par excellence, showed unexpected muscle by hitting two home runs in the first game of the doubleheader. Wills also figured in the Mets' first ever triple play. In the sixth inning of the second game on May 30, Willie Davis hit a line drive to shortstop Elio Chacón. The Venezuelan flipped to Charlie Neal to double up Wills; Neal then threw to Gil Hodges at first to erase Jim Gilliam to complete the hat trick. Hodges gave the fans something else to cheer. With his home run in the first game, Gil tied Kiner for tenth on the all-time list with 369.

Vin Scully, the Dodgers' red-headed, wry-witted announcer was pleas-antly surprised when a bleacher bum at the Polo Grounders shouted out his name. Then he heard: "Hey, Scully, who the hell needs you. Gwan back to Los Angeles."[20] George Weiss would have disagreed. The first day crowd of 55,704 was the largest in the major leagues so far. The total gate for the three-game series between the Dodgers and Mets was 155, 879. There was something to be said for reinventing tradition.

And so the month of May ended for the New York clubs, rivals from across the Macombs Dam Bridge. Casey Stengel, the erstwhile "managerial genius," so anxious to prove himself after his firing by Dan Topping two years earlier, had been unable to summon the acumen that had resulted in ten pennants and seven World Series championships between 1949 and 1960. For Stengel, redemption would come, not from on-the-field victories, but from the unaccountable devotion bestowed by the Polo Grounds' fans on his lovably hapless Mets.

The bungling Mets would continue to lose spectacularly, all the while basking in the glow of their sublime ineptness. For the Yankees, the rest of the season would be a long and painful slog toward another pennant. There would be no Maris-Mantle home run derby. It was Stengel's Mets, not Maris' Yankees, that tugged at the hearts of New Yorkers in 1962. The world, or at least its baseball equivalent, was being turned upside down.

Part II: A World Turned Upside Down

6

"How Long Can This Go On?"

At mid-morning on Friday, June 1, 1962, Willie Mays stepped out of the penumbra of the center field clubhouse at the Polo Grounds and walked down the steps into the sunshine of Coogan's Bluff. At the first sighting of the "Say Hey Kid," the bleacher fans erupted in cheers. Mays acknowledged the crowd and then sauntered forward to greet the reporters and camera men, mingling together in center field. As Willie fielded questions from reporters, 400 feet away the Mets were taking batting practice. Suddenly, a drive by Charlie Neal rocketed toward the group, threatening to decapitate an unsuspecting scribe. Willie, without uttering a word of warning, stepped deftly around the reporter and speared the ball.

In his younger days on the Giants, Willie — just a grown-up kid himself — often played stickball with the local boys on the streets of Harlem. But that was then; he was now, at $90,000 a year, the best paid player in the game. Mays' day began with a visit to his lawyer (he had been divorced earlier in the year), and then he strolled for a haircut from old pal Joe Walker at his barbershop on 155th Street. Willie admitted to being a little nervous about his return to the Polo Grounds; the tension had been growing ever since the Giants left Philadelphia. When it was San Francisco's turn at batting practice, the nervousness showed; he bunted the first pitch foul. Mays gradually loosened up. He parked the fifth pitch in the upper deck in left field. He hit the seventh offering clear over the roof in left-center field. Willie had already taken his fielding practice — and scored Good Samaritan points.

The game that Mays played with so much ease came less naturally to the members of the New York Metropolitan Club. The Mets had not won a game since beating the Milwaukee Braves at County Stadium on May 20. The Mets could hit a bit. Hobie Landrith (.353), Richie Ashburn (.350), Frank Thomas (.322) and Gil Hodges (.312) all topped the .300 mark. But with the exception of Thomas, none was an everyday performer. Hodges was still hobbled by a knee injury incurred that spring. But more than the hitting, it was poor pitching, leaky defense, and atrocious base running that plagued the Mets. The accumulation of these sins was reflected in the pitching records: Roger Craig (2–7), Al Jackson (2–6), Jay Hook (3–5) and Craig Anderson (3–4). Furthermore, the Stengel men had not won a game at the Polo Grounds since their extra inning victory over the Chicago Cubs on May 16.

The league-leading San Francisco Giants, on the other hand, were a formidable assemblage of power, speed, and pitching, as reflected by their 35–15 record. First baseman Orlando Cepeda (.350) was pacing the National League in hitting. Outfielder Felipe Alou (.331) and slick fielding third baseman Jim Davenport (.319) were among the league leaders. Cepeda led the league in RBIs with 49 and Mays led in home runs with 16. Also on hand were former American League batting champion Harvey Kuenn, slugging catcher Ed Bailey, and the hulking outfielder-first baseman, Willie McCovey, supposedly coveted by George Weiss. The Giants mound corps presented the Mets' hitters with a daunting array of talent: Jack Sanford, Billy O'Dell, Billy Pierce, and the young Dominican, Juan Marichal. Stu Miller, an All-Star the previous year, was in the bullpen. If there was a weakness in the lineup, it was at second base, where young Chuck Hiller held forth. But the much talked about trade that would send Charlie Neal to San Francisco for the disgruntled McCovey had yet to materialize.

During the opening game of the series on Friday, a fan ran into the Mets' dugout and had to be evicted by security. Who knows, maybe Casey should've given him a tryout. The Mets absorbed a 9–6 pounding from the Giants, their 12th consecutive defeat. Willie McCovey had two home runs and three RBIs against loser Roger Craig. Willie Mays, wearing a protective helmet this season for the first time in his career (under orders from manager Al Dark), blasted his 17th round tripper, adding to his National League lead. The big blow, however, came from the bat of Jim Davenport. His grand slam highlighted a five-run seventh inning. The winning pitcher was veteran left hander Billy Pierce. A native of Detroit, Michigan, Pierce had last pitched at the Polo Grounds in the annual *Esquire* Scholastic East-West Game in 1944. Pierce's catcher on the West team that year was a Tilden, Nebraska, native named Richie Ashburn. Returning to the Polo Grounds after 18 years, Pierce retired Ashburn in his only plate appearance, but surrendered Rod Kanehl's first major league home run.

Before the first game of Saturday's doubleheader on June 2, Mets announcer Ralph Kiner introduced the visiting players. Willie Mays was the last to emerge from the Giants' dugout, and, of course, received the biggest applause. Besides Willie, the only other current Giants players with ties to the Polo Grounds were pitchers Mike McCormick and Stu Miller, neither of whom had been stars at the time. More familiar to the fans were Giants manager Al Dark and coaches Whitey Lockman, Larry Jansen, and Wes Westrum. The introductions over, Dark and company saddled the Mets with their 13th consecutive defeat, 10–1. As the Mets headed for the center field clubhouse to change for the second game, the public address system followed their progress with strains of *Aida*'s triumphal march. If this was intended to inspire the Mets, it clearly failed. In the second game, Stengel and company went down to their 14th straight loss, 6–4, despite out-hitting the mighty Giants, 12–8 (one of those hits was Willie May's 18th home run). The Mets' ineptness in the field seemed to be contagious. Mays allowed a Richie Ashburn grounder to go through his legs for an error.

On June 3, the Sunday crowd of 34,102 fans witnessed a 6–1 Giants victory and the Mets' 15th consecutive loss. Willie Mays, greeted by a chorus of boos in his first at-bat, had the fans on their feet cheering with his 19th homer off lefty Bob Miller in the sixth. The crushing blow, however, was Miller's bases loaded walk to rival pitcher Juan Marichal in the seventh inning. The neighborhood around the Polo Grounds, once populated by European immigrants, was now largely Spanish-speaking. The Dominican dandy and his compatriots, Felipe and brother Matty Alou, were delighted with the Spanish language billboards in Nueva York (*cerveza fresca*—fresh beer). The Dominicans had plenty of reason to raise a glass after the game. Marichal notched his eighth victory and eighth complete game, the latter equaling the entire output of the Mets' staff. The Mets' only consolation was at the box office. Total attendance for the weekend series with the Giants was 118, 845. The Mets management showed its appreciation by taking out a quarter page ad in the New York dailies expressing their "love" for the fans. The ad read: "Never in sports history has there been such a heart-warming demonstration of loyalty and affection as we have received from the Met fan ... Our fans have shown that they love us and we love them." Standing amidst the lengthening shadows of Coogan's Bluff, the Old Perfessor marveled at the Mets' fans gluttony for punishment. "How long," he muttered, "can this go on?"[1]

While the San Francisco Giants were carving out a two and a half game lead over the Los Angeles Dodgers, courtesy of the Mets, on the other side of the continent the Yankees were at Chavez Ravine, becoming acquainted with Dodger Stadium, the new home of the Los Angeles Angels. The Angels, it seems, were the model for George Weiss' New York Mets. General Manager Fred Hamey had constructed a team composed of veteran sluggers, which had made a respectable showing by finishing eighth in the first year of American League expansion in 1961. The sluggers were still there in 1962: leftfielder Leon ("Daddy Wags") Wagner was tied for second in the league in home runs and tied for third in RBIs. Manager Bill Rigney also had a group of good young players, including second baseman Billy Moran, shortstop Jim Fregosi, and pitchers Ken McBride, Dean Chance, and Bo Belinsky. Bo already had a no-hit game under his belt. The Angels (24–20) were currently in fifth place in the tight American League race, just two and a half games behind pace-setting Cleveland, and a game and a half behind the second place Yankees.

Joining the Yankees in Los Angeles was Mickey Mantle. The Switcher had flown in from Dallas, where he had been nursing his torn right thigh muscle and sprained left knee. His bat was sorely needed in the lineup. Despite being absent since May 18, Mickey was still the Yankees' leading hitter at .315. Clete Boyer was batting a surprising .311, but Roger Maris (.267), Elston Howard (.252), Moose Skowron (.228), and Yogi Berra (.178) were not exactly frightening opposing pitchers. Maris had eight home runs—half as much as the league leader, Jim Gentile of the Baltimore Orioles. Roger obviously missed the protection afforded by having Mantle batting in front of him. But Mickey wasn't coming back to the lineup anytime soon. Ralph Houk insisted that he would not play him until he was ready for full-time work. Nor would he use him as a pinch-hitter, even though Yankee pinch-hitters were hitting 3–43 (.070) since Mickey went on the disabled list. In any case, it was good to have the Mick back on the bench and in the clubhouse. He would be of "therapeutic, inspirational value" to the club, said Houk.[2]

The New York Spanish language newspaper, *El Diario*, ran ads featuring Luis Arroyo doing testimonials for "Wonder Bread." The Yankees, meanwhile, were wondering when their premier relief pitcher would be rejoining the club. Little Louie was in Ponce, Puerto Rico, nursing his sore arm. Also disturbing to Houk were the travails of his ace pitcher, Whitey Ford. The 1961 Cy Young Award winner was bothered by tendonitis in his left shoulder. Healthy or not, none of the Yankee starters was having a particularly good season at this stage. Ralph Terry was 5–4, and Bill Stafford, 4–3. Luckily, the off-season acquisition, Marshall Bridges, had emerged as something of the "new Luis Arroyo" in the bullpen.

Jim Bouton remained the lone rookie on the veteran staff. Born on March 3, 1939, in Newark, New Jersey, James Alan Bouton had grown up in the Bergen County community of Rochelle Park. His father, George, was a former national diving champ who had played semi-pro ball with the Nutley Iron Dukes and fought in the Golden Gloves. In his teens, Jim's family relocated to the south side of Chicago. Undersized and unheralded, he spent most of his sophomore year at Bloom Township High School throwing in the bullpen. They called him "Warmup Bouton." After two years on the varsity, he enrolled at the University of Western Michigan in Kalamazoo, where, although still undersized, he caught the attention of major league scouts. On Thanksgiving Day 1958, he signed a $30,000 bonus contract with the Yankees (negotiated by his father, a salesman). Bouton had several pitches—fastball, curve, and knuckler—and, like Bill Stafford, exhibited excellent poise on the mound. In the minors he began to put weight on his six-foot frame, while adding speed to his fastball.

Bouton made the most of his opportunity that spring, beating out veterans Robin Roberts and Tex Clevenger. Pitching coach Johnny Sain marveled, "I never had to show him a thing."[3] Although he had hurled the first Yankee shutout of the season against Washington on May 5, Bouton was known only to a small cluster of knowledgeable Yankee fans in early June. By the end of the month, his name would be familiar from coast to coast.

In their initial contest at Chavez Ravine on Friday night, June 1, the Bombers faced the Angels' controversial lefthander, Bo Belinsky. If Bouton was still a relative unknown at the time, the Angels' lefty was not. Robert Belinsky was born December 7, 1936, in New York City, but grew up in Trenton, New Jersey. Belinsky didn't play on his high school baseball team—"not my dish," he said. He was too busy hanging around pool halls. His pitching skills were noticed by the Baltimore Orioles; he kicked around the Orioles' chain for years, before being drafted by the Angels in December 1961. Bo reported nine days late to camp, holding out for more money. Once signed, he headed straight for Bill Rigney's doghouse, with complaints ranging from the clubhouse cuisine ("a bad scene") to his bad luck at not being drafted by the Mets. Casey Stengel should've been so lucky. On May 6, 1962, Belinsky pitched a no-hitter against his former employers, the Orioles. Bo was soon equally famous for his off-the-field shenanigans in and around Hollywood. "I'm no dinging prize," he admitted, but you know how the Baseball Bonnies are." His curfew-breaking exploits with the "Bonnies" did nothing to endear him to either Hamey or Rigney, but for a news-starved media he was the perfect antidote to the colorless Roger Maris. Jim Murray, writing in the *Los Angeles Times*, saw Bo as "a welcome breath of old-time lunacy in a sport which is getting more like bond-selling all the time."[4]

Roger Maris and the other bond-selling Yankees, together with the notorious Bo Belinsky, lured 51,584 fans to Chavez Ravine, the largest night crowd thus far that season in Los Angeles (including Dodgers games) and the largest gate in the American League to date. With Clete Boyer leading off, Maris in center field and batting third, and Elston Howard in the clean-up spot, the Yanks dug in for their first look at the controversial rookie. Belinsky retired Boyer and Bobby Richardson, walked Maris, and then struck out Howard as the Chavez Ravine crowd roared its approval. There was little else to cheer about from there on. The Bombers jumped on Belinsky for ten hits in eight innings, on route to a 6–2 victory. Ralph Terry went all the way for his sixth win. The teams then split the next two games. The total gate for the three-game series at Chavez Ravine was 146,623; colorless or not, Maris and company were still the biggest draw in baseball this side of Casey Stengel. Most importantly, Ralph Houk's charges left for New York still tied with the Cleveland Indians for first place in the American League standings.

"I've got to get a different team," Casey Stengel exclaimed. The frustration was setting in. During his heyday with the New York Yankees, Stengel always seemed to acquire the player he needed. Be it a starter or role player, George Weiss always managed to come through. This wasn't proving to be the case with the Mets in 1962; there was no Kansas City Athletics team willing to trade a Maris, Terry, or Boyer. "It's strange," the Old Perfessor wondered, "they can't get me on the phone. I'm supposed to be a very famous man."[5] The very famous Casey and his woebegone club, having concluded their series with the Giants, hopped on the team bus and crossed over the George Washington Bridge on the way to Philadelphia. The June 15th trading deadline was approaching, and as the Mets headed south on the New Jersey Turnpike, Weiss was working feverishly to clinch a deal that would provide the team with some semblance of respectability. But the only addition to the Mets' entourage on the trip to Philly was ten-year-old Gary Landrith, son of the club's catcher. The youngster was thrilled to be accompanying his father on a road trip for the first time. The trip would be more memorable than young Gary could've possibly imagined.

On Wednesday, June 6, the Mets dropped a doubleheader to the Phils at Connie Mack Stadium. In the first game, the multi-named Cal McLish beat the Mets, 2–0, thus becoming the first National League hurler to hold them scoreless. Curiously, for all their mishaps, the Mets were the last National League club to avoid being shut out in 1962. The 2–1 defeat in game two to Art Mahaffey made it 17 losses in a row, breaking the old record for New York teams set by the 1944 Brooklyn Dodgers. The luckless Mets flew out of Philly and landed later that night at O'Hare Airport in Chicago, with Gary Landrith on board—but not his father. Hobie Landrith was on the Mets' "no fly list," having been sent by Weiss to the Baltimore Orioles to complete the trade a month earlier for Marv Throneberry. Young Gary lingered at O'Hare for several hours before finally catching a flight to Detroit to join his grandparents.

In Chicago, the Mets were slated for a five-game series against the Cubs. Bruins owner Phil Wrigley was still sticking with his rotating "college of coaches" (Elvin Tappe, Charlie Metro, and the current head man, Lou Klein). G.M. John Holland, however, had made a historic addition to the coaching staff. On May 29, he hired Buck O'Neil as the first black coach on a major league team. O'Neil, 50, was a former Negro Leagues player and manager for the Kansas City Monarchs. He had been a Chicago scout since 1956 and was responsible for signing most of the black players in the Cubs' organization, including the club's star player, Ernie Banks. O'Neil, Holland hastened to add, wouldn't be part of the "college of coaches"—that is, he would not be managing the team—although Buck might do so in the future. Managing or not, O'Neil's presence was a welcome event for the team's black players. When Banks went to the hospital after a beaning in late May, Buck was the only member of the Cubs' management to visit him.

The big news for the mainstream media wasn't the Cubs' hiring of Buck O'Neil. The Mets had finally won a game! On Friday, June 8, the Mets' losing streak came to a merciful end with a 4–3 victory in the first game of a doubleheader. It was not pretty. An error at first base by Ernie Banks set up the winning sacrifice fly by Jim Hickman in the ninth inning. The victor was Jay Hook, the same Hook who won the Mets' first game ever at Pittsburgh on April 23.

The next day the *Chicago Tribune* ran a photo of Casey Stengel, hands folded, face turned toward the heavens, in a prayer of thanks. Indeed, the heavens seemed to be smiling on Ol' Casey. The Polo Grounders lost the second game of the Friday doubleheader, but came back on Saturday to beat the Cubs, 11–6. In winning, the Stengel men set a club record with 16 hits. On Sunday, June 10, the Mets came close to their third doubleheader sweep. They won the first game, 2–1, Ken McKenzie saving the game for Roger Craig. But in game two, with two outs in the ninth, Rod Kanehl booted an easy ground ball. Banks followed with a three-run homer to tie the game. The Bruins went on to win it in the tenth against McKenzie. Still, there was something to crow about; it wasn't everyday that the Mets won a series.

Unfortunately, as in the previous month, a good showing against a Midwestern opponent was followed by a discouraging trip to the Texas plains. Things started out well enough. At Houston on June 11, Al Jackson went all the way on a seven-hitter as the Mets won, 3–1 (their first victory over the Colt .45s). That made it four out of six since games since breaking their 17-game losing streak in Chicago on June 8. There was little opportunity for celebration, however. The Mets were soon reminded as to why the Houston city fathers were busy building a domed stadium; they and the small Monday crowd of 8,820 fans were eaten alive by insects. After two consecutive defeats on June 13 and 14, Stengel and company left the insects and humidity to the Texans and scurried back to the Polo Grounds and their ever-forgiving fans.

Ralph Houk and his men flew back from Los Angeles tied with the Cleveland Indians for first place in the American League standings. From June 6 to June 12, the Yankees played host to the Indians, Orioles, and Tigers. Thus far, the surprising Indians were shaping up as the biggest pretender to the American League crown—and the Bronx Bombers rose to the challenge. On June 6, Ralph Terry shut out the Tribe, 5–0. He gave up just four hits, while striking out ten. Roger Maris snapped a 0–0 tie in the sixth inning with his ninth homer against loser Jim (Mudcat) Grant. The following day, Bill Stafford needed just 93 pitches to 29 batters in a 4–0 Yankee triumph. Maris hit his tenth homer in the fourth against loser Jim Perry. The Bombers now had sole possession of first place. Minnesota moved up to second as Cleveland dropped to third.

The Yankees' opening day opponents, the Baltimore Orioles, were the next to arrive at the Bronx. On Friday, June 8, as the Mets were breaking their 17-game losing streak in Chicago, the Yankees squeaked by the O's in the opening game of their series in the Bronx. The 1–0 victory was the club's third consecutive shutout victory. Whitey Ford started the game, but retired after only one inning with a recurrence of tendonitis. Jim Coates replaced him and pitched eight scoreless innings of relief.

On Saturday, Jaipur won the final leg of racing's Triple Crown, the Belmont Stakes, by a nose, with the legendary Willie Shoemaker on his back. Earlier that day against the Orioles, the Yankees garnered their fourth victory in a row, although their consecutive scoreless inning streak was stopped at 28 and two-thirds. On Sunday, June 10, the Yankee game had competition from the Puerto Rican Day Parade. The annual fiesta was declared "the best yet,"[6] as an estimated crowd of 450,000 watched 50,000 marchers cover the distance from 44th Street to 88th Street. Everything was proceeding splendidly when a 1927 Studebaker, hauling a float with six beauty queens, broke down at 64th Street. The jolt sent the señoritas flying from their perch to the float deck below. Meanwhile, the Yankees absorbed a jolt of their own, losing both ends of a doubleheader to the Orioles. The peripatetic Hobie Landrith, discarded by the Mets because of his supposed defensive deficiencies, threw out three Yankee runners that afternoon.

On Monday, June 11, the Yankees lost their third consecutive game to the Orioles, 5–3, in a game marred by a frightful beaning. In the top of the fourth inning, with the count 1–0, Bud Daley hit young Orioles outfielder John (Boog) Powell on the top of the helmet, the ball caroming about a hundred feet down the third base line. Powell fell on his back, his legs and knees lifted into the air. He remained on the field for a full five minutes, before being removed to Lenox Hill Hospital for observation. In the bottom of the inning, O's pitcher Robin Roberts, cast off by the Yankees a month earlier, threw a ball that sailed close to Roger Maris' head. Maris, enraged, started for the mound with bat in hand. Hobie Landrith, standing at home plate, said something to Maris. The Yankee right fielder wheeled around and pushed in Landrith's facemask. The 16,483 fans rose to their feet as the two benches spilled onto the field. Plate umpire Charlie Berry seemed to have restored order, when rival managers Ralph Houk and Billy Hitchcock engaged in a shouting match. The two lunged at each other, throwing aimless punches until the New York City police, led by Lieutenant Barney Toner, broke up the scene for good. Houk and Hitchcock were banished from the dugout. Daley and Roberts didn't receive so much as a warning.

The Yankees played the Detroit Tigers the next day, June 12, winning 2–1 to regain their first-place lead over Minnesota. But the off-the-field conversation remained focused on the previous day's rhubarb. Boog Powell was diagnosed with contusions of the head, but thankfully no concussion. Questioned by reporters, Charlie Berry explained why he hadn't tossed Daley and Roberts out of the game. He didn't believe that either pitcher had intentionally thrown at Powell or Maris. Indeed, Roberts, a gentleman of the first order, was known throughout his illustrious career for his pinpoint control. He hit only 40 batters in 14 years. Meanwhile, Ralph Houk claimed that he had been provoked by Hitchcock. The O's' manager, claimed the Major, had accused Daley of deliberately hitting Powell. One observer was happy just to see the Yankees show some emotion. Writing in the *New York Daily News*, sports columnist Jimmy Powers remarked: "It was a real, old-fashioned, down-to-earth baseball scene ... a reassurance that baseball has not degenerated to the point where its heroes play mechanical ball, moving like robots, only to shower and hurry to board meetings of corporations." Powers, who was no fan of Maris, added, "Idols with spirit were becoming almost extinct in baseball."[7] The Mets, unwittingly, were about to produce a new "idol" of their own.

Sunday, June 17, was Camera Day at the Polo Grounds. The Old Perfessor, of course, was the favorite target of shutterbugs. "Everyone wants this face," chortled Casey as the fans milled around the first and third base box seats, snapping away. At one point, Stengel turned the tables on his admirers. He grabbed a camera from a fan and starting taking their pictures. "Now smile pretty," he coaxed, as his acolytes warmed to his charm.[8] There was nothing pretty about the Mets. By the time Sunday rolled around that weekend, the Stengel men had already lost twice to the Chicago Cubs, 5–1 and 6–3. Ernie Banks homered in both Friday's and Saturday's games, his 16th and 17th round trippers of the season. On Sunday, once the cameras were put away and the real action began, the Mets would lose as no other team could lose. About to unfold was a comedy of errors of mythical proportions. At its center was the recently acquired first baseman, Marv Throneberry.

Marvin Eugene Throneberry (his initials spelled "MET") was born on September 2, 1933, in Collierville, Tennessee. Marv was the second member of his family to play in the major leagues. His older brother, Faye, was a major league outfielder with the Boston Red Sox, Washington Senators, and Los Angeles Angels. Marv was signed by the Yankee organization in 1952 and played parts of three seasons under Casey as an understudy to Bill Skowron. In December 1959 he was traded to the Kansas City Athletics in the trade that sent Roger Maris to New York. From there he was shipped to Baltimore, which dispatched him to the Mets on May 9, 1962.

With Gil Hodges hobbled by a knee injury, Casey gave him a chance to start. Throneberry was no Gil Hodges, either at bat or in the field. But in three hours of madcap action, this thickly-built fellow with a freckled bald head would be transformed into the kind of living legend that only baseball can create.

For "Marvelous Marv," the day's adventurers began with his errant play in the field. In the first inning of the first game of the doubleheader on June 17, the Cubs' Don Landrum led off for the visitors with a walk against loser Al Jackson. Ken Hubbs struck out, and Landrum, trying to steal, was caught in a rundown between first and second. The runner was declared safe, however, when Throneberry obstructed Landrum's path as he dashed back to first. This opened the flood gates. Ernie Banks walked and Ron Santo followed with a triple, driving in two runs. The young Cubs outfielder Lou Brock, not known for his power, then became the first major leaguer to hit a ball into the left-center field bleachers at the Polo Grounds, a distance of 460 feet. Thanks in part to Throneberry, what could have been a scoreless inning had turned into a 4–0 deficit. But as it turned out, Marv was just getting started.

The Mets struck right back in the bottom of the inning. Richie Ashburn led off with a bunt single and was sacrificed to second by Elio Chacón. Gene Woodling, the ex–Yankee left fielder recently acquired from the Washington Senators, then walked. Frank Thomas singled to center, scoring Ashburn. Up came Throneberry with a chance to redeem himself after the first inning fiasco. He swung at a pitch from right-hander Glen Hobbie and hit a drive to deep right. Marv lumbered around the diamond to third as Woodling and Thomas scored. His moment of glory was soon dashed, however. Ernie Banks asked for the ball and stepped on first on an appeal play. Umpire Dusty Boggess called Throneberry out for failing to touch the bag. Casey came out to protest — and was stopped dead in his tracks. Marv, the umpires told him, hadn't touched second base either. When the next batter, Charlie Neal, hit a home run, Marv's folly loomed even larger. Instead of a potentially big rally, the Mets managed only to knot the game at 4–4. In the bottom of the ninth, with the Cubs leading 8–7 and the winning run on base, Throneberry — who else?— struck out to end the game. Joe McDonald, the Mets' statistician, could only shake his head in wonder as he looked over Marv's stats for the day:

At bats: 5   Hits: 0   RBIs: 2   Errors: 3

No other sport so proudly and precisely records its failures as major

Marv Throneberry, Mets first baseman and Polo Grounds favorite, pretending to field a ball. Playing against the Chicago Cubs on June 17, 1962, his stats read: five at-bats, no hits, two RBIs. Throneberry drove in two runs with a triple, but was called for failing to touch the bases. He also made three errors that day. It helped make "Marvelous Marv" a living legend.

league baseball. No other American sport makes such a fetish of futility. The scorecard gives us a pitcher's walks, wild pitches, balks, and hit batsmen (and that's not counting his times at bat, which can be horrendous in the extreme). By contrast, pro football merely records a quarterback's interceptions; the game records successes not failures. Moreover, with its compressed schedule, 60-minute clock, and precise hash marks, the gridiron is all business. It has no time or room for sentiment, and therefore, none of the self-deprecation or the sense of the absurd, which characterizes baseball. No other sport but baseball could have invented Marvelous Marv Throneberry; no other fans could have created the Marv Throneberry fan club. And Marv, tutored by the media-savvy Richie Ashburn (who had the locker next to him), learned to make the most of his misfortunes on the diamond, playing the lovable patsy to the hilt. As Arthur Daley of *The New York Times* later put it, Throneberry's "only crime was to steal more newspaper space than he really deserved."[9]

The same could be said of the team in general. The Mets hadn't won a game at home in over a month. The Milwaukee Braves followed the Cubs into the Polo Grounds and extended the Mets' current losing streak to seven games with a 7–1 victory on June 18. Hank Aaron duplicated Lou Brock's feat by planting a Jay Hook pitch 460 feet, this time into the left field bleachers (Aaron's teammate Joe Adcock was the last to do it in 1953). The next day, the Mets finally ended their losing streak, with a 6–5 win over the Braves. Gene Woodling hit his first round tripper as a member of the Mets. But the Stengel men soon returned to their losing ways, dropping both ends of a doubleheader to the Braves on June 20.

The Mets ended their miserable homestand on what, for them, was a high note by splitting four games with the Houston Colt .45's June 21 to 24. On Friday, June 22, Al Jackson shut out the Colts, 2–0. It was his (and the team's) second shutout victory, the first coming against Philadelphia on April 29. Richie Ashburn hit a rare home run leading off the first against Dick (Turk) Farrell. The Colts inflicted a 16–3 drubbing on the Mets on Saturday, the Polo Grounders giving up a whopping 17 hits and committing six errors — three by the Marvelous One. The Mets exacted sweet revenge on Saturday, June 23. The hero of the day for the Mets was the unlikeliest slugger of them all. Richie Ashburn had never hit more than four home runs in one season. On this afternoon, he hit two in leading the Mets to a 13–2 win. When Sunday's game was rained out, Ashburn rested. In the Polo Grounds clubhouse, Richie lit his English pipe and savored his recent power display.

The team had played .500 ball (3–3) since defeating the Milwaukee Braves at the Polo Grounds on June 19. But the mantle of mediocrity didn't sit well on the shoulders of the Mets. Abject failure seemed to be more their style.

While Marv Throneberry was being enshrined in the pantheon of Polo Grounds legends, the "corporate" Yankees were laboring through their longest road trip of the month. Between June 15 and June 25, Ralph Houk and his not-so-merry men hauled their suitcases to Cleveland, Baltimore, and Detroit. Houk was encouraged by the return of Luis Arroyo from Puerto Rico — although it would take some time for him to round into shape. But the Major was still bedeviled by his pitching staff. Whitey Ford was still out with his ailing left shoulder. Columnist Jimmy Powers could not find "a satisfactory explanation for the brittleness, the lack of muscular strength and stamina, in our modern pitchers." Neither could the Yankees' team physician, Dr. Sidney Gaynor. Asked about Ford's eventual return to health, Gaynor shrugged and answered, "Who can tell about these things."[10] Who indeed!

The visit to Cleveland wasn't a pleasant one. On Friday, June 15, the New Yorkers were shut out by the Indians' Jim (Mudcat) Grant. The loss, their fourth in a row, left the Bombers clinging to first place by a single percentage point over the Minnesota Twins, and three percentage points over Cleveland. On Saturday, June 16, Tito Francona banged Yankee pitching for five hits in a 10–9 Indians win. Ralph Houk, giving in to temptation, inserted Mickey Mantle into the game as a pinch-hitter in the eighth inning. It was Mickey's first appearance since May 18. The 50,254 fans who came out on Ladies Night saw the mighty Mick hit a 400-foot shot, which cleared the railed fence in right-center field at Municipal Stadium, and landed in the Indians' bullpen for a three-run homer. It was too little, too late.

On Sunday, June 17, as Marv Throneberry was burnishing his legend at the Polo Grounds, the Yankees lost both ends of a doubleheader at Cleveland. A crowd of 70, 918, the largest crowd at Municipal Stadium since the 1954 pennant-winning season, witnessed the thrashing. The twin losses left the Yankees in third place in the American League standings, three games behind the league-leading Indians, and a game shy of the second-place Minnesota Twins. In past years, these losses would've been regarded as simply a temporary setback for the Bombers. But there was now a growing sense around the league that the Yankees could be taken. "They may beat you, but they won't scare you to death," wrote Gordon Cobbledick in the *Cleveland Plain Dealer*. Meanwhile, pennant fever was starting to infect the Indians. "Everyone is thinking at least a little about it," admitted Tito Francona.[11]

Flying into Baltimore, the Yankees faced the Orioles for the first time since the rhubarb at Yankee Stadium on June 11. The series was mercifully played without incident. On June 19, the Bombers lost their fifth in a row, this time to righty Chuck Estrada. Brooks Robinson broke a 1–1 tie in the sixth with a home run off Ralph Terry, on route to a 3–1 Oriole win, as Yogi Berra made his first appearance of the season behind the plate. Meanwhile, Bill Skowron was at the Pascack Valley Hospital in Westwood, New Jersey, tending to his six-year-old son, who had been burned in the face and chest when a gasoline-propelled model airplane exploded.

The Yankees finally broke their five-game losing streak with a 3–0 victory on June 21. Whitey Ford, making his first start in almost two weeks, left after eight and two-thirds innings with a blister. Bill Skowron, back from New Jersey, hit his tenth homer off loser Steve Barber in support of Ford. The Yankees were now three games behind Cleveland as they headed for Detroit for the final five games of their road trip from June 22 to 25.

Like the Yankees, the Tigers were without the services of their star player. Al Kaline, a Baltimore native, was a Gold Glove-winning outfielder, who in 1955, at age 20, became the youngest player ever to win a batting crown. Kaline had been sidelined since May 26 with a broken collar bone, suffered making the last putout in a Tiger victory over the Bombers at Yankee Stadium.

Al joked that he was becoming an "expert" on the Kennedy Administration, since he did nothing all day but read the papers.[12] In fact, his recuperation was anything but enjoyable. He was unable to button his shirts or knot a tie without the help of his wife, Louise. Without the services of Kaline, with the previous year's batting champ Norm Cash and top slugger Rocky Colavito mired in slumps, and their best pitcher Frank Lary nursing a sore arm, the Bengals were fighting to stay out of the second division after a second-place finish in 1961.

In the opener at Tiger Stadium on June 22, the Yankees lost, 6–4, to lefty Hank Aguirre. The worst hitting pitcher in the American League (Sandy Koufax held that distinction in the National League), Aguirre singled in a run to help his own cause. Mickey Mantle made his first start since May 18 in right field, as the Yanks dropped to fourth place. The next day, the two teams played the first day-night doubleheader in Detroit history. The Yankees arrived at Tiger Stadium at 11 A.M., intending to return to their hotel after the first game for dinner. A rain delay, however, played havoc with their plans. After finally nailing down an 8–4 victory, the club settled for an improvised meal of ham sandwiches in the visitors' clubhouse. The Tigers, on the other hand, enjoyed a buffet spread consisting of chicken, turkey, ham, potato salad, cottage cheese, onions, radishes, olives, rolls, and chocolate cake. After losing, 5–4, to the well-fed Tigers in the nightcap, the exhausted Yanks finally made their way back to their hotel at midnight. They were back at Tiger Stadium the next morning for what proved to be one of the most memorable games of the entire 1962 season.

This nationally televised game on Sunday, June 24, promised a duel between two of the American League's best pitchers: the Yankees' "Bullet Bob" Turley and the Tigers' "Yankee Killer," Frank Lary. Instead, fans at Tiger Stadium sat through an exhausting 36-minute first inning. The Yankees scored six runs off the sore-armed Lary, including a three-run homer by Clete Boyer. Turley didn't fare much better. He lasted just one-third of an inning after yielding a three-run shot to the Tigers' Purnal Goldy. At this point, Turley could have showered, hailed a taxi to the airport, taken a jet to New York, changed planes, and landed in Los Angeles before the final out was made. The contest lasted 22 innings and took exactly seven hours to complete.

The Yankees chased Lary in the second, adding one run for a 7–3 lead. The Tigers, however, nibbled away with three runs in the third and a single run in the sixth. There the scoring stopped. The CBS national telecast, with Dizzy Dean and Pee Wee Reese, signed off after the tenth inning. WPIX-Channel 11 in New York remained on the air as the parade of relievers continued, inning after inning, hour after hour. The Yanks' Tex Clevenger threw shutout ball from the seventh to the 12th frames—surviving one scary moment. In the 11th, the Tigers' Rocky Colavito tripled (he went 7-for-ten on the day, raising his average from .268 to .287). Ralph Houk ordered intentional walks to Norm Cash and Dick McAuliffe. With the bases loaded and both the infield and outfield drawn in, Chico Fernández hit a soft liner to left field that Johnny Blanchard smothered for the third out. Bud Daley relieved Clevenger and blanked the Tigers in the 13th, 14th, and 15th innings. In the bottom of the 16th, Houk sent young Jim Bouton to the mound. Bouton pitched the last seven innings for the Yankees, yielding just three hits and walking none. Terry Fox of the Tigers did him one better, hurling eight shutout innings.

The concession stands closed down at 8:15 P.M. per Michigan state law — not that they had much left to sell. The 34,520 fans, most of whom stayed to the bitter end, consumed approximately 41,000 bottles of beer, 34,520 sodas, and 32,260 hot dogs. For the starving masses there were 15 minutes to go. In the top of the 22nd inning, Phil Regan came in to relieve Terry Fox for the Tigers. Regan walked Roger Maris and then faced rookie Jack Reed, who had taken over in center field for Mickey Mantle in the seventh inning. Reed hit a Regan offering over the left field fence, the first Yankee runs in 19 innings, to decide the game. The line score read

New York: 9 runs, 20 hits, 4 errors
Detroit: 7 runs, 19 hits, 3 errors

The game ended at exactly 8:30 P.M., seven hours after plate umpire Bill McKinley's cry of "play ball." Together, the Yankees and Tigers shattered the previous record of 4:58.

The contest was exhausting for everyone involved. Plate umpire Bill McKinley didn't leave the field during the entire game and had just one cup of water in seven hours. The Yankees used all of their players except for Luis Arroyo, Whitey Ford, Rollie Sheldon, and Ralph Terry. Arroyo, recovering from his sore arm, warmed up 11 times in the bullpen. Whitey Ford ended up with a cramped left hand. He kept the Yankee pitching chart that day and recorded all 316 pitches thrown by Yankee hurlers. Yogi Berra caught every single one of them. "One of the most amazing feats I've ever seen," marveled Ralph Houk. One of the available catchers, Elston Howard, had pinch-hit for Marshall Bridges in the seventh inning. Johnny Blanchard was available to spell Berra, but he played the entire game in left field. Yogi took it all in stride. "My legs feel fine," he said, before departing for an Italian meal at a friend's house. Equally matter of fact was the winning pitcher, Jim Bouton. "They tell me it was seven innings. I wasn't tired at all. I guess I could have gone another inning or so."[13]

The Yankees needed just 2:24 to beat the Tigers in the final game of the series on Monday, June 25. Whitey Ford, recovered from his hand cramps, went 8 and two-third innings before a twinge in his left shoulder forced his removal from the game. The Yankees departed for New York, tied with Los Angeles for third place in the American League standings, 2 and a half games behind Cleveland and a game and a half games in back of Minnesota.

The New York Mets, safely anchored in last place, embarked on an 11-game road trip. On Monday, June 25, Lou Niss' charges left the Polo Grounds on a bus at 10:15 A.M. for Newark Airport. Their chartered United Airlines flight lifted up into the New Jersey sky at 11 A.M. and landed at Pittsburgh at 12:30 P.M. It took another two hours for the players to check into the Pittsburgh Hilton, retrieve their bags, and claim their rooms. There were six hours to kill before the bus arrived to take them to Forbes Field. For a veteran like Gil Hodges, there was only one way to alleviate the tedium: sleep. It's what got players through road trips." The Mets, unfortunately, took Hodges' advise too much to heart. They proceeded to sleepwalk their way through the Pittsburgh series, dropping all three games to the Pirates June 25 to 27.

Witnessing the debacle at Forbes Field on June 26 was none other than Branch Wesley Rickey. With reporters' notebooks eagerly opened before him, Rickey proceeded to expounded on a number of topics, including the Mets. After observing the Metropolitans' ineptness first hand, "the Mahatma" pointedly criticized George Weiss' decision to go after "established players of mediocre talent" in the National League expansion draft. The Mets' front office, he noted, "deadens its feelings to realities" by putting its faith in "anesthetic players."

Having dismissed the Mets, the Mahatma returned to what had long been his greatest concern — the diminishing popularity of major league baseball. Professional football, he said, was supplanting baseball as the nation's most popular spectator sport. To restore fan interest, Rickey once again recommended the establishment of a third major loop. The four current expansion clubs, together with four brand new clubs (presumably situated in cities once part of the defunct Continental Baseball League) would thus create a third major league. This would result in a "greater intercontinental apportionment of teams." The Mahatma continued with his impromptu dissertation. The pennant winners of the three leagues, he said, would qualify for the World Series, games to be played on a rotating basis. The interest generated by this arrangement, the Mahatma believed, would be enormous. Finding players to stock a new league, Rickey insisted, was not a problem. There was "talent to burn."[14] Actually, the Mets had recently found some young talent of their own — and in the Yankees' backyard, no less. On June 28, George Weiss announced the signing of Ed Kranepool, a 17-year-old phenom out of James Monroe High School in the Bronx, to a $75,000 bonus contract.

Before one thinks of the life of the major league ballplayer as glamorous, one might have considered the plight of the Mets. On Thursday, June 28, at 9 A.M. Eastern Standard Time, the Stengel men took off from Pittsburgh and landed at O'Hare Airport in Chicago. They then boarded a non-stop jet to Los Angeles. The players found diverse ways of passing the time on the long flight to the West Coast. The brainy Ken McKenzie was immersed in reading. Richie Ashburn held forth on the prospects of the Republican Party. Eventually, most players dozed off to sleep. Arriving at Los Angeles Airport later that morning, the players stumbled to their rooms. That night, the weary Mets dropped a 5–4 decision to the Los Angeles Dodgers at Chavez Ravine. Unmercifully, the game took 14 innings and 4:09 to play. Maury Wills, taking aim at Ty Cobb's all-time record, stole his 41st base, off Al Jackson. The game featured something rarely seen in major league baseball — an all–Jewish battery. The Angelinos' Norm Sherry caught his brother, Larry Sherry. The following night, the Polo Grounders, finally receiving a full night's rest, broke a four-game losing streak with a 10–4 victory.

Winning wasn't exactly the Stengel men's forte. They were much more spectacular in defeat. On the last day of the month, Brooklyn native Sandy Koufax threw the first no-hitter of the National League season, beating the Mets, 5–0. It was not a perfect game — Koufax yielded five walks while striking out 13. But this imperfection meant little in the end. When it was over, and the celebration had begun in the Dodger clubhouse, a teammate shouted above the din, "Remember, Sandy, curfew is 5 A.M." — a reference to the playboy antics of the Angels' no-hit pitcher Bo Belinsky.[15] Casey Stengel would've given anything for that kind of pitching talent–to hell with the curfew.

The New York Yankees closed out the month of June with a short homestand against the Minnesota Twins and Los Angeles Angels. The Bombers took two out of three from the Twins. They dropped the first contest, a Tuesday night game on June 26 and a shutout loss to Twins ace Camilo Pascual. The game was notable for the first appearance of Luis Arroyo in more than a month. He pitched one inning, gave up no hits or walks, and struck out one. Home runs by Roger Maris (numbers 13 and 14) then helped the Yankees to two consecutive victories over the Twins.

Before the final tilt on Thursday, the Yankees sent veteran outfielder Bob Cerv to Houston for cash. A Nebraska native, Cerv had his best season with the Kansas City Athletics in 1958, swatting 38 home runs — still a club record. But he was originally and forever a Yankee. This was his third and last tour of duty with the club.

The Yankee teammate that would miss Cerv the most was Roger Maris. The two men were neighbors in the Kansas City suburbs and shared an apartment during the season in Jackson Heights, Queens. Jackson Heights was established early in the 20th century as a middle class retreat for New Yorkers, taking advantage of the newly completed 59th Street Bridge to escape from Brooklyn and Lower Manhattan. The term "garden apartment" was invented in Jackson Heights. Maris' teammates found havens in Bergen County, New Jersey, or Nassau County, Long Island (and in Yogi Berra's case, the Essex County, New Jersey, community of Montclair). Meanwhile, the two Midwesterners Maris and Cerv, with no families around them, found their own escape from the maddening crowd: TV, gin rummy, and when Mickey Mantle was around, "hillbilly" records. Unlike Casey Stengel, neither was likely to be seen rubbing shoulders with reporters and fellow athletes at Toots Shor's. Now, Cerv was gone.

The Yanks split the last two games of June with the Angels. Whitey Ford won the first game on Friday, June 29, twirling a four-hitter for a 6–3 win. The game did not start out as auspiciously for Ford. The first batter, Albie Pearson put his five-foot, five-inch 140 pound frame into Whitey's third pitch and sent it into the right field stands for a home run. But four Angels errors and nifty defensive work by Tresh, Richardson, and Mantle, sunk the visitors. On the last day of the month, the visitors turned the tables on the Yankees, winning 5–3, marking their first win ever at Yankee Stadium. Maris hit his 15th home run in the losing cause. As July approached, the Yankees, after two months of mediocre play (29–26) were in second place behind Mel McGaha's Cleveland Indians.

So the month of June ended. The Mets were still in last place, unable to swing that magical trade that might vault them into a semblance of respectability. The Yankees, after dipping into fourth place, had crawled back up to second. Bad times would continue for Casey Stengel in July. Meanwhile, Mickey Mantle would finally return to the Yankees—good news for Roger Maris, who had yet to crack the top five among the league leaders in home runs. In fact, Mantle, Maris and the rest of the Yankees were about to have their best month of the season.

7

"She Must Have Seen Us Play"

George Steinbrenner was in a buoyant mood as he celebrated his 32nd birthday on July 4, 1962. He had recently signed Ohio State All-American Jerry Lucas to his Cleveland Pipers club in the fledgling American Basketball Association, taking Lucas right from under the noses of the National Basketball Association's Cincinnati Royals. The ABA was teetering on financial bankruptcy, but Steinbrenner himself seemingly could not lose. His champion Pipers, led by their current star, Dick Barnett, and their star to be, Jerry Lucas, would likely be absorbed into the more established NBA.

The Cleveland shipbuilder's habit of hiring and firing personnel had not endeared him to the Cleveland press. There had also been a celebrated feud between himself and the owner of the San Francisco franchise. But neither the chattering of the sportswriters nor the carping of fellow owners troubled him particularly. Steinbrenner had already set his sights well beyond the shores of Lake Erie.

Meanwhile, the present owners of the New York Yankees, Dan Topping and Del Webb, saw their team stuck in a tight race in their quest for another American League pennant. After splitting a Sunday doubleheader with the Angels on July 1, the standings read:

New York	40–32	.556	_____
Los Angeles	42–34	.553	_____
Cleveland	41–34	.547	½ behind
Minnesota	43–36	.544	½ behind

The situation could very well have been worse for Ralph Houk and company. Mickey Mantle, Whitey Ford, and Luis Arroyo had all missed substantial portions of the season due to injuries. Roger Maris was only just beginning to get untracked. Elston Howard, Bill Skowron, John Blanchard, and the 37-year-old Yogi Berra were all having subpar seasons at the plate. Although

Ralph Terry had won his tenth game on Sunday, the pitching was still a point of concern for the Major. Still, despite all these problems, the Yankees remained in the hunt for a 20th world championship.

The Angels left town and the Yankees welcomed the Kansas City Athletics to the Bronx. In the opener on July 2, Roger Maris, Mickey Mantle and Héctor López all hit round trippers in an 8–4 victory that saw Luis Arroyo finally win his first game of the season. The home run barrage continued the next day. The M&M Boys connected for two homers apiece in an 8–7 win. Maris now had six in his last eight games. The Yankees then split a July 4th doubleheader with the A's. Mantle added two more home runs, passing Duke Snider on the all-time list with 389. Maris chipped in with a solo blast, his 19th of the year, allowing him to crack the top five in home runs in the American League, just four behind league leader Leon Wagner. Despite the home run fest, the Houk men left for Minneapolis in second place, a half-game behind the Los Angeles Angels, who on the Fourth of July slipped past them into first place by sweeping the lowly Washington Senators.

Casey and the Mets had less cause for optimism as the team's plane tilted its nose upward from Los Angeles Airport and headed north Sunday night for San Francisco. The loss to the Dodgers in the getaway game on July 1 left the Mets deep in the National League cellar, six games behind the ninth-place Cubs. If that wasn't enough, their schedule now called for 25 consecutive games against first-division clubs. On the flight to San Francisco, Frank Thomas once again did the serving honors. His teammates didn't make it easy for him. Richie Ashburn and his group wanted franks and beans. Gil Hodges was part of another contingent that held out for chicken. Meanwhile, the stewardess, relieved of her duties, began collecting Mets autographs on an airline sick bag. "She must have seen us play," quipped one player.[1]

San Francisco was a balmy 67 degrees with clear skies that July 2, the perfect place for a light breakfast and an afternoon stroll. By game time that night, the weather had turned windy and chilly at Candlestick Park. Chilled though they were, the Mets played spoilers, dropping the Giants to second place behind Los Angeles with an 8–5 victory. The next night, the Mets registered enough misjudged fly balls and missed grounders to ensure a 10–1 loss to the Giants. Orlando Cepeda hit a high pop between first base and the mound. Marv Throneberry came in to make the play — then let the ball drop in front of him. Casey Stengel wasn't on hand to witness this train wreck. He had flown 80 miles east to Stockton in an effort to recruit University of Santa Clara pitcher Bob Garibaldi. The Mets welcomed back Casey by dropping both ends of the doubleheader on July 4. Willie McCovey, still in a Giants uniform despite George Weiss' best efforts, drove in seven runs in the first game. Meanwhile, young Garibaldi spurned the charms of the Old Perfessor and signed a $150,000 bonus contract with the Giants.

Having completed their miserable 2–9 road trip, the Mets boarded a plane for New York at 11 P.M., Pacific Coast Time. They arrived home at 7:10 A.M. A tired Rod Kanehl returned to his Jersey City flat (low-paid Mets couldn't afford the luxury of Bergen Country). Kanehl and his teammates logged 15 hours and ten minutes in airplanes; seven hours and eight minutes in buses; five hours and 17 minutes waiting to board planes or buses; and 33 hours and 21 minutes playing baseball. The hardships of the expansion era schedule would be a major item on the agenda when team representative Richie Ashburn and his fellow player reps met at Chicago prior to the first of the All-Star Games on July 10.

The New York Yankees ended the first half of the 1962 season with a three-game sweep of the Minnesota Twins at Metropolitan Stadium. On July 6, Mickey Mantle and Roger Maris both hit two home runs to pace the Yankee victory. It was the second time that they had turned the feat in four games. Mantle had now homered in four consecutive at-bats, going back to the two he hit in the second game of the Fourth of July doubleheader against Kansas City. The home run barrage wasn't enough to keep the Bombers in first place, though, as the Cleveland Indians took over the top spot by half a game. The Yankees, led by the pitching of Bill Stafford and Whitey Ford, won the remaining two games of the series against the Twins on July 7 and 8. The two wins put them on top once again in the American League standings. The Tribe dropped to second, following a doubleheader loss to the Chicago White Sox on July 8.

The Yankees concluded the first half of the season with a 46–33 record. Mickey Mantle, Roger Maris, Elston Howard, Bobby Richardson, and Tom Tresh now headed for Washington, D.C. They had been chosen by their peers to represent the American League in the first All-Star Game of the year. Whitey Ford and Ralph Terry were also going to Washington.. They had been selected for the pitching staff by Ralph Houk, who would manage the American League squad.

On the south end of the Macombs Dam Bridge, the first half season in New York Mets history came to a close with two victories in four tries against the St. Louis Cardinals. On Friday, July 6, the Polo Grounders won for the first time ever against the Redbirds. Gil Hodges and Rod Kanehl supplied home runs in a 10–3 rout. For Gil, it was the 370th of his career, allowing him to pass Ralph Kiner on the all-time list. Among the 14,515 spectators cheering at the Polo Grounds was Joan Whitney Payson, who had just returned from her annual European vacation.

On Saturday, the Mets extended their winning streak to two games, beating the Cards, 5–4, in the first game of a doubleheader. Marv Throneberry turned from goat to hero, hitting a two-run homer to pace the win. Throneberry homered again in the second game, but a Stan Musial clout, with two out in the eighth inning, sent the home team down to defeat, 3–2. On Sunday, July 8, the Mets ended a difficult first half of the season by enduring a 15–1 beating at the hands of the Redbirds. Musial hit three consecutive home runs, four in all going back to his last at-bat in the previous day's doubleheader.

The Mets were 23–59, safely in last place, 31 and a half games behind the league-leading San Francisco Giants. Casey Stengel and Richie Ashburn headed for the All-Star Game in Washington on July 10. Whitey was the Mets' sole selection on the National League squad. Casey's nominal role was to coach third base. His real role was to entertain.

Richie Ashburn, the Mets player representative, was one of the 16 major league player reps who met at the Statler Hilton Hotel in Washington the day before the All-Star Game. Presiding over the meeting were the Yankees' Bob Turley (American League) and the Pittsburgh Pirates' Bob Friend (National League). Other National League team player reps included Dallas Green of the Philadelphia Phillies, Harvey Kuenn of the San Francisco Giants, and Sandy Koufax of the Los Angeles Dodgers. Among the American League delegation were Brooks Robinson of the Baltimore Orioles, Early Wynn of the Chicago White Sox, and Jim Bunning of the Detroit Tigers. The players had gathered to express their displeasure at "the 162 game monstrosity," which, as both Yankees and Mets players could attest, had created a bizarre and brutal schedule.[2] In response, the Players' Association presented several demands to the team owners:

1. No more night games on the last date of a series ("getaway games"), which had teams landing at 4 A.M. in the next city and playing a game later that night.
2. Elimination of day-night doubleheaders.
3. Allowing for more open dates by cutting the schedule to 153 or 156 games.

The idea of playing a reduced schedule wasn't new. Before relinquishing control of the Chicago White Sox, Bill Veeck had proposed a 156-game interleague schedule, with 40 of the 156 games played against opponents in the rival league. Ford Frick wasn't willing to endorse interleague play, but he favored a reduction in games. So did American League president Joe Cronin. The big stumbling block was the National League, where the crusty Warren Giles vehemently opposed any changes in the status quo. Los Angeles Dodgers G.M. Buzzie Bavasi also held to the status quo; team owner Walter O'Malley stood to lose 7 to 9 Dodgers home games and an equal number from his renters, the Angels, as a result of a reduced schedule. Many American League owners balked at a schedule that would have them play fewer games against the New York Yankees. The New York-Cleveland series at Municipal Stadium on June 15–17, for example, had drawn 170,000 customers, one-third of the Indians' season gate by the All-Star break.

The players' pension board (which included the Mets' Richie Ashburn) met with a group of the owners (Joan Payson was represented by Donald Grant) on July 9. The players made their pitch for a shortened schedule. The owners countered by demanding the elimination of the second All-Star Game, which brought them few profits. But the players insisted that it continue because the revenue went into the players' pension fund. The meeting concluded without any chance of altering the schedule in the near future.

The players weren't the only ones demanding changes in the game. By 1962 criticism of the National Pastime had become, well, a pastime. Letters to *The Sporting News*, the "Bible of Baseball," abounded with suggestions for improving the game, some quite ingenious. The expansion to ten teams in each league, it was argued, created more also-rans and, consequently, deadened fan interest. In response, Robert Ricelli of San Jose, California, suggested breaking up the majors into three loops, with six teams each. Another complaint involved the increasingly long games. To deal with this problem, Ralph Busher of Roselle, New Jersey, came up with something like the equivalent of the "mercy rule," suggesting that games be automatically ended if one team was leading by 13 runs after five innings.[3] In short, it wasn't just Casey's Mets who, with their improbable popularity, were threatening to turn the game upside down. Radical change was in the air in the baseball world. Players, fans, and pundits all debated the future of the game. But those who controlled the game refused to heed its call.

There was at least one area of major league baseball in which change was readily accepted. New, multi-sport, municipally funded stadiums were planned for St. Louis, Cincinnati, Pittsburgh, and Philadelphia, replacing the aging, privately financed ballparks of the pre-expansion age. The first of these to be built was District of Columbia Stadium in Washington, D.C., the site of the 32nd major league All-Star Game. The new park was lavishly praised, President Kennedy hailing it as an "enduring symbol of the American belief in the importance of physical fitness."[4] The $24 million stadium eschewed any of the dimensional eccentricity associated with the New York ballparks. It featured a symmetrical playing field: 335 feet down the foul lines, 385 feet in the power alleys, and 410 feet to dead center field. There were no pillars or posts to obstruct the view. Another novel feature was the lack of a lower outfield deck. The highest seats were 115 feet above the field, affording a panoramic view of both the stadium and the nation's capital. The lowest viewing point was in the mezzanine area, 40 feet above the playing area. (Roger Maris presumably would have less to fear from flying objects).

Casey Stengel hadn't been particularly successful as an All-Star manager, and the American League hadn't done much better since his departure. The National League squad had won 11 of the last 16 contests. The lifetime record stood at American League 16 wins, National League 14, giving the Nationals a chance to tie things up with victories here in Washington and at Chicago on July 30.

Writing in *Pageant Magazine*, Jackie Robinson put his finger on the reason for the recent dominance of the National League: the reluctance of the American League to sign black players. At Washington, the National League was represented by ten black players, four of whom were Latins. The American League had just three black players, including Elston Howard of the Yankees. (The Latins on the American squad — Camilo Pascual, Luis Aparicio, and the California-born Hank Aguirre — were not considered to be "tan" players, either by the mainstream or black press). However, there was one big difference in 1962. Minnesota Twins catcher Earl Battey and Los Angeles Angels left fielder Leon Wagner were starting for the Americans. The black Cuban, Minnie Miñoso, had graced many an American League squad in the past, and African Americans were "proud of him" representing their race. But as the *Pittsburgh Courier* pointed out, this was the first time that a "native son" had been on the starting team since Cleveland's Larry Doby in 1950.[5]

Mel Allen, the "voice of the Yankees," and Yogi Berra's childhood friend, Joe Garagiola, were doing the play-by-play in a nationwide telecast on NBC-TV. A live crowd of 45,480, the largest in Washington sports history, was at the game, including President Kennedy. In throwing out the first ball, JFK became the only chief executive to "pitch" at both the old Griffith Stadium and the new DC showcase. The biggest applause of the afternoon went to the 41-year-old Stan Musial. "The Man" was enjoying a late revival in his long career. With a .333 average, he was the fourth leading batter in the National League. There was also a "noisy demonstration" for Casey Stengel. The Old Perfessor was called over to the President's box before the game. After chatting with Kennedy for a couple of minutes, he excused himself by saying, "I have to get back, Mr. President because I'm not working for myself today."[6] JFK laughed in approval.

The pre-game festivities over, the Nationals continued their mastery over the Americans, winning 3–1. Stan Musial and the Dodgers' Maury Wills were the senior circuit stars. With the score tied 0–0 in the top of the sixth, Musial, playing his 22nd All-Star Game, opened with a single. National League manager Fred Hutchinson sent in Wills to run for him. Wills, who had already pilfered 46 bases and was making a serious run at Ty Cobb's all-time record, promptly stole second. He came home on a single by Dick Groat.

American League manager Ralph Houk switched Mantle and Maris in the outfield, placing the Mick in right to compensate for his healing groin and knee injuries. Maris was robbed of an extra base hit in the sixth, Willie Mays leaping high into the air to spear his drive at the 410-foot mark. It was, Ralph Houk later said, the turning point of the game.

While the major leagues' first All-Star Game of 1962 was being played in Washington, the National Basketball Association's Board of Governors was meeting at the Hotel Roosevelt on Madison and 45th Street. Commissioner Maurice Podoloff emerged from the conference and announced that the Cleveland Pipers had been admitted as the fifth team in the NBA's Eastern Division. All that Pipers owner George Steinbrenner needed to do now was to come up with the $250,000 entrance fee, and his "stormy tenure" in the ABA would come to an end. To be sure, the NBA was hardly in the class of Major League Baseball. Most arenas were so small that the league still scheduled doubleheaders at Madison Square Garden, with the Knickerbockers playing the first game against a team like the Boston Celtics; and a team like the Syracuse Nationals taking on the Cincinnati Royals in the second game. But for Steinbrenner, being the owner of the ABA champion was somewhat like being the emperor of the North Pole. In joining the NBA, and taking Jerry Lucas and Dick Barnett with him, he was making the jump to the big time.

As George Steinbrenner was celebrating his good fortune, the New York Yankees were at Chavez Ravine playing the Los Angeles Angels. On July 12, a crowd of 48,259 cheered the home team to a 5–4 victory. Ted Bowsfield and Dean Chance combined to conquer Whitey Ford in a swift-paced 1:48. The loss left the Yankees a mere .004 points ahead of the second-place Cleveland Indians, who beat the Baltimore Orioles to keep pace with the Bombers. Robin Roberts started for Baltimore and gave up just one run in seven innings of work, but wasn't involved in the decision. Roberts had prospered with the Orioles. He had stopped trying to get by with his fastball and had begun to change speeds. His ERA was a sparkling 2.80. Hobie Landrith, traded a month earlier by the Mets for Marv Throneberry, had homered in three of Roberts' victories.

A Cleveland loss to Baltimore on July 13 allowed the Yankees to cling to the lead, despite a second straight loss to the Angels. Houk and his men had a one-game lead over the Indians, and a game and a half advantage over the pesky Angels, as they lifted off from the West Coast and headed east to Kansas City.

The return of Casey Stengel to major league baseball was a welcome event, not just to New York metropolitan fans, but for the other nine National League clubs as well. Visiting clubs received 27.5 cents for every paid customer at the Polo Grounds; business was especially brisk July 12 to 14, as the Los

Angeles Dodgers made their return to Coogan's Bluff. It was not, unfortunately, so profitable for the Mets in the win column. They dropped three straight to start the second half of the season. On July 12 they were blanked, 3–0. Sandy Koufax won his 14th game, although he departed after seven innings with a sore finger. Larry Sherry, the other Jewish pitcher on the club, completed the shutout. Former Dodger Roger Craig lost his 12th. There was only one consolation for the Mets: Maury Wills didn't steal any bases.

July 13 was Old Timers' Day at the Polo Grounds. Old and current Dodgers—Jackie Robinson, Roy Campanella, Ralph Branca, Duke Snider, Gil Hodges and the oldest living Dodger, 82-year-old Jack Desher—mixed with a sprinkling of Giant heroes of old—Bill Terry, Frankie Frisch, and the man who had hit "the shot heard 'round the world," Bobby Thomson, attended the event. Casey Stengel represented both teams. Ford Frick, Warren Giles, and Donald Grant were all on hand. The Old Timers' exhibition game lasted one inning and ended in a 1–1 tie, but overflowed with nostalgia. Thomson strode to the plate and Ralph Branca came in to face him to wild cheers. This time around, Branca induced Thomson to pop to left-center. Settling under it, Duke Snider cradled the ball and then proceeded to jump up and down, waving his arms as if it were the last game of the 1951 playoff between the Dodgers and Giants. The old Brooklyn faithful joined in the joyful moment, while the Giants' fans looked on unimpressed. For one short moment, history had been rewritten.

Meanwhile, the Mets continued to act from their old script, losing 5–4 to Don Drysdale. Al Jackson was the victim of a Ron Fairly home run that decided the contest in the ninth. July 14 brought the final insult, the Dodgers bombing the Mets, 17–3. Winning pitcher Stan Williams got into the act with a home run in the sixth. The spray-hitting Richie Ashburn, suddenly possessed of muscles, parked a pitch into the upper deck in right field in the fourth off Williams for his sixth homer of the year.

Mel Allen's voice, thick as molasses, and Red Barber's staccato delivery were as familiar to Yankee fans as the crack of Mickey Mantle's bat. Lindsey Nelson and Bob Murphy added their Kentucky and Oklahoma vocal colorings to the Mets' telecasts. But there was a 56-year-old resident of Staten Island, who arguably had an even larger following, at least on radio. His name was Buck Canel. Eloy Canel was born in Buenos Aires in 1906 to parents of Spanish and Scotch Irish descent. Canel's father came from Asturias, a Gaelic outpost in western Spain; he joked that he was "Celtic on both sides."[7] Raised in Staten Island, Buck started out as a correspondent for the Associated Press in 1931, later moving on to *Agence France Presse*. But his métier was sports, primarily boxing and baseball. Broadcasting on the predominantly Spanish language station WHOM, Canel reached millions of *fánaticos* in the Caribbean, Mexico, and Central America. Canel's huge audience was expected to be even bigger than usual as the San Francisco Giants came into town. The Giants had one of the largest contingents of Latin American players in the major leagues.

The influx of athletics from Latin America, both in the baseball and horse racing world, hadn't gone unnoticed. What explained the growing talent from south of the border? Were Americans growing soft? Were they benumbed by an excess of consumer goods? According to *The Sporting News*, America's youth was "losing interest in the game."[7] The car, the drive-in restaurant, et cetera were all intruding on the lives of youngsters between 15 and 17 years— the age during which an earlier generation had been seen competing on the sandlots. The result was a dramatic increase in the number of international players.

Willie Mays was the undisputed star of the San Francisco Giants, one of the biggest draws in the major leagues. But international players easily out-numbered native-born blacks on the San Francisco roster. They included Orlando Cepeda (who had led the National League in home runs and RBIs in 1961) and José Pagán, both of Puerto Rico, and the Dominican trio of Juan Marichal and Felipe and Matty Alou. All of these men were regarded as black players in the racial categorization of the time. But for Latin Americans, black and white, tuning in to Buck Canel's broadcasts on WHOM, their color was a secondary matter. The Spanish–speaking players were a source of cultural pride throughout Latin America. Not even Fidel Castro could keep Cubans from cheering for the Spanish–speaking contingent, as they came in to the Polo Grounds to do battle with the Mets in a Sunday doubleheader on July 15, 1962.

Jay Hook, winner of the first Mets game back on April 23, had a repu-tation of being the Mets "stopper." He lived up to that reputation, holding the Latin American bats silent as he out-dueled Billy Pierce, 5–3. Hook went the distance, handing the Giants their first loss at the Polo Grounds since 1957. The Giants came back in game two to beat the Mets, 9–8. The Latin American bats accounted for half of the San Francisco runs. Juan Marichal, usually a starter, notched his first save of the season. The following day, the Giants bade Coogan's Bluff goodbye, sneaking by the Stengel men, 3–2. Bob Garibaldi, the bonus baby whom Casey Stengel had tried to lure on the last west coast trip, stopped a Mets rally in the ninth with the tying run on base. It was a typical snake-bit day for the Mets. In the bottom of the seventh, Marv Throneberry took off from first on a hit-and-run play. Charlie Neal hit a ball to the right side of the infield, straight at Throneberry. Marv tried to elude the ball's path, but his feet became tangled and tumbled to the ground. He crawled to second base just ahead of the throw. Instead of landing on third, Marvelous Marv remained on second as Giants pitcher (and former

Yankee) Don Larsen struck out Jim Hickman and induced Richie Ashburn to foul out, to end the threat. In the dugout, Casey Stengel threw up his arms in frustration.

Buck Canel's Latin American fans had plenty more to cheer for as Roberto Clemente and the Pittsburgh Pirates came into town. The miserable homestand ended for the Mets with a doubleheader loss to the Bucs on July 18. The second game finished at 12:28 A.M., a heartbreaking tenth-inning loss. Although the Mets had gone 1–7 at the Polo Grounds since the All-Star break, the public's love affair with Casey Stengel remained undiminished. In fact, as Tommy Holmes put it in the *New York Herald Tribune*, Casey had attained a "higher wave of popularity in an atmosphere of failure."[8] It was indeed a world turned upside down.

While Casey's Mets were entertaining the Dodgers, Giants, and Pirates at the Polo Grounds, Ralph Houk's Yankees were flying eastward from Los Angeles. In Kansas City on July 15, the largest crowd that year at Municipal Stadium (34,865) saw the Yanks take two from the lowly Athletics. Things were looking up again for the Yankees. They left Kansas City for Boston, three and a half games ahead of the slumping Cleveland Indians and the surprising Los Angeles Angels, who were tied for second.

Under the eight-team setup that existed before 1961, the New York Yankees and Boston Red Sox played each other 22 times each season. Their schedules alternated between games versus the eastern teams—themselves, Baltimore and Washington—and contests against the western teams—Cleveland, Detroit, Chicago, and Kansas City. The old schedule was rational, and more leisurely—a product of the railway age. By comparison, the expansion schedule, exacerbated by the speed of jet travel, was a crazy quilt. The two old rivals hadn't met since May 17, two months and 57 games earlier.

The New York-Boston rivalry wasn't the same as it had been in the days of DiMaggio and Williams. Still, one question —"Can the Yankees be had?"[9]— was circulating around the American League in 1962. The young Bosox, 6–2 on their current road trip, were eager to test themselves against the defending world champions. It was no contest. The Yankees took three straight at Fenway Park. On July 17, the Bombers squeaked by the Red Sox, 1–0, in a game that lasted 2:18. Ralph Terry went all the way on a four-hitter for his 12th victory of the season. The six-foot, three-inch Terry out-dueled the six-foot, eight-inch Gene Conley (9–8 but pitching much better than his record indicated). After a lopsided victory at Fenway, it was back to Yankee Stadium for a 12-game homestand that would take the Bombers to the second All-Star Game.

No one personified the futility of the first month of the Mets' existence better than Don Zimmer. Before being traded to the Cincinnati Reds on May

7, Zim had hit .077 for the Polo Grounders, managing just four hits in 52 at-bats, with one double and a single run batted in. Actually, the trade to the Reds was a homecoming of sorts. Zim graduated from Western Hills School in Cincinnati, which also produced current Boston Red Sox catcher Russ Nixon (the catcher in all of those pictures of Roger Maris hitting his 61st home run). There was yet another Western Hills alumnus on his way to the majors, a second baseman in the Reds' farm system named Pete Rose. The days when Zim was touted as the best prospect in the Brooklyn Dodger chain were long gone. He was now a utility man on manager Fred Hutchinson's bench. The night before, he delivered a pinch RBI single in the Reds' 4–3 victory over the Los Angeles Dodgers. Zimmer, however, didn't see any action in the Reds' four-game series with the Mets at Crosley Field from July 20 to 22. Then again, his services were hardly required, as the Redlegs took all four games. The Polo Grounders left Cincinnati with their season record at 24–70.

Frank Thomas came about his nickname — "the Big Donkey" — honestly. On the charter flight from Cincinnati to Milwaukee, Thomas once again took on the role of airline attendant. This time, there were complications. One of the flight attendants dropped a container with ten trays, creating a temporary shortage in meals. Road secretary Lou Niss instructed Thomas to serve the players first. The Mets' 60-year-old trainer, Gus Mauch took umbrage at this violation of the pecking order and got into a heated argument with Thomas. "If it wasn't for your age," growled Thomas, "I'd ..."[10]

Arriving in Milwaukee, the Mets ran into another Mets alumnus. Like Don Zimmer, Gus Bell had endured a tough time as a Met, hitting just .149 in 101 at-bats, with just six RBIs. But Bell had since prospered as a part-time outfielder and pinch-hitter with the Braves. In the opening game of the series on July 23, the Kentuckian came through with a pinch single in the ninth, sending the game into extra innings. The Braves won it in the 12th inning. But Casey Stengel wasn't there to see it. He was in Kansas City attending the funeral of his brother, Grant. Cookie Lavagetto managed the team in his absence and introduced a new keystone combination: Charlie Neal shifted over to shortstop, allowing Rod Kanehl to patrol second base — gamely if not gracefully. The results of this move were not readily apparent, as Bell's new team wrenched two more victories from the Mets. On the final day of the series on July 25, the Braves' Warren Spahn beat the Polo Grounders for his 319th career victory. He also hit a home run, the 31st of his career, a new record for National League pitchers. The Mets now headed for St. Louis and a rendezvous with another old-timer, Stan (the Man) Musial.

The Yankees' fortunes had risen dramatically with the reappearance of Mickey Mantle in the lineup on June 22. During his absence, the club had played .500 ball (15–15) and fallen to fourth place in the American League standings. Since returning, Mickey had hit .371 (36–97), with 25 RBIs. The Yankees were 22–8 during that period. They were now once again in first place, three games in front of Los Angeles, five ahead of Minnesota, and seven games above the fading Cleveland Indians. The Yankees would finish the month of July at home in the Bronx, with series against the Washington Senators, Boston Red Sox, and Chicago White Sox.

On July 20 and 21 the Bombers turned back the Nats in two closely-played games. Roger Maris' 24th home run was the decisive blow in the second contest. Saturday, July 21, was family day at Yankee Stadium. About 20 wives and 40 children streamed onto the field before the game. The youngest, eight-month old Scotty Slabodan, stayed in the dugout with his proud grandpa, Ralph Houk. During his pre-game show, Red Barber, the Yankees' play-by-play announcer, turned the mike over to Scotty's grandmother, Bette Houk, who carried on in his place as "mistress of ceremonies."[11]

The doubleheader on Sunday, July 22, saw a reversal of fortunes. The lowly Senators beat the Yankees twice in two rapidly played games (the times were 2:12 and 2:14). Jim Bouton and Luis Arroyo were on the receiving end of the Nats' surprising assault on Yankee pitching. After completing their series with the Senators, the Yankees flew to Utica, New York. They stayed there overnight, and the next day, drove to Cooperstown to play the Milwaukee Braves in the annual Hall of Fame Game. They watched as Bill McKechnie, Edd Roush, Bob Feller, and Jackie Robinson were received into baseball's Valhalla. The skies, which had been threatening rain all morning, finally emptied themselves on the throng. The game between the Yankees and Braves was postponed because of rain. Houk's wet and weary bunch headed back to New York.

While the Milwaukee Braves—formerly the Boston Braves—were hosting the Mets July 24 to 26 at County Stadium, the Yankees were in the Bronx entertaining the now sole occupants of Beantown, the Boston Red Sox. This was a very different club from the Ted Williams–led outfits of the late 1940s that had challenged Joe DiMaggio's Yankees for supremacy in the American League. Pinky Higgins' club was safely ensconced in the second division. Higgins did have some fine veteran players in third baseman Frank Malzone, first baseman Pete Runnels, catcher Russ Nixon, and center fielder Gary Geiger. He also had a group of good young pitchers, such as starters Bill Monbouquette, Earl Wilson, and the huge reliever, Dick Radatz (nicknamed "the Monster"). A month earlier, Wilson had thrown a no-hitter — the first black American Leaguer ever to do so. Veteran Gene Conley was enjoying a fine season — even if it didn't show in the won-loss column. The Bosox also had some promising hitters, including second baseman Chuck Schilling, catcher

Jim Pagliaroni, and right fielder Lu Clinton. Finally, there was the heir apparent to the retired Ted Williams, the Long Island-born left fielder, Carl Yastremzski.

Long Island, New York had experienced billion dollar growth in the 1950s. With a combined population of 2,084,904, Nassau and Suffolk Counties would've ranked as the fourth largest city in the United States in 1962, richer than 32 of the 50 states of the Union. Nassau and Suffolk were more than just suburban appendages to New York City. Gross income had increased 300 percent during the decade, the two counties producing an annual income of $3.76 billion a year. The building of Levittown in the late 1940s had been followed by a mass migration from Brooklyn, Manhattan, and the Bronx, and nurtured the culture of consumption that characterized post–World War II America. The number of family-owned cars on Long Island rose from 340,592 to 789,539 by 1961. Eighty-six percent of residents owned TV sets; 13 percent had air conditioners, with the numbers growing every day. The pressure of suburban construction was inexorable. In the past decade, agricultural acreage decreased from 150,680 to 97,182.

Carl Yastremzski was born in a very different Long Island, before Levittown, and before the mass migration from New York City. His father, Carl, Sr. and his mother, Hattie, worked a 60-acre potato farm in the small Suffolk County community of Bridgehampton. Young Carl himself had spent many a day moving irrigation pipes and storing bushel baskets filled with potatoes. The Red Sox signed him out of Notre Dame University in 1958, and, after a stellar year at Minneapolis (where he hit .339), Yaz was deemed the successor to Ted Williams. In his rookie year in 1961, the dark-haired farm boy with the piercing dark eyes and prominent nose hit .266, with 11 home runs and 80 RBIs. The Bombers could've used his glove in left field, and his left-handed bat would have been a natural for the short right field fence at Yankee Stadium. In fact, Yaz had been given a tryout by the Yankees. If things had gone differently, he might've become Yankees property. But Yaz was put off at being made to suit up with the batboys on his visit to the Stadium, and his father was further miffed when he was denied entry into the park to see his son work out. So it was Boston, six hours away from Bridgehampton, which became his baseball address.

Carl Yastremzski and his Boston teammates didn't fare well in the Bronx from July 24 to 26, dropping three of four games to the Yankees. On July 24, they were beaten, 5–3. Whitey Ford, utilizing a snappy curve and hard fastball, struck out eight of the first 15 Red Sox he faced. Whitey's shoulder stiffened in the late innings, so Marshall Bridges mopped up, in a game that flew by in 2:09. On July 25, the Yankees and Red Sox played one of those infamous day-night doubleheaders. In game one, Earl Wilson won for the first time since no-hitting the Angels (and Bo Belinsky) on June 26. Bridges, clearly Luis Arroyo's replacement in the bullpen, won the second game for the Yankees in relief.

The getaway game of the series, on July 26, began normally enough. The Yankees, who had defeated Gene Conley the previous week, 1–0, in Boston, beat up on him for ten hits and eight runs in the third inning of a 13–3 romp. Clete Boyer led off the third with a single and came back later in the inning to hit a two-run homer (his 13th of the year). Carl Yastremszki contributed to the deluge by dropping a fly ball in the sun; he had forgotten to take his sunglasses when he ran out on the field. Jim Bouton was the recipient of this bounty, with 2 and two-thirds innings of relief help from Bob Turley. With that, the Red Sox took off for Newark Airport and a flight to Washington. That is, all of the Red Sox, except two. Conley and reserve infielder Pumpsie Green never made it over the George Washington Bridge into New Jersey.

Conley and Green made an odd couple, a "Mutt and Jeff" pairing. Conley, the tallest player in the league at six-foot, eight inches, was originally signed by the Boston Braves and followed them to Milwaukee, where for a while in the 1950s he was a dependable third or fourth starter behind Warren Spahn and Lew Burdette. Conley was traded to Philadelphia in 1960, and a year later was sent to the Red Sox for the six-foot, seven-inch Frank Sullivan, in what, to this day, must be the trade featuring the tallest players in the major leagues. During the off-season, "Daddy Longlegs" was a backup center and forward on the Red Auerbach–led Boston Celtic championship teams of the late 1950s and sixties. Conley had pitched well for the Red Sox so far in 1962; some even thought he should be an All-Star choice. But the Red Sox had not scored a run for him in 23 innings.

Pumpsie Green, despite his modest major league credentials, was the most controversial major leaguer since Jackie Robinson. Boston was the last segregated team in the major leagues in 1959. Green, a shortstop and second baseman, had hit well in Florida and was expected to be the Red Sox's first black player. Boston, however, sent the Berkeley, California, native to its Triple-A farm team at Minneapolis for more seasoning. Owner Tom Yawkey was soon assailed by civil rights groups, claiming discrimination, which Yawkey vehemently denied. Green finally came up to Boston in July 1959, marking the final integration of all major league teams. Playing behind Chuck Schilling at second and Eddie Bressoud at shortstop, Green saw little action in 1962. But for black culture, his presence on the team was no less important than if he had been a star of Ted Williams' magnitude.

Leaving the Stadium on Thursday, July 26, the Red Sox' team bus became stuck in traffic on the Cross Bronx Expressway. For 15 minutes, the Red Sox sat at the same block in the stifling summer New York heat. Conley had to go

Yankee Stadium, the Bronx, New York. On July 26, the Boston Red Sox left the Stadium after an afternoon game, and became stuck in traffic on the Cross Bronx Expressway. Pitcher Gene Conley and infielder Pumpsie Green jumped the bus and went AWOL. Conley reportedly went to Idlewild Airport and tried to board a plane to Israel. "I want to see Bethlehem," he supposedly said.

to the bathroom and asked permission to step off the bus. Green did the same, and the two disappeared into the wilds of New York City. Twenty seven hours later, on the evening of July 28, Pumpsie turned up at the Statler Hilton Hotel in Washington and went promptly to bed, missing the doubleheader against the Senators. He met the next day with a fuming manager Pinky Higgins, who fined him $1,000 — a stiff penalty for a player making less than $10,000 a year. Green was sorry for what he had done, but couldn't explain why he did it. Conley, meanwhile, remained AWOL for another 41 hours. According to one account, he was last seen at 3 P.M. on Friday in the lobby of the Commodore Hotel. Chris Kieran of the *New York Daily News* reported that Conley had been picked up by a cab at Al Schacht's Restaurant at 102 East 52 Street at 2:45 P.M., and asked to be taken to Idlewild Airport. "I want to see Bethlehem," he supposedly told the cabbie. Conley subsequently tried to book a flight to Israel on El Al Airlines, but was denied admission on the plane for lack of a passport. News photographers finally caught up with him, barefoot and downcast, at his trailer park home in the Boston suburb of Foxboro on Saturday, July 28. Conley paid a high price for his gallivanting, a $2,000 fine — the highest since Ted Williams was assessed $5,000 in 1955.[12]

In a telegram to manager Pinky Higgins, Conley apologized, saying, "I am sorry for the way I have handled things, but I'm tired and have other plans. Thank you for everything, Mike."[13] It wasn't the first time that a Boston player had gone AWOL. Jackie Jensen, the American League's MVP in 1958, hated flying, and had retired after the 1959 season. He returned in 1961, but had a change of heart and left the team for Lake Tahoe, Nevada, without explanation. Although travel in the railroad age wasn't glamorous by any stretch of the imagination, the Jet Age and Major League Baseball's recent expansion to ten clubs presented additional trials—less leisurely travel and odd scheduling. Teams jumped from city to city at dizzying speeds. Seen in this light, it seemed understandable that Conley or Green would want to escape the incessant pressure. Curiously, while Conley's wandering was well documented in the mainstream press, and provided a measure of mirth in the dog days of summer, the black press remained scrupulously silent on Green. For a people still trying to gain full equality in America's National Pastime, Pumpsie's behavior was a source of embarrassment, not amusement.

The New York Mets touched down on the banks of the Mississippi on July 27 for a four-game set with the St. Louis Cardinals. Casey, well-traveled as a player (he toiled for the Giants, Dodgers, Pirates, and Braves) had somehow avoided donning a Cardinals uniform. Stengel, however, had vivid memories of St. Louis, some good and some bad. He recalled the days of traveling between New York and St. Louis in the railway era. Train rides from the east coast to the middle of the country took "all day and all night, and most of the next day." In these days before air conditioned cars, players would strip naked and wrap themselves in sheets rather than ruin their clothes with grime and sweat. But the Old Perfessor also had warm memories of St. Louis. It was in St. Louis in the early 1920s that Charles Dillon Stengel wooed his future wife, Edna Lawson.

The little lefty, Al Jackson, finally put the Mets on the winning side of the ledger by shutting out the Cardinals, 1–0, in the first game of a doubleheader on Friday, July 27. Jackson was responsible for all of the club's three shutout victories. The Mets had the Cards beaten in the second game too, but lost a heartbreaker on a three-run homer in the eighth inning. On the plus side, the new keystone combination of Rod Kanehl and Charlie Neal turned over three double plays in the doubleheader. On Saturday, the Mets came back to win, 9–8, over the Redbirds. This was one of those games where the Old Perfessor's managerial genius may have played a role in the victory. St. Louis starter Curt Simmons' best pitch was a screwball, which was most effective against right-handed hitters. Knowing that the screwie was less effective against lefty batters, and remembering that Gene Woodling could handle left handed pitching, Casey sent the 40-year-old veteran to the plate in the fifth inning. Woodling hit a pinch home run to put the Mets ahead to stay.

After the game, the Mets celebrated Casey Stengel's 73rd birthday, with George Weiss coming into town especially for the occasion. The birthday celebration continued the next day, as Casey sampled a birthday cake between games of the Sunday doubleheader. There was nothing else to celebrate, as the Mets dropped both contests to the home team Cardinals. That was it for the Mets in July.

They ended the month with an overall record of 26–76. Their manager had just turned 73. Their most popular player, Gil Hodges, was in the hospital with kidney stones and suffering from a possible season-ending knee injury. The veterans Weiss had traded — Don Zimmer, Gus Bell, Hobie Landrith — were prospering on other teams. The team had no hot prospects coming out of the minors, although Rod Kanehl was proving a pleasant surprise. The one major signee, bonus baby Ed Kranepool, was being farmed out for seasoning after a short trial on the bench.

There was one potential bit of good news. One of the Polo Grounds ushers had a son serving in the military in Texas. The son's army team had a terrific young pitcher named Jerry Koosman. Perhaps the Mets might want to give him a look?

Conley and Green weren't the only ones making headlines in the summer of 1962. Bill Veeck, facing yet another leg amputation, had relinquished his ownership of the Chicago White Sox. Nevertheless, he continued to stir controversy; his autobiography, *Veeck as in Wreck*, came out in July. In it, Veeck lamented the state of the National Pastime. A major league game, he groused, was nothing more than a "tableau ... singularly lacking in drama." Twenty minutes of every hour of a game was taken up with the pitcher holding the ball and peering at home plate. Veeck, the man who had given baseball the exploding scoreboard, placed surnames on players' uniforms, and sent a midget to bat, also had ideas for speeding up the game. The plate, he suggested, should be widened. Only two strikes and three balls should be allowed to the hitter. He also suggested that the majors increase its pool of potential players by subsidizing college baseball.[14]

Veeck being Veeck, he couldn't help but heap venom on his favorite bête noir, Yankee co-owner Del Webb. In his book, Veeck accused Webb of being a sinister string puller who had prevented him and Chicago G.M. Hank Greenberg from obtaining the new franchise in Los Angeles. Webb, Veeck alleged, had wanted the stadium building contract for his construction company. On the field, Veeck's former club, the White Sox, and Webb's present club, the Yankees, played a four-game series in the Bronx July 27 to 29. Dale Long, reacquired from the Senators two weeks earlier, hit a 3–1 pitch from

Turk Lown in the bottom of the 12th inning to give the Yanks a 4–3 victory in the opening game of the series on Friday night.

Saturday, July 28, was Old Timers' Day at Yankee Stadium. The main event was a reenactment of the 1937 classic, played at the Stadium and won by the American League, 8–3. This was the fateful All-Star Game in which a drive from the bat of Earl Averill of the Cleveland Indians had broken the toe of the St. Louis Cardinals' ace, Dizzy Dean. Dean, the last major league pitcher to win 30 games in a season, was never the same pitcher again. Averill was present at the Stadium along with 1937 American League All-Stars Joe DiMaggio, Hank Greenberg, Jimmie Foxx, and Roger (Doc) Cramer. Dean was also present, along with National League All-Stars Bill Terry and Gabby Hartnett, among others. The recent inductees into the Baseball Hall of Fame — Bill McKechnie, Edd Roush, Bob Feller, and Jackie Robinson — were introduced to the Stadium crowd and received a generous ovation from the fans. The members of the Yankees' 200-homer club were also recognized. Joe DiMaggio, Bill Dickey, Yogi Berra, and Mickey Mantle received certificates. The widows of Babe Ruth and Lou Gehrig received silver framed certificates.

The festivities over, the crowd of 52,038 settled in for a close 4–3 Yankee victory over the White Sox. Johnny Blanchard provided the heroics that afternoon with a three-run homer in the seventh inning, following Mickey Mantle's 21st round tripper of the year. Jim Bouton cut off a Pale Hose rally in the ninth. He relieved the struggling Luis Arroyo and threw just three pitches to end the game. The Yankees and White Sox ended their July schedule by splitting a Sunday doubleheader. The Sox's Juan Pizarro, the losing pitcher in the first game, came back to win game two in relief.

The end of July saw a series of roster changes. The Yankees optioned a slumping Joe Pepitone to Richmond to make room on the roster for the imminent return of Tony Kubek. A more serious roster problem concerned Mickey Mantle. He aggravated his injury from the previous month, and his participation in the second All-Star Game at Chicago on July 30, not to mention the rest of the season, was thrown into doubt.

Roger Maris was sitting at the large center table in the visitors' clubhouse at Chicago's Wrigley Field on Monday, July 30, perspiration dripping down his face. Mickey Mantle was a few feet away, having just finished eating a sandwich — a concoction of rye bread, cheese, sliced beef, tomatoes, and relish spread. Mickey was now slowly unwrapping the yards of protective tape from his tender knees. Around them were their jubilant American League teammates, who had finally beaten the National Leaguers in All-Star Game play after five consecutive defeats. Neither Mantle nor Maris had played much of a role in the scoring. Mickey sat out the game; his May 18 injury was acting up again. Roger had one hit, a double in the ninth after the contest was already decided in the American League's favor. He also made two fine catches, one against the ivy in right field to help preserve the American League's lead. He had been booed every time he came to bat, but at least he had escaped injury at the hands of the Wrigley Field fans. At one point, a peach sailed over his shoulder. He was a "marked man" indeed.

That same day, the National Basketball Association Board of Governors met at New York's Roosevelt Hotel. They decided to rescind their invitation to the ABA's Cleveland Pipers. George Steinbrenner had been unable to raise the $250,000 needed to secure the Pipers' entry into the NBA. Steinbrenner's vault into big time sports ownership would be postponed for another decade. Meanwhile, in New York, the high (the Topping-Webb Yankees) and the low (Joan Payson's Mets) continued their unlikely rivalry for the hearts and pocketbooks of the Metropolitan area fans.

8

"What Did Belinsky Say Today?"

The New York Mets began their August schedule with a five-day, seven-game homestand versus the Philadelphia Phillies and Cincinnati Reds. While Casey and the Mets soldiered on at the Polo Grounds, team owner Joan Payson was at her cottage at Saratoga Springs tending to her Greentree Stable, which she co-owned with her brother, Jock Whitney. Each year, between July 30 and August 25, the small upstate spa resort of Saratoga Springs was the center of the racing world in the northeast. Mohawk Airlines was running five special weekend flights from Idlewild Airport to Albany; from there, special buses shuttled horse racing enthusiasts to Saratoga. Belmont Racetrack had closed in deference to the occasion, but racing fans could enjoy one last week of betting at Monmouth Park in Oceanport, New Jersey, where the big attraction was "Jaipur," the last year's Belmont Stakes winner, ridden by Willie Shoemaker.

Had she been in her private box at the Polo Grounds in early August, Joan Payson would have witnessed a dazzling display of power hitting by Frank Thomas— all of it, unfortunately, in vain. On Wednesday night, August 1, Thomas hit two home runs (one a grand slam) and drove in six runs in an 11–9 loss to Philadelphia. On Thursday night, Thomas again hit two home runs (numbers 22 and 23 of the season) and Marv Throneberry added two of his own, but the result was the same. The Quakers' Art Mahaffey absorbed the Mets' power barrage, pitching a five-hitter, striking out 12, and smacking a grand slam of his own in a 9–4 Phillies victory.

The action continued on the southern end of the Macombs Dam Bridge with a five-game set between the Mets and the Cincinnati Reds. On Friday, August 3, Frank Thomas hit two home runs for the third consecutive game (numbers 24 and 25). Marv Throneberry added his eighth. But the Mets lost their fifth game in a row, 8–6. On Saturday, "Carry Back" won the $57,400 Whitney Stakes at Saratoga Race Track. Back in New York, Joan Payson's Mets also came up winners that day. The Stengel men, who had beaten every team except Cincinnati, finally broke the spell by sweeping both ends of a double-header from the Reds. Round trippers by Throneberry and Charlie Neal paced a 9–1 victory in game one. Thomas' 26th home run, coming in the 14th inning, gave the Mets a 3–2 win in the nightcap. Cincinnati badly needed to win these games against the Mets, in order to keep pace with Los Angeles and San Francisco in the National League pennant race. After the second loss to the Mets, an enraged Reds manager, Fred Hutchinson, remained in the vis-iting dugout, steaming. Running into Hutchinson later that night at Toots Shor's, Casey Stengel couldn't help baiting "the Bear." "You sat so long in that dugout," Casey quipped, "that I thought you were going to apply for a job as groundskeeper." Later on, Hutchinson accepted a ride back to his hotel from Stengel. But when he saw the company car with "METS" emblazoned on the door, Hutch changed his mind. "I'll walk," he growled, and then stum-bled down the sidewalk.[1]

Hutchinson's humor was no better the next day, May 5, as Casey's team beat the Redlegs for the third consecutive time in the first game of a Sunday doubleheader. Rookie Rick Herrscher, called up from Syracuse on July 31 (after the release of Vinegar Bend Mizell), hit his first major league home run to win it. The Mets then reverted to form, losing the second game, but the five-game series against the Reds allowed the Mets to surpass the entire season attendance of the 1957 New York Giants. To date, 667,161 customers had passed through the turnstiles to see the Stengel men, compared to 653,923 for the Willie Mays-led Giants in their last year at the Polo Grounds. There was good news on another front. Gil Hodges had just been released from Roo-sevelt Hospital following his kidney stone surgery. He would visit his mother in Petersburg, Indiana, before rejoining the team on the West Coast against the Dodgers and Giants.

Major league ballplayers didn't travel in the same social circles as the Whitneys, Vanderbilts, and Woodwards that ruled the racing world of Saratoga. Still, the modern ballplayer was increasingly more coddled and bet-ter paid than his "rowdy and rough-hewn" predecessors of yesteryear.[2] The Marises and Mantles on the Yankees—and the Ashburns and Hodgeses on the Mets—enjoyed benefits unbeknownst to players of Casey Stengel's era. The M&M Boys walked about the Yankee Stadium clubhouse on wall-to wall-carpeting. In the past, players submitted their aching joints and muscles to trainers wielding nothing more than bottles of Sloan's liniment. By 1962, Mets trainer Gus Mauch, his assistant Lynn Lischer, and their fellow practioners were equipped with the best that science and technology could offer — diathermy machines, whirlpool baths, and infra-red lamps. And it wasn't just the ballplayers enjoying the new era of abundance. On trips to Los Angeles to play the Angels, manager Ralph Houk might occupy a suite at the Sheraton West that was recently vacated by a Texas oil millionaire.

The growing gap between the modern player and the average fan didn't sit well with longtime observers of the sport. Years earlier, the players might be found patronizing the same neighborhood watering hole frequented by the bleacher fan. But the times were changing. Stanley Frank, writing in *Sports Illustrated*, complained that the "amiable eccentric" of yore — the Rabbit Maranvilles, Dizzy Deans, and Pepper Martins— had been supplanted by players as "impersonal as motorcycle cops." Frank blamed the lack of colorful characters in baseball, in part, on the pension system. A current player with 20 years of service, he noted, stood to make $700 a month at age 65. A five-year man would receive $112.50 at age 50.[3] This kind of money wasn't enough to allow ballplayers to rub elbows with Joan Payson Whitney at Saratoga's races, but it was enough to curb their enthusiasm for on-the-field high jinks. Yet, it was more than just a question of money or relative luxury that determined their behavior. Modern pop psychology, a la David Riesman's *The Lonely Crowd*, was applied to the modern ballplayer. "Maris' run for Ruth's record," wrote Bill Veeck, "was a godsend to the American League." It saved the junior circuit from an otherwise "disastrous year." But, said Veeck, "his personable impact was unbelievably slight." Baseball was crying out for colorful characters, but Maris wanted to "submerge himself," not stand out. For Veeck, Roger emblemized the conformity that had characterized the country in the era of the Cold War,[4] a lack of spirit and individualism that had made baseball so entertaining.

The financial opportunities available to the modern ballplayer — especially if, like Maris or Mantle, he was white — roused the envy of the members of the Fourth Estate. The previous December, the M&M Boys had cashed in on their record-breaking home run spree of 1961 with a six-figure endorsement deal in men's outwear. A sportswriter approached Roger during spring training and, with thinly veiled contempt, remarked, "I bet you weigh 380 pounds now with your money belt on."[5] The writers yearned for colorful, somewhat naïve characters to mold stories around — someone like Bo Belinsky. When Belinsky complained that he wasn't able to bet on games in the majors as he had in the minors, *The Sporting News* called on Angels officials to discipline him. The loose-lipped Bo, however, had his defenders in some corners of the press. For all his loony behavior, Bo represented a throwback to an earlier age. He represented a sentimental attachment to a less sophisticated age and player — and the mythologizing possibilities it suggested.

On the first day of August, Roger Maris had 24 home runs, fifth best in the American League, and six behind the leader, Norm Cash of Detroit. Neither Maris nor Mickey Mantle were shattering records in 1962, but their club, after a torrid July, was threatening to make a shambles of the American League race. Ralph Houk's men were now six games in front of their nearest competitor, Bo Belinsky's Angels, and six and one-half games ahead of the Minnesota Twins. The Cleveland Indians, who had wrested the lead from the Yankees in June, lost nine in a row in mid-July and were now ten games behind the Bombers. Tito Francona's pennant aspirations had been premature.

About the only thing the Yankees had failed to do was to no-hit the opposition. In Chicago on Wednesday, the first day of August, Bill Monbouquette of the Boston Red Sox became the third American League pitcher (after Belinsky and fellow Bosox Earl Wilson) to throw a no-hitter. Six hundred fifty miles away, the biggest crowd ever at the nation's capital, 48,147, saw the Yankees beat the lowly Nats twice in a doubleheader for a sweep of the three-game series begun on July 31. Mickey Mantle, still nursing the knee injury suffered on May 19, sat out the entire series.

From Washington, Ralph Houk and company flew to Chicago for a three-game series against the White Sox. Comiskey Park, home of the Pale Hose, was located about three and a half miles south of the Loop, 20 minutes by car and ten minutes by subway and el train transportation. The old and shabby Comiskey had undergone a dramatic transformation after Bill Veeck took over the club reins in 1959. The ballpark was painted inside and out, new ticket booths installed, and new entrances created to alleviate the human traffic. There was now a picnic area under the left field stands. The stadium's most salient feature was the exploding scoreboard, premiered by Veeck in 1960, but not all of his experiments worked so well. The current ownership had unloaded most of the grizzled veterans acquired by Veeck, but after a fine April start, Al López's club had played sub–.500 ball and was mired in seventh place.

The Chicago series from August 3 to 5 marked the long-awaited return of Tony Kubek after ten months in military service. PFC Kubek, who earned $124 a month (with a $90 home allowance) during his stint for Uncle Sam, joined the team after a short visit to his off-season home at Milwaukee. Tony was feeling "clumsy" after his long layoff and uncertain about his status on the team. Tom Tresh had done an admirable job at the position in his absence, making the All-Star squad as a rookie, and Ralph Houk refused to tip his hand as to who his shortstop of the future would be. Would Kubek play shortstop? "I wish I knew," Kubek answered.[6] In the meantime, Tony watched from the bench as his teammates, after winning the series opener in Chicago, dropped the next two games to the White Sox, both one-run decisions. Despite losing two of three at Comiskey, the Yankees still enjoyed a solid five-game lead over the second-place Twins in what, at one time, had been a close pennant race. But the major league season was a marathon, not a sprint. Houk and company had a punishing schedule in August: 36 games, with just two days off. If anyone was going to catch them, this would be the month to do it.

As the Yankees were flying back to New York on Sunday, August 5, the world was learning of the death of Marilyn Monroe. The Hollywood sex god-

dess, last seen in New York on May 19 at the JFK birthday gala at Madison Square Garden, had succumbed in Los Angeles to an apparent overdose of sleeping pills. As fate would have it, Casey and the Mets were arriving in Los Angeles for a series with the Dodgers. The Dodgers were currently in first place in the National League standings, enjoying a four and a half game lead over the second-place San Francisco Giants, and a whopping ten games over the third-place Cincinnati Reds. Despite their comfortable lead, not all was well with the Dodgers. Lefty Sandy Koufax had been sidelined since July 17 with a mysterious circulation problem in his throwing hand. Alston's other aces, Don Drysdale and Johnny Podres, had little problem with the Mets at "Chevy's Ravine"[7]— as Casey Stengel called it — on August 6 and 7.

Tony Kubek, Yankee shortstop. Kubek played his first game of the season on August 7 after returning from military service (this was the height of the Cold War). Yankee manager Ralph Houk worried about the absence of his shortstop. He worried for nothing. Tony reclaimed the shortstop position and hit .314 on the season. His replacement, Tom Tresh, shifted to left field and won the Rookie of the Year Award.

Moving on to San Francisco, on Wednesday night, August 8, the Mets finally won their 30th game of the season, beating Al Dark's Giants at Candlestick Park. Roger Craig went all the way for his seventh victory (against 17 loses) in a 5–2 win. The Mets' infield of Félix Mantilla, Charlie Neal, Rod Kanehl, and Marv Throneberry turned over five double plays in support of Craig. One of Casey Stengel's season-long complaints had been the inability of the Mets to erase base runners. But since switching to the keystone combination of Neal and Kanehl, the Mets had made 27 double plays in 17 games. Inevitably, the next day the Mets reverted to type. Fielding lapses contributed mightily to a 7–1 defeat. The Giants' winner, Jack Sanford, won his 15th game of the season, his fifth against the Polo Grounders. There were quite a few National League pitchers zeroing in on 20 wins—thanks, in great part, to the expansion Mets.

The Mets had won three of five games against the Cincinnati Reds the previous week at the Polo Grounds, and hoped for continued success at Crosley Field. Instead, they dropped all three games to the Redlegs August 10 to 12, thus losing all 11 contests at Cincinnati in 1962. At least the Mets were good copy. Casey Stengel was trying to convert the shy catcher, Choo Choo Coleman, into a take-charge guy. After one particular play in which Coleman had been less than assertive, Casey admonished Choo Choo, saying, "You ain't playing for Syracuse. Thousands of people are here. You got to yell to the pitcher, 'Cover first.'" The young catcher mulled over this piece of fatherly advice and responded, "I figured they should know what to do up here."[8] If only it were so easy.

Between August 6 and August 12, the Yankees were home entertaining the Minnesota Twins, Baltimore Orioles, and Detroit Tigers. Ralph Houk, sick of hearing how the Yankees played in an easier league, lashed out against his team's critics in an article in the August edition of the *Saturday Evening Post*. The National League was not better balanced or stronger than the American League, argued the Major. Winning pennants had "never been easy" and in fact, with the surge of the Minnesota Twins and Los Angeles Angels, the loop was now stronger than ever.[9] The Angels, he pointed out, had All-Star starters in Leon Wagner and Billy Moran. And then there were the Minnesota Twins, the former Washington Senators, who were playing in their second season in the Twin Cities and were one of the biggest surprises of the 1962 season. The team had plenty of power, supplied foremost by one of the most feared sluggers in the game, Harmon Killebrew. The "Killer," a mild-mannered, stocky powerhouse of a man, was currently second in home runs with 29 (five more than Roger Maris) and second in runs batted in with 77. His teammate, rookie Rich Rollins, was batting .311 (fourth in the league) and tied for third in RBIs with 75. Another teammate, the flashy-fielding Puerto Rican first baseman, Vic Power, was currently fifth in the American League batting race at .305. The Twins also had another Gold Glover and slugger in catcher Earl Battey.

The biggest improvement on the Twins, according to the *Minneapolis Star's* Dick Gordon, was the "kid infield."[10] Second baseman Bernie Allen, 23, had chased Billy Martin into retirement. At short, Zoilo Versalles was fast becoming the best at his position in the American League. Rich Rollins was a revelation at third. Anchoring the infield was the ageless veteran, Vic Power, whose ability to scoop errant throws had helped raise the confidence of his young diamond mates. Rollins claimed that Vic's fielding had saved him seven errors in the first two weeks of the season. What made the Twins' challenge to the Yankee hegemony questionable was its pitching. The staff was led by the Cuban curve ball specialist, Camilo Pascual, and the promising lefthander, Jim Kaat. But Pascual, who logged dozens of inning in the Cuban Winter League, was often sidelined with arm woes while third starter Jack Kralick was inconsistent. In the meantime, manager Sam Mele was praised for his deft handling of the relief corps. The series at Yankee Stadium beginning on August 6 would test the mettle of the young Twins.

The Twins set out to prove Houk right about the increase in competition in the American League. They beat the Yankees in the series opener at the Stadium, 5–4, handing the Bombers their third consecutive defeat. Mickey Mantle, whose tales of woe began with an injury against the Twins in a game on May 18, returned to the lineup for only the second time in eight days. He contributed a long double in an eighth inning rally. Roger Maris added his 25th home run, all for nothing. The next day, August 7, Tony Kubek played his first game of the 1962 season, but in left field. Kubek made his debut a memorable one, homering off Camilo Pascual in the first inning with two on. The Yankees proceeded to rack up 18 hits off three Twins hurlers and coasted to a 14–1 victory. Tom Tresh, still ensconced at shortstop, hit two home runs. With the Yankee' lead again up to five games over the Twins, so much for the increased competition in the American League.

Next on tap were the Baltimore Orioles. Due to the idiosyncratic scheduling, the Yankees and Orioles had not faced each other since their encounter on June 21 at Memorial Stadium. Not much had changed for "the Flock." The Orioles were playing .500 ball then and were playing .500 ball now. The loss to military service of shortstop Ron Hansen and pitcher Steve Barber, coupled with injuries to catcher Gus Triandos, had all taken their toll on Billy Hitchcock's team. The Birds split a doubleheader with the Yankees on Wednesday, August 8, both one-run games. The Yankees won the first contest on a single by Moose Skowron off Milt Pappas with two outs in the ninth. Marshall Bridges, who threw one pitch for a game-ending double play, was the winner. Jim Bouton lost the second game, hurt by sloppy fielding from an unexpected source. Clete Boyer made two errors in opening the door to a four-run Oriole sixth inning.

The Yankee home stand ended with four games against the Detroit Tigers from August 10 to 12. What a difference a year makes. On August 10, 1961, the Tigers were in second place in the American League standings, three games behind the mighty Yankees. Now, a year later, Bob Scheffing's team was in seventh place, two games under .500 and a distant 13 games behind the Yankees. Al Kaline had come back on July 23, after missing 57 games due to the broken clavicle incurred at the Stadium in late May. Norm Cash, the league's batting champ the previous year at .361, was contending for the league lead in home runs but was nowhere near the .300 mark. The Yankee Killer, Frank Lary, a 23-game winner the year before, had been victimized by a sore arm. Rookie standouts Jake Wood and Steve Boros were suffering through the sophomore jinx. The Bombers began the series by splitting two blowouts with the Bengals; they ended the series with two closely played victories. On Saturday night, August 11, Roger Maris tied the game with his 26th home run in the sixth inning off Jim Bunning, and then won it with a run-scoring single in the tenth against reliever Terry Fox.

With that, the Yankees packed their bags for a tour that would keep them living out of suitcases until August 27. They were still holding the Minnesota Twins and Los Angeles Angels at bay; the two young challengers were both five games out of the first spot. But the wheel would turn again.

Parks commissioner Robert Moses was stirring up controversy on Long Island with his plan to build a highway across Fire Island. Things were going much better for Moses in New York City, as work continued on another of his pet projects, the Flushing Meadows Stadium. With the new stadium nearly half completed, the club was expected to make its debut in Queens in April 1963. George Weiss had good reason to look to the future. The current Mets were 30–86, 47 and a half games behind the first-place Los Angeles Dodgers. Although the season had a month and a half to go, they were already mathematically eliminated from the National League pennant race. Even the low man on the totem pole in the American League, the Washington Senators, had won 15 more games than Casey's Mets. Since the expansion Senators had tied for ninth the previous year with the Kansas City Athletics, the Stengel men were poised to become the first major league club in the modern era to finish in tenth place.

There were many frustrating nights for the Mets on their side of the Macombs Dam Bridge, but none more gallant than that of Tuesday, August 14. Al Jackson soldiered on for 15 innings before succumbing to the Philadelphia Phillies, 3–1. Jackson was heroic in his duel with Quaker starter Dallas Green, who went the first ten innings. The little lefty threw 215 pitches and didn't allow a Phillies runner as far as second base from the fifth to the 14th inning. Jackson's undoing had something to do with the fact that Marv Throneberry, not Gil Hodges, was playing behind him at first base. In the top of the 15th, the Phils' Bob Oldis opened with a single to right. Rubén Amaro then walked. With runners on first and second, Tony González hit a ground ball to Throneberry. Marv let the ball go through his legs for a two-base error, loading the bases. Mel Roach then placed a single through the drawn-in infield for two runs to doom Jackson. The Mets had one last chance in the bottom of the 15th inning. With one out and Joe Christopher on base, Marvelous Marv — who else? — fouled out to the catcher. The Mets extended their current losing streak to seven in a row, dropping a doubleheader the next day to the Phils. The Quakers departed down the New Jersey Turnpike to Philly, and the St. Louis Cardinals came into town.

The Mets, having demonstrated little of brilliance on the field, prepared to honor a member of the opposition instead, the Cards' Stan Musial. To understand why the Mets did so requires entering into a very different America from that of today. As a society, we tend to regard diversity and multiculturalism as a product of the last 30 or 40 years, strictly an outgrowth of affirmative action. But the truth is that Americans have always been acutely conscious of ethnic differences — as Major League Baseball can attest. For many years, *The Baseball Digest* in its yearly spring training survey provided information on the ethnic heritage of big league players. Surveying the March 1962 edition indicated that the Yankees' Phil Linz was of German descent. His rival for the vacated shortstop job, Tom Tresh was of Ukranian origin. On the Mets, Ray Daviault was acknowledged to be French Canadian and Jim Hickman Scotch-Irish. Feature stories on Bo Belinsky didn't neglect to inform the reader that the zany left hander was of Polish descent. Today we place relatively little importance on the origins of players of European descent. They are simply described as "white." This was not the case 50 years ago. European heritage was much more celebrated, and in a case like Musial's, transcended uniform. Stan the Man was a drawing card on the road, and not just because of his potent bat. There were thousands upon thousands of Polish-Americans throughout the United States who were proud of the accomplishment of their native son. On "Stan Musial Night" at the Polo Grounds that Saturday night, August 18, three Polish bands performed while three Polish girls and one Polish boy presented flowers to Musial's mother, wife, and three daughters.

In our present vitriolic and violent sports world, it would be unthinkable to honor a member of an opposition team. Over the years, Stan Musial had caused so much misery for the hometown team. He had 47 career homers at the Polo Grounds. But Stan the Man transcended both ethnic boundaries and hometown loyalties. He was described glowingly in the New York press as the vestige of "a vanishing breed ... a gentleman professional in and out of uniform."[11] He wasn't, in other words, Roger Maris. Musial was showered with gifts — although, in violation of the "strict liturgical patterns" of the ritual, he wasn't given a car. Dick Young of the *New York Daily News* presented him with a portable typewriter on behalf of the members of the New York chapter of the Baseball Writers' Association of America. Stan also received golf clubs, a hunting gun, and from Ted Williams— his only contemporary peer in the hitting department — a fishing rod. Musial had directed that all cash gifts be donated to the Stan Musial Scholarship Fund at Columbia College (Yogi Berra had a similar endowment at Columbia, as did Lou Gehrig).

A tearful Stan accepted a handkerchief from his mother and thanked Major League Baseball for bringing baseball back to New York, "where I like to play."[12] George Weiss, no sentimentalist, had his own reasons for all of this heartwarming promotion. As with the Mets' logo, Gil Hodges, Casey Stengel, and Miss Rheingold, Kathy Kersh — whose image graced the back cover of the *Mets Yearbook*— Musial helped give this last-place expansion team a measure of (invented) tradition. But it wasn't all about summoning the past; Weiss looked to the future as well. One of the principal speakers on "Stan Musial Night" was John T. Clancy, Queens borough president. Queens, in the form of the Flushing Meadows Stadium, represented the future home of a revitalized Mets team.

Stan Musial Night wasn't the only celebration under the Macombs Dam Bridge that weekend. Saturday, August 18, was also Family Day at the Polo Grounds. The children of the Mets' players took the field along with their dads. Reggie Jackson, aged four, made like Maury Wills and tried for home. Al's son veered off for the dugout, not to be seen again. Reggie must've been watching his father's team play. The Mets were swept by the Cardinals.

The homestand continued against the Pittsburgh Pirates. The Bucs, who had tied a record by starting the season with a ten-game winning streak, had played just .500 ball in May and dropped out of pennant contention. They were currently in fourth place, 11 games behind league-leading Los Angeles. Roberto Clemente was hitting .325 and Bob Skinner .323, but the club suffered from a lack of pitching depth and had trouble beating the top teams in the league. Beating the Mets was another question altogether; Pittsburgh led the season series 10–1 as they arrived at the Polo Grounds for two consecutive doubleheaders on August 20 and 21. The Mets won only the last of the four games, with Marv Throneberry's three-run homer in the bottom of the ninth off Bucs bullpen ace Elroy Face providing the margin of victory. Throneberry had just entered the game after coaching at first base in the seventh and eighth innings. Solly Hemus had been ejected from the game for arguing a call in the fifth. Casey Stengel took over his duties for one inning before giving way to Throneberry. Marvelous Marv as first base coach made for particularly strange theater.

With the Flushing Meadows Stadium apparently well on the way toward completion, the Mets welcomed back the former Polo Grounds tenants, the Giants, for what was expected to be the last time on August 22 and 23. In the first game, the Mets defeated the Giants, 5–4. The winning run came in on an RBI single by Charlie Neal in the eighth inning off Bob Garibaldi. There was a measure of retribution for Casey Stengel, Garibaldi having spurned the Mets' offer, taking a $125,000 bonus from the Giants instead. The bespectacled Yalie, Ken McKenzie, earned the victory. Thus far, McKenzie had the only winning record on the Mets' staff at 5–4. The following night, San Francisco took the second and last game of the series, 2–1, behind the five-hit pitching of Juan Marichal. None of the Giants' sluggers—Mays, Cepeda, or McCovey—figured in the victory. The Giants scored the winning run in the tenth inning off losing pitcher Al Jackson on an RBI single by second baseman Ernie Bowman. Bowman, who came into the game hitting .188, provided the initial Giant run with his first major league homer in the fifth.

The Houston Colt .45s had outplayed the Mets on the ballfield so far in 1962, but the Colts couldn't match the Stengel men when in it came to public relations. The Colts were merely a mediocre expansion team; unlike the Mets, they never achieved legendary status. There were several reasons for this. Before 1962, Houston had been a Triple-A city in the American Association with no historical antecedents of significance. The Colts had no ghosts to conjure like the Mets did with the longtime Giants manager John McGraw or the Giants' star outfielder, Mel Ott. The Houston city fathers were building a domed stadium the likes of which had never been seen. But their present arena was not the showcase for nostalgia that the Polo Grounds was. It evoked no memories of great catches or famous home runs—at least none that had captured the imagination beyond the Texas border. Furthermore, the Colts didn't have Casey Stengel to rouse the faithful and inspire the quills of a press corps eager for myth-making. Houston G.M. Paul Richards was a native of Texas (he was born near Dallas), but neither he nor field manager Harry Craft helped turn the turnstiles at the Houston park. Finally, the Colts had no players on their roster that generated any deep-felt affection from the fans. By contrast, the Los Angeles Dodgers' visit to the Polo Grounds featured a tribute to the former Dodger and current Mets darling, Gil Hodges.

Gil Hodges' homecoming, as gratifying as it was personally for him after four years in Los Angeles, had been a disappointment on the field. Gil's troubles had started in spring training, after a game against the White Sox in Sarasota. He slept most of the way back to St. Petersburg, his left leg braced against the seat in front of him. When he awoke, he couldn't straighten the leg. The injury, later diagnosed as a deterioration of cartilage behind the left knee, had reduced him to a part-time performer. On July 7, Hodges' knee problems had been overshadowed by an attack of kidney stones that sent him to Roosevelt Hospital. It was a wrenching experience. According to the attending physician, Gil "required four times the amount of demorol and morphine given an ordinary man to put him to sleep."[13] By the time he was released later in the month, a pale and worn Hodges was well under his playing weight. But as the astute George Weiss understood, on a team as inept in the field as the Mets, Gil was still vitally important for evoking a sense of tradition — and spurring ticket sales.

On a sultry mid-summer Friday evening, August 24, a crowd of 39,741 showed up for Gil Hodges Night. Mets announcer Lindsey Nelson served as master of ceremonies. With Joan Payson busy at Saratoga, Donald Grant represented the brass. The gifts included 100,000 in trading stamps; a case of champagne; a complete wardrobe for himself, his wife Joan, and his son and two daughters (Gilly, Irene, and Cindy); a year's supply of coffee; a complete home work bench; and two radios. Grant also presented Gil with a commemorative plaque. Duke Snider surprised his ex–Brooklyn teammate with a shotgun, presented on behalf of all of the Dodger players. The Mets gave Gil a baby blue golf caddy cart, which Richie Ashburn cheerfully drove to home plate from the center field clubhouse. Cash donations were directed to the Gil Hodges Foundation's "dollars for scholars" program.

Unfortunately, the festivities were almost marred by tragedy. Dodgers coach Leo Durocher had a bad reaction after receiving a penicillin injection in the clubhouse just before the game. A frantic call for help was carried over the public address system. Dr. Wade Hastings, a physician from Malone, New York, heard the call from his seat in section 15 and headed for the clubhouse. He got lost twice before arrival. If he had been three or four more minutes, Durocher would have died.

The festivities over, the Mets continued the celebration by rising up to beat the Angelinos, 6–3. The Stengel men chased Dodger ace Don Drysdale (22–7) with three runs in the eighth, on RBIs by Gene Woodling, Rod Kanehl, and winning pitcher Jay Hook. The Mets' first three runs off Drysdale came in on solo homers by Choo Choo Coleman, Ron Kanehl, and Marv Throneberry. (A member of the Throneberry Fan Club danced on the Mets' dugout and ran a bell in celebration before being shooed away by park police.) In winning, the Polo Grounders reduced the Dodgers' lead over the second-place Giants to two and a half games. On Saturday August 25, the last day of racing at Saratoga, "Outing Class," a two-year-old colt owned by Joan Payson's Greentree stable, was the surprise winner of the $117, 500 Hopeful Stakes. Payson's baseball club wasn't quite so fortunate. The Dodgers saddled Roger Craig with his 21st loss of the season in an 8–2 victory over the Polo Grounders. The final game of the series was even worse for Casey and the Mets, a 16–5 pasting. Maury Wills reached base four times and stole three bases, stretching his season total to 72. Craig Anderson ran his losing streak to 13 straight games. With that, the Mets headed for the George Washington

Bridge and a trip down the New Jersey Turnpike to Philadelphia. They would conclude their August schedule in the City of Brotherly Love.

While the New York Mets were stoking the flames of nostalgia at the Polo Grounds, the New York Yankees were on a journey that took them to the Pacific Coast and then back across country to the Chesapeake Bay. The trip began in the middle of the country, in the Minneapolis suburb of Blooming-ton, with four games against the Minnesota Twins August 13 to 16. This was a crucial series for Sam Mele and the Twins. They were currently in third place, six and a half games behind the Yankees with a chance to move up in the standings. The Twins started out well, beating the Yankees in the opening game of the series, 6–4. Harmon Killebrew provided five of the six runs against Jim Bouton and Bud Daley. But the Yankees came back to take two of the remaining three games to maintain their lead, Whitey Ford and Ralph Terry winning their 13th and 17th games, respectively. The Bombers departed after dropping a 9–8 slugfest that saw Marshall Bridges lose his first game of the season.

Roger Maris claimed that the difference between hitting a home run and hitting a single was "a question of one-eighth of an inch." If the batter hit the ball on the hard under-part of the bat, the ball would be gone. If the batter missed by one-eighth, the result was a line drive. Maris had enjoyed little success hitting homers at Metropolitan Stadium in 1961, getting only one of his 61 homers there. He hit none in the four games in this current visit to Bloomington. But the presence of the M&M Boys in the Twin Cities made for overwhelming success at the box office. Attendance for the series was 156,168, bringing in $500,000 in four days. The Yankees received 30 cents per dollar, so they left the Twin Cities pocketing $45,000 (or close to $300,000 in today's money).

Back in spring training, Ralph Houk hoped that either Tom Tresh or Phil Linz would be able to fill the shortstop position until Tony Kubek returned from military service. The Major's prayers were more than fulfilled. Tresh was having a banner year, making the American League All-Star squad as a rookie. On August 14, he hit his 15th home run and tying him with Frank Crosetti for most home runs by a Yankee shortstop in one season. Tresh, however, wouldn't have too many more opportunities to extend his record. As the Yankees were departing the Twin Cities area, Ralph Houk announced that Kubek would be returning permanently to the shortstop position. Tony, he stressed was the better fielder of the two. As for Tresh, the Major had every reason to believe that the youngster, who had shown surprising power at bat, would make a smooth transition to left field. The new lineup made its debut in a five-game series at Kansas City August 17 to 20.

The Athletics' original owner, Arnold Johnson, died in 1960, and the following year, the club passed into the hands of Charles O. Finley. The 43-year-old Finley had made his name in the Chicago insurance business and considered himself something of a self-made man. With considerable aplomb, he proceeded to make over his new possession. Finley spent $480,000 to improve Municipal Stadium. He had the stadium painted a light color and installed lights to brighten the entire area outside. Inside, he had the seats repainted, some citrus yellow, others turquoise. Picnic grounds were installed behind left field. The new stadium scoreboard featured a fireworks display as well as a "Fan-a-Gram," which provided messages to the patrons during the game. The fans, with little to cheer for on the field, were treated to other technological marvels. A compressed air device blew the dust off home plate and a "jack-rabbit basket" popped out of the ground and proffered new balls to the home plate umpire. Actually, many of these "innovations"—the lighting of the stadium, the fireworks display, the jack-rabbit basket—had originally been the creation of Bill Veeck at Chicago. These acts of piracy did not escape the attention of Veeck, who quipped, "If I ever run out of ideas, [Finley's] gonna be in trouble."[14]

The lineup fielded by the A's included a number of ex–Yankees, including two starters, first baseman Norm Siebern and second baseman Jerry Lumpe. The club also had two prize rookies in left fielder Manny Jiménez and third baseman Ed Charles. Jiménez was currently second in the American League batting race at .323, and Siebern and Lumpe were also in the running with identical .302 averages. Siebern, who two years earlier had been traded by George Weiss to Kansas City for Roger Maris, was second in the American League with 84 RBIs. The A's pitching, however, was spotty at best and a major reason for the team's ninth-place standing, 18 and a half games behind the Yankees.

But the effects of the punishing August schedule were beginning to catch up with Ralph Houk and company. They dropped three of five games to Kansas City. On August 18, Whitey Ford lost the first game of a doubleheader, 5–4. With the bullpen overworked, more pressure was placed on the starters to finish games. Whitey went the distance, giving up 16 hits in 8 and two-thirds innings. The two teams produced a total of 22 hits (including home runs by Mickey Mantle, Roger Maris, and Tom Tresh) as well as five walks—all in 2:35.

The next day's temperature was brutal: 103 degrees. The New Yorkers also sizzled, burying the A's, 21–7. Elston Howard had eight RBIs and Mickey Mantle, seven. The two teams must've been anxious to leave the heat; the contest took just 2:27 to play. With that, the Bombers left Kansas City for Los Angeles, holding a four-game lead over the Angels.

Albie Pearson, the five-foot, five-inch centerfielder for the Los Angeles

Angels, had a theory regarding Roger Maris' precipitous decline in home run production in 1962. Maris had "set his sights too low," said Pearson. When sportswriters asked him in spring training whether he would equal or approach his previous year's total of 61 home runs, Roger might have said he would hit 55 to 60 home runs. Instead, he spoke of hitting 30 to 40 home runs. Low expectations, in Albie's estimate, had resulted in lower home run totals. Widely derided as an overpaid flash in the pan, Maris was almost perversely happy to be out of the limelight. "I'm glad I didn't break Ruth's record in 154 games," he told *Look* magazine. In 1961, the chase of Ruth's record gave him no peace; he was trailed everywhere by a horde of reporters. A year later, he walked the hotel lobbies undisturbed. Roger, the small town boy, sought solace in anonymity, the kind that could only come by disappearing into relative mediocrity. Clearly, he was no Bo Belinsky — when Pearson arrived home from the ballpark, his wife greeted him by asking, "What did Belinsky say today?"[15]

Roger Maris and Bo Belinsky were both in the spotlight when the second-place Angels hosted the league-leading Yankees before 50,830 fans at Chavez Ravine on Tuesday night, August 21. The Yankees and Angels were tied 4–4 through nine innings. Belinsky slogged through 8 and a third innings, giving up five hits and six walks, before retiring without a decision. The Angels, after sending Bill Stafford to an early shower in the fifth, were held in check by Jim Bouton through the sixth, seventh, and eighth innings. The rookie right-hander gave up no hits and fanned five Angels before yielding the tying run in the ninth, which sent the game into extra innings. The tie was short-lived. In the top of the tenth, with sudden fury, the New Yorkers erupted for seven runs against ex–Yankee Ryne Duren and Jack Spring for an 11–4 triumph. The Yankees then split the final two games at Chavez Ravine, allowing them to maintain a five-game lead over the Angels.

Since the getaway game went 13 innings (a 5–4 loss), New Yorkers' plane left late from Los Angeles. Jetting cross-country, Ralph Houk and his charges arrived in Baltimore at 6 A.M., Friday morning, August 24. After a few hours of sleep, they boarded the bus to Memorial Stadium for a twi-night doubleheader against Billy Hitchcock's Orioles. Such was the plight of the major league ballplayer in the new age of expansion.

Roger Maris' salary received a hefty dose of attention in the mainstream press. But perhaps the real revelation was the dramatic rise in salaries of black players. "The Year of the Big Money"— that's what *Ebony* called the 1962 baseball season. According to the magazine's tabulation, there were, at present, a record 85 black players in the major leagues with a combined income in excess of $500,000. The ten highest-paid players averaged $50,000 per annum (by contrast, Jackie Robinson's highest salary was $42,500 in 1953). Together, blacks made up 21 percent of the $8.75 million spent by big league owners on player payroll in 1962 (almost $2 million), versus 19 percent on spent on white players.[16] Of course, there needs to be an understanding of who was considered to be a "Negro" (or "tan") player. The list of the top ten best-paid black players at the time was headed by Willie Mays at $90,000 a year. But it also included Orlando Cepeda of the San Francisco Giants, Roberto Clemente of the Pittsburgh Pirates, and Minnie Miñoso of the St. Louis Cardinals. In 1962, a full decade before affirmative action categories appeared in the U.S. Census, there was a general consensus as to the racial categorization of Latin American players. High salaried Hispanic players, such as Camilo Pascual, Luis Aparicio, and Luis Arroyo, were considered white and didn't figure in these statistics.

The spectacular rise in black salaries was a modest, but significant sign of a world being turned upside down. But the higher earnings of Mays, Aaron and company must be contrasted with the lack of black salaried players on the other end of the pay scale. There were, in fact, relatively few black journeyman players in the major leagues. Indeed, even 16 summers after Branch Rickey brought Jackie Robinson to the Brooklyn Dodgers, the presence of blacks on major league squads couldn't be taken for granted. The Baltimore Orioles came to Florida with just two black players in 1962: rookie Earl Robinson and Dominican–born infielder Ozzie Virgil (once the first black on the Detroit Tigers). The Orioles had been one of the teams that joined Dan Topping's Yankees in providing integrated rooming facilities for their clubs. But Robinson, a former $50,000 bonus baby with the Los Angeles Dodgers, refused to live with his white teammates in the McAllister Hotel. In late June of 1962, the Orioles farmed out Robinson to Triple-A Rochester. His demotion to the minors meant that there were no longer any black players on the team (Virgil having long since departed). In 1962, the year in which Jackie Robinson was elected to the Baseball Hall of Fame in Cooperstown, the Baltimore situation seemed to many blacks as nothing less than a giant step backward. *Jet Magazine* charged that Earl Robinson's demotion was a blatant act of racial discrimination.

Orioles G.M. Larry MacPhail vigorous denied the allegation, claiming that the decision to demote Earl Robinson had been made strictly on merit. Curiously, there were people in the black press who supported MacPhail and the Orioles— and not Robinson — on this issue. Wendell Smith of the *Pittsburgh Courier*, who had been one of the leading critics of racially discriminatory practices in spring training camps in Florida the past two years, saw "no justification" for the claims of racial bias. The people making those claims, scoffed Smith, were "just stupid." No team, he argued, had been "more tolerant or understanding" than Baltimore. If anything, Robinson had "shirked his responsibility" by refusing to room with his teammates in Miami. The Orioles, Smith continued, had perfectly legitimate reasons for sending him down: he had an injured throwing arm. Robinson "can carry the ball faster back to the infield than he can throw it." The Orioles, said Wendell Smith, were the real "victims of bigotry.[17] In any case, whether there was bias on the part of the club or not, the fact remains that there were no black players in Orioles uniform during the entire series between Baltimore and New York August 24 to 26.

Thus far, the New York Yankees hadn't compiled a good record in doubleheaders in 1962. Exhausted from their coast to coast journey, they would now be forced to play five games against the Orioles— including two consecutive doubleheaders. Ralph Houk and company would lose all five at Memorial Stadium. In the first game of the Friday doubleheader on August 24, ex–Met Hobie Landrith delivered the big blow with a two-run triple off the left field wall against Jim Bouton. The second game was a 14–2 pasting, the Yankees' worst loss since falling to the Boston Red Sox, 14–4, on May 15. The misery continued with a twin loss on Saturday. The final game on Sunday, August 26, was a form of vindication for Yankee castoff Robin Roberts, who defeated Whitey Ford, 2–1. It was Roberts' second victory over his ex-teammates, the first coming on June 11, when the beaning of Boog Powell resulted in the bench clearing melee at Yankee Stadium. Relying on his new "let up" pitch to complement his fast ball, Roberts went all the way for a five-hitter. He threw 105 pitches, all but 28 for strikes, and yielded only two walks— both to Mickey Mantle. After retiring Moose Skowron for the last out, the usually composed Roberts jumped in the air and performed a neat pirouette before landing once again on the ground. Victory, to say the least, was sweet.

For the Yankees it had been a bitter turn of events. Done in, as much, by the brutal schedule as the opposition, they had dropped 11 of 16 road games. Their lead, which had stood at five and a half games over Los Angeles at the start of the road trip on August 13, was now just three games over the Angels and Minnesota Twins. The two young clubs were tied for second behind the Yankees. Yogi Berra was out of action, having had a nail torn off his finger on Friday against the Orioles. Joining Yogi on the sidelines was Tony Kubek, who had suffered a spike wound on his left foot. The tired and injured warriors made their way up the East Coast to New York to thankfully end the month in their own beds.

Shibe Park, the home of the Philadelphia Phillies, had been repainted and refurnished after the co-tenant Philadelphia Athletics moved to Kansas City in 1955. The re-named Connie Mack Stadium (capacity 33,608) was only 20 minutes from city center. But as in New York, parking was difficult and inconvenient. Inside, the ballpark had its share of culinary pleasures. The house specialty was the hoagie, the Philadelphia-South Jersey version of a hero sandwich. The hoagie received its name from the workers on nearby Hog Island during World War II. It cost 50 cents. No beer was sold at the ballpark, but many patrons brought their own brew anyway. Popcorn was sold in cone-shaped cardboard containers. When empty, they became very handy megaphones, helping to make the Phillies' fans the worst boo birds in the National League.

There really wasn't all that much to boo when playing the Mets. The Phillies took three of four from the Stengel men to end the August schedule. They finished 8–26 on the month, bringing their season record to 34–102. On August 29, there occurred an incident, which in retrospect might have had consequences years later. In the bottom of the tenth, with two outs, Charlie Neal, playing third base, threw wide of first on a grounder by Don Demeter. The next batter, Frank Torre (Joe Torre's brother), stepped back quickly from a low, inside delivery by Jay Hook, claiming he had been hit by the pitch. Umpire Stan Landes said, "Prove it."[18] Torre asked for the ball and demonstrated a black smudge of shoe polish, whereupon Landes awarded him first base. Hook then walked Clay Dalrymple to fill the bases. The light-hitting shortstop, Bobby Wine, followed with a two-run single to left to end the ballgame. It marked the 100th loss of the season for the New York Mets, the first New York club to lose that many since 1912, when the New York Yankees were still called the Highlanders. But again, the incident with Torre may have paid dividends years later. The injured Gil Hodges was in the dugout that day observing the play. One can imagine that he filed it away for a later day — a day in October 1969 when he, not Casey Stengel — was manager of the New York Mets, and the hitter was J.C. Martin.

On August 26, Minnesota Twins lefthander Jack Kralick became the fourth American League pitcher to throw a no-hitter in 1962, beating the Kansas City Athletics, 1–0. The Yankees, meanwhile, finished the month of August in Cleveland. In the opener on August 27, the Bombers broke their six-game losing streak, blanking the Indians, 5–0. Mickey Mantle had four hits and Bobby Richardson made two circus catches to pace Ralph Terry's 19th win. The following night, the Yankees nipped the Tribe, 2–1, in an abbreviated (five-inning) game. Mantle's homer off Mudcat Grant provided all the scoring needed as Bill Stafford upped his record to 11–8. Then the bottom fell out again. On August 29, Cleveland swept the Yankees, 3–2 and 9–5. After playing the entire month with just two days off, the Yankees had seen their lead cut to just two games over the Minnesota Twins and three games over the Los Angeles Angels. Ralph Houk refused to panic. He pointed out that the unusual concentration of dates — at one point, 17 games in 14 days —

wouldn't be repeated in September. The Yankees would have six open dates in September — giving the Major plenty of opportunity to rest the pitching staff. Houk ultimately counted on the Yankees' vast pennant race experience to make the difference over the upstart Angels and Twins. Flashing an impish grin, the Major said, "The closer they get to us, the tougher it gets on them."[19]

If only Joan Payson could say the same about the Mets! All the Stengel men had to look forward to in September was another month in which the endless losing was shrouded in a thick mist of nostalgia.

9

"Come Ona My House"

For Ralph Houk, the trip to the Bronx would be considerably smoother on Labor Day weekend, 1962. A few days earlier on August 29, two touring cars, one traveling westward carrying New York Governor Nelson A. Rockefeller, and another moving in an eastwardly direction bearing New Jersey governor Richard Hughes, arrived at the midpoint of the Hudson River. Together, the two state governors presided over an hour-long ceremony to mark the opening of the new, six-lane lower deck of the George Washington Bridge. The $145 million addition made the GWB the only 14-lane vehicular crossing in the world. As 3,000 guests looked on (including special guest Linda Ferla of Bergenfield), Hughes and Rockefeller cut the ceremonial tape. Gold curtains were lowered, revealing the two state seals with the word WELCOME emblazoned above them.

At the Stadium, the Yankees laid down the welcome mat for the Kansas City Athletics, their opponents on Friday, Saturday, and Sunday of Labor Day weekend. The A's had a somewhat symbiotic relationship with the Yankees. In 1953, club owners Dan Topping and Del Webb sold Yankee Stadium to Arnold Johnson, a Chicago businessman. Johnson bought the Kansas City Athletics in 1955, and, facing a conflict of interest, sold the Yankee Stadium Corporation to John William Cox of Chicago. In July 1962, Cox gave his shares of the ballpark to his alma mater, Rice University in Houston, Texas. Yankee Stadium was now in Confederate hands, so to speak. As Yankee general manager, George Weiss had engineered numerous trades with the A's between 1955 and 1959, in the process putting Roger Maris, Ralph Terry, Clete Boyer, and Héctor López in pinstripes.

The current Yankees had no trouble dispatching the Kansas City Athletics. On the last day of August, they beat Kansas City, 5–1. The Bombers collected 15 hits, including two by winning pitcher Whitey Ford. Tom Tresh shined with a home run and two singles. Tony Kubek was back in the lineup at shortstop, but Roger Maris was sidelined with a strained shoulder muscle suffered sliding head first at Baltimore the previous week. Before the game, the "Little Fellas" League took the field. PS 71 beat PS 54 for the league championship. Mike Landi and Mickey Nagy hit consecutive homers in the first innings to pace the victory. Was Roy Hamey watching?

On September 1, Ralph Terry beat Kansas City, 3–1, and became the first 20-game winner in the American League in 1962. It was an economical performance; Terry needed just 105 pitches to dispatch the A's. Elston Howard's triple and two RBIs paced the victory. The Bombers ended the series with a 2–1 victory over the Midwesterners. The winning run came in the bottom of the ninth, Bobby Richardson's double sending his keystone partner, Tony Kubek, home with the winning run. Jim Bouton and Bud Daley combined for a seven-hitter, with Daley earning credit for the victory against his former teammates. With that, the Yankees took the season series from the A's, 13–5, eight of those victories coming in the Bronx. The Yankee had a four-game lead over the Minnesota Twins and a four and a half game lead against their Labor Day opponents, the Los Angeles Angels.

The Angels might have drawn closer to the Yankees by this time had Bo Belinsky retained his first half-season form. Belinsky wasn't the same pitcher he had been during the Yankees' last visit to Los Angeles in mid–July. Slowed by arm woes, he had won only one game since June and sported an unimpressive 8–9 record. Whether spectacular or merely mediocre, Belinsky was never too far from controversy. Bo's reputation as a man about town had been tarnished by a lawsuit filed by a Hollywood starlet, who claimed he had struck her during an all-night fling on June 13. It was rumored that the Angels, sick of his escapades, were engineering a trade that would send him to the Kansas City Athletics for a minor player. Belinsky called the Angels management "stupid" for acquiring so little for him in return. Bo (nicknamed "the Prince" by his teammates) also struck back against those critical of his lifestyle. The Yankees, he told the *New York Post*'s Leonard Schecter, were no "holy rollers." He added, "There have been escapades in Los Angeles. They're just human. They come into a hip town and things happen."[1] [Note: Leonard Schecter would later serve as editor on Jim Bouton's groundbreaking book, *Ball Four*].

Bo's extra-curricular troubles were compounded on the field. The Yankees took the first game of the Labor Day doubleheader against the Angels, 8–2, rocking Belinsky for seven runs on eight hits in six innings. Roger Maris, Tom Tresh, and Elston Howard had two RBIs apiece, Howard hitting his 16th home run of the year. This was a must-win series for the Los Angeles Angels, and they didn't give up without a fight. They came back to take the second game, 6–5. Trailing by five going into the eighth, the Angels scored two runs on an Albie Pearson home run, and then added four more tallies in the ninth versus Jim Coates and Luis Arroyo for the victory. On Tuesday, September 4, the Angels triumphed yet again, 7–6. Whitey Ford was cruising along with a 4–0 lead when the Angels struck for six runs, sending Ford to the showers. Lee Thomas, a former Yankee farmhand, delivered the big blow, a two-run homer. The New York lead was now cut to two and a half games over the second-place Twins, who, with sluggers Bob Allison, Harmon Killebrew, and Earl Battey teeing off, were beating up the Washington Senators. The Angels were three and a half out. To add to the day's torment, Mickey Mantle was out with a muscle strain incurred on his last swing in batting practice.

Ralph Houk was beloved by his players, but not as much by the local sports writers who bemoaned his increasingly dull press conferences; the scribes reserved their affection for Casey Stengel. The Old Perfessor was out of town, but luckily Bo Belinsky was around to make news. Ford Frick, responding to the trade rumors involving Belinsky, announced that he would veto any trade by Los Angeles sending Bo to the Athletics. Belinsky was summoned by the commissioner to his New York offices and interrogated about the matter. The playboy-pitcher was back with the Angels on Thursday, September 6, watching his teammates drop the last game of the series to the Yankees, 6–5. It was a tough loss for manager Bill Rigney and company. The Angels broke a 1–1 tie with three runs in the top of the seventh, sending Ralph Terry to the showers. But the Bombers struck back in the bottom of the frame with four runs of their own to take the lead. It wasn't pretty: the Yankees capitalized on two errors to beat Belinsky's party-mate Dean Chance, 6–5. Tom Tresh, who had recently become a father, drove in the tying and winning runs. The season series was over between the Angels and Yankees, with Ralph Houk and company squeaking by, 10–8.

Far from the Bronx at Amarillo, Jim Bouton and Phil Linz had heard stories about how the Yankees ran away with the pennant every year, cashing in their World Series checks before the season was even over. But Linz, in the thick of a pennant race, "didn't feel that way now." The *Minneapolis Star*'s Charles Johnson smelled change in the air, predicting, "This is the year to beat the Yankees."[2] The Bombers, in fact, had just a three-game lead over the second-place Minnesota Twins. Still, Houk and company were in an enviable position, having no more games to play against their closest competitors. The Angels and Twins, meanwhile, would go head-to-head two more times in September, leaving the Yankees to pick up the spoils. With the expansion of the major league rosters, the club welcomed back Joe Pepitone from Richmond, along with third baseman Jake Gibbs and pitcher Al Downing. Fred Hamey, concerned with the uneven state of the team's pitching, purchased veteran righthander Hal (Skinny) Brown from the Baltimore Orioles for the $20,000 waiver price.

Gene Conley's last appearance in New York had ended with one of the most memorable events of that — or any — season. But "Long Gene" had returned to the good graces of Boston manager Pinky Higgins after his disappearing act on the Cross Bronx Express on July 25 with fellow absentee Pumpsie Green. Facing the Yankees on Friday, September 7, at the Stadium, Conley lost a heartbreaker, as the Boston Red Sox fell to the Yankees, 5–4. The tall right-hander was nursing a 3–2 lead going into the seventh, when home runs by Bill Skowron and Tony Kubek sent him to the showers. New York beat Boston again on Saturday, 6–1. The winner was Whitey Ford, now 15–7. Ford, hit by a Don Schwall pitch, gave way to Jim Coates after five innings of work. Bobby Richardson had a single, double, and a triple. His 180 hits led the American League. The Boston Red Sox suddenly rose up to smite the Yankees on Sunday, September 9, taking both ends of the doubleheader, 9–3 and 5–4. Carl Yastremszki started things for the Bosox in the top of the first against Skinny Brown. Eddie Bressoud (taken by Houston as the first player taken in the National League expansion draft the previous October and since traded to the Red Sox) then homered in the third to send Brown to the showers, spoiling his debut in pinstripes.

The second game of the doubleheader on September 9 was so unusual that, it is safe to say, we shall never see its like again. The Yanks were leading 3–2 going into the top of the seventh inning, when Boston centerfielder Gary Geiger homered off Jim Bouton. Marshall Bridges came on to replace him. Pinky Higgins, hoping to preserve the lead, turned the game over to his ace reliever, Dick Radatz, in the bottom of the seventh. Higgins was reasonably confident of victory; the six-foot, five-inch, 240 pound Radatz (nicknamed "the Monster") was the American League leader in saves. But after two were out, Tony Kubek singled against Radatz and then stole second. Bobby Richardson walked. With runners on first and second, Tom Tresh lashed a single to tie the game. The Yanks threatened once again against the Monster in the bottom of ninth. Tony Kubek doubled. Bobby Richardson then sent a bouncer over second. Shortstop Eddie Bressoud was late with his throw to first. Kubek, a daring runner all afternoon, sped for home. Tony beat the throw, and the game would have been over right then and there, but he missed the plate and was tagged out by catcher Bob Tillman. With that, the game went into extra innings.

For nine innings, Radatz and Bridges (nicknamed "the Fox" because of his propensity for telling tall tales) battled each other to a standstill, neither allowing the opposition to score. Finally, in the top of the 16th, Bob Tillman led off with a double. Chuck Schilling struck out, but a wild pitch by Bridges put Tillman on third. Yankee discard Billy Gardner then sent a squeeze bunt straight toward Bridges. Overeager, the Yankee lefty tripped over his own feet, falling flat on his face. The ball rolled by him as Tillman lumbered home for a 5–4 Boston victory. Four hours and 33 minutes after it started, the contest was finally over. The line score read:

	IP	H	R	ER	BB	SO
Radatz	9	7	1	1	1	9
Bridges	9	4	1	1	5	8

These individual performances would've been the envy of many a starting pitcher. Radatz earned credit for the victory. Chet Nichols, who pitched the bottom of the 16th, picked up the save. Bridges, of course, was the losing pitcher. Yogi Berra caught all 16 innings for the Yankees. Before anointing any present-day hurler as the greatest reliever of all-time, one might pause to consider the way in which Ralph Houk and Pinky Higgins utilized their two aces on that afternoon at Yankee Stadium. Can any reasonable comparison be made between this heroic (if foolhardy) age of relief pitching and the current therapeutic era of pitch counts?

In keeping with the helter-skelter 1962 baseball schedule, the New York Mets spent the Labor Day weekend in St. Louis, then flew east to Pittsburgh for a three-game series, before dashing west again to finish their ten-game road trip at Houston. None of these clubs was going anywhere this season. The first of September found the Cardinals in fifth place, 15 and a half games behind the pace-setting Los Angeles Dodgers; the Pirates were a little better, in fourth place, nine games out; Houston was 38 games out, but in eighth place, above the Chicago Cubs and the Mets, who were 55 and a half games behind. The real contest in the National League was on the West Coast between the first-place Dodgers and the second-place San Francisco Giants, who trailed by two and a half games. The two teams squared off for four games at Dodger Stadium on September 3 to 6, the Giants pitting the power hitting of Willie Mays, Orlando Cepeda, and Willie McCovey against the speed of Maury Wills and Willie Davis. The Giants won three of the four games at Chavez Ravine, cutting the Dodger lead to a game and a half .

Meanwhile, Casey Stengel and company were knocking about like pinballs between the Ohio and Mississippi Rivers and the Texas plains, losing all the while. Of the ten contests played on the road between August 31 and September 9, the Mets won only one — the getaway game against St. Louis on September 2. Jim Hickman's RBI single and brilliant catch paved the way to a 4–3 victory. Frank Thomas added his 30th home run for the Polo Grounders. Hickman, who had three home runs on the road trip, had developed into one of the few genuine assets for the Mets. Success in the big leagues had its rewards. Hickman would return to his home at Henning, Tennessee (population 490), after the season — but not to his off-season job, inhaling the noxious fumes at the cotton mill. His Mets future assured, he would be going quail hunting and breathing fresh air instead.

For Casey Stengel, the recent Mets road trip was the same compendium of negative statistics, oddities, and sheer bad luck that had characterized the club all season. Craig Anderson lost his 14th and 15th games in a row. Richie Ashburn crashed into the outfield wall at Forbes Field in Pittsburgh on Labor Day, and, although continuing to play, had no memory of the last four innings afterward. He was examined by Pirate team physician Dr. Joseph Finegold (who had treated Tony Kubek after he was hit in the throat in the seventh game of the 1960 World Series). Whitey, said Finegold, was "playing on nothing but reflex."[3] X-ray photos of Ashburn mercifully showed no trace of a concussion. At Houston, the Mets succumbed to a squadron of mosquitoes and the pesky bats of the "pea-shooting" Colt .45s. The getaway game on September 9 was called off due to local curfew rules at 7:07 P.M. Central Time, sparing Anderson of what might have been his 16th straight loss of the season. Four months earlier, on May 10, the Stengel men had returned to New York from Chicago in ninth place. In the early morning of September 10, they deplaned in New York from Texas, mathematically eliminated from ninth place.

A few weeks earlier, Roger Maris had responded to his critics in an article in *Sport* magazine. He did not, he insisted, ignore fan mail; he had answered an average of 30 letters a day during the winter. As for rumors that he exited awards dinners early, that, he insisted, had been blown out of proportion. It occurred just once — with the permission of the promoters. As for giving a kid an autograph signed with an "X" instead of his name in spring training at Fort Lauderdale, it was just a joke, he said. He had called the kid right back and signed his ball for him. No, Roger didn't hate all writers; there were good ones and bad ones, although he insisted that the latter were "out to get me." Should he consider taking a Dale Carnegie course to counter his "surly slugger image?"[4]

September 10 was Maris' 28th birthday. On this date, the New York Yankees began their last road trip of the 1962 season. The Bombers left New York in first place, two and a half games ahead of second-place Minnesota and four games over third-place Los Angeles. Unlike the glorious year of 1961, no Yankee was listed among the league leading hitters. Maris was tied with Baltimore's Jim Gentile for fifth in the home run race, six behind the pace-setting Harmon Killebrew of the Twins. Among the pitchers, only Ralph Terry ranked among the league leaders. If not as spectacular as 1961, the New Yorkers were at least consistent. They had gone 7–4 in their recent homestead and would duplicate that record on the road against Detroit, Cleveland, Boston, and Washington.

The happiest news for Ralph Houk on this Western swing was the return of Mickey Mantle. The club had played .500 ball during the six games he missed earlier in September with an abdominal muscle strain. At Tiger Stadium on September 10, Mantle unleashed a 420-foot blast to center field for his 400th career home run, putting him in seventh place behind Stan Musial on the all-time list. The Yankees won that game and the next one the following night. On September 11, Yogi Berra hit the 350th home run of his career. The Bombers took the season series from the Tigers, 11–7. Moving on to Cleveland, Houk and company played a single game at Municipal Stadium on September 12. Mantle starred once again, helping Whitey Ford to his 16th win, with a three-run shot off Pedro Ramos. For Cleveland, the heady days of June, when they swept four straight from the Yankees to take over first place, were now a distant memory. Although they took the season series from New York (11–7), it was small consolation for their seventh-place position. Manager Mel McGaha's days were said to be numbered.

From Cleveland, the Yankees flew east to Boston to finish their season series with the Red Sox. They dropped two of three to the Bosox at Fenway Park. Bill Monbouquette and Gene Conley administered the defeats. In their lone victory on September 15, young Jim Bouton evened his record at 7–7. The Bombers left Boston leading the Minnesota Twins by just three games, with just ten more left to play. The Twins had won four straight at home, including a 12–2 pounding of the Indians, in which Harmon Killebrew had hit two homers and driven in five runs. But, for Minnesota, it was too little, too late. The Twins were undone by their relatively poor home record at Municipal Stadium (41–34). Meanwhile, the Bombers had two more stops left on their road tour: Washington and Chicago.

While the Yankees were on the road against Detroit, Cleveland, and Boston from September 10 to 16, the New York Mets were at home against the Cincinnati Reds and the Milwaukee Braves. Due to one of those bedeviling scheduling quirks, the Milwaukee Braves came in for only one final game at the Polo Grounds on September 10. The Braves, in sixth place, 20 and a half games out, and losers of nine of their last ten games, found the old horseshoe-shaped ballpark a congenial environment. They stayed around just long enough to saddle the Mets with their 110th loss of the season. Eddie Mathews and Hank Aaron homered for the visitors. Bob Miller (AKA Robert L. Miller) lost his 12th game in a row to tie a record set by Russ Miller for the 1928 Philadelphia Phillies.

George Weiss, when riding high as the Yankees G.M. in the early 1950s, had sneered at Bill Veeck's publicity gimmicks with the lowly St. Louis Browns. It was beneath the dignity of the mighty Yankees. Now, like the A's' Charlie Finley, Weiss dipped deeply into Veeck's bag of tricks. The game between the Braves and the Mets on September 10 was preceded by the following extravagances: "hit the flag with the fungo," "throw the ball into the basket," and the *piece de resistance*: "the blind wheel barrow race" between Rod Kanehl and Milwaukee coach Andy Pafko, a former Dodger outfielder.[5] It was all more worthy of a carnival than a baseball club. But in this strange world turned upside down, carnival combined with nostalgia was the Mets' main drawing card.

On September 12, the New York Knickerbockers opened their 1962–63 season camp at Upsala College in East Orange, New Jersey. Missing from the Knicks' camp was Gene Conley, acquired by the Knicks in a trade with the Boston Celtics. The lanky Conley was still employed as a pitcher with the Boston Red Sox and would report following the end of the baseball season. That same day, the Mets went on a tour of their future ballpark at Flushing Meadows. On September 14, play resumed at the Polo Grounds as the Stengel men played host to the Cincinnati Reds.

Don Zimmer and his Reds teammates still had a glimmer of hope, five games in back of the league-leaders. But the Stengel men had experienced some of their biggest success of the season at home against Fred Hutchinson's club, and prepared to play the spoiler once again. The opening game of the series on Friday, September 14, saw the Mets defeat an exhausted Reds team, 10–9 (the club had flown twice across the country in the past few days). Roger Craig, the Mets' number one starter, won his eighth game — in relief. The Mets, even in defeat, continued to set new standards. Vada Pinson's inside-the-park homer in the seventh was the 187th home run surrendered by the Mets' pitching corps, setting a new National League record. The Reds evened matters with the Mets the next day, winning 9–6. It was Cincinnati's 93rd victory of the season, equaling the Reds' previous year's mark as National League champions. The Mets, however, came back on September 16 to take the rubber game, 8–3. Roger Craig started this time and won his ninth game. Marv Throneberry (who hit his 15th homer the day before) swatted his 16th in support of Craig, to the delight of the crowd. The Reds left town six games out of first place, their pennant hopes dashed for good. Casey Stengel actually felt a little sorry for Fred Hutchinson. He told Hutch, "If we had beat those guys (i.e. Dodgers and Giants) like we beat you, all you guys would be right up there right now."[6] The Bear's response went unpublished.

The Yankees were a team composed of Midwesterners; among the front-line players, only Whitey Ford was a native New Yorker. In 1962 none of these Midwesterners was more important to the team than Ralph Terry. The tall right-hander was born at Big Cabin, Oklahoma, in the northeastern part of the state on January 9, 1936. He started out throwing corn cobs, and then rocks, on his grandmother's farm, sharpening his aim on the family rooster.

Spotting his talent, the old lady gave him a baseball. Terry starred at Chelsea High School, where he attracted the attention of Tom Greenwade, who several years earlier had signed Mickey Mantle to a big league contract with the New York Yankees. The six-foot, three-inch, 195 pound Terry played parts of two seasons with the Yankees, before being traded to the Kansas City Athletics on June 15, 1957. He was a throw-in in the blockbuster trade, engineered by George Weiss mainly to get rid of Billy Martin following the infamous Copacabana incident. Receiving a chance to start regularly, Terry developed as a pitcher in Kansas City. In May 1959, Weiss reacquired Terry, along with Héctor López. He pitched well for the Yankees in 1960, but his misfortune to be the victim of Bill Mazeroski'S dramatic lead off home run in the ninth inning of the seventh game of the 1960 World Series. it was a loss that in all probability cost Casey Stengel his job as Yankee manager.

On September 18, Ralph Terry won his 22nd game of the season, beating the Washington Senators at District of Columbia Stadium. Terry thus became the first Yankee right-hander to win that many games since 1928. Mickey Mantle hit two home runs and drove in five runs in the 7–1 victory. He also made a spectacular catch of a Chuck Hinton drive in deep center field. The losing pitcher was Tom Cheney, who a week earlier, had struck out 21 batters in a 16-inning game. The Twins kept pace with the Yankees thanks to a victory over the Detroit Tigers. The fearsome Harmon Killebrew hit two home runs at Bloomington, raising his league-leading total to 42. At Washington on September 19, a bases-loaded walk to Roger Maris in the ninth inning allowed Houk and company to increase their lead to four games over Minnesota. A homer by Detroit's Al Kaline off starter Jim Kaat had doomed the Twins to a 5–1 defeat.

Casey Stengel made his major league debut with the Brooklyn Dodgers on September 17, 1912. It took place at old Washington Park, located on Third Avenue between First and Third Streets. Casey had four hits that day in a 7–3 victory over the Boston Braves. Surveying the game's statistics, it was easy to see why scribes and other observers complained about the state of the modern game. On that afternoon at Washington Park, the Dodgers and Braves combined for 22 hits, six walks, and two wild pitches. The game took just 1:45 to play. "Yessir, those were the days," Casey exclaimed. "The ball was deader then, outfielders used to play closer in and there were many more throws to the plate." Asked if the game was better then or now, he paused and then answered: "I'd have to see it again before I'd make a decision."[7] Baseball's many critics didn't need a time machine to figure out what was wrong with the game. Football, it was noted, created the "illusion of high powered action"— dashes in and out of the huddle, and plays handled with snap and decision. (This was, of course, before instant replay eliminated the huddle altogether, extending the illusion of speed even further). Major league baseball, by contrast, was "infested with pointless loafing."[8] Quick decision-making under pressure was the measure of competitive team sports everywhere — everywhere, that is, except baseball. The average game in 1905 was 1:49 in length; at present it was 2:41. Casey's Mets, it was noted, averaged 2:54 to lose.

Winning not being their forte, the Mets turned to their most prized commodity to attract customers to the Polo Grounds. The club announced that it would commemorate the Old Perfessor's 50th anniversary in Major League Baseball prior to the game between the Mets and the Houston Colt .45s on Tuesday, September 18. A sparse crowd of 3,670 showed up on a chilly night at the Polo Grounds to honor Casey Stengel for his "service to baseball."[9] Between games of the doubleheader, Donald Grant, Warren Giles, and, in another elegiac gesture, Blanche McGraw (the widow of John J. McGraw) gathered at home plate with Stengel. A long, white table-clothed table was set astride home plate, groaning with gifts. They included a golden key to City Hall, an achievement medal from the Brooklyn Rotary Club, a silver bowl from the Mets, and a tape recorder from the New York Baseball Writer's Association. Giles gave Casey a cocktail shaker on behalf of the National League; this was the same man (Giles) who had fined him $500 in April for posing with Miss Rheingold amid assorted alcoholic beverages.

The colorless Colts played the party wreckers, beating the Mets in both ends of the doubleheader. To add insult to injury, Houston catcher Merrit Ranew, not a power hitter of note, hit a home run, allowing the Stengel men to surpass the 1956 Kansas City Athletics for most round trippers allowed in a season: 188. The days were getting shorter and the nights becoming cooler, but on September 20, Gil Hodges tried to revive some of the spirit of youth and played for the first time since July 14. It was to no avail. Harry Craft and his Colt .45s terminated their fruitful relationship with the Mets, beating them twice, despite Frank Thomas' 31st and 32rd home runs. The second loss on this bleak and chilly night was the 115th of the season, a new National League record for futility.

It was only appropriate in this upside down world of 1962 that Marv Throneberry should be the winner of the Howard Clothes home run hitting contest. Marvelous Marv received a $7,000 cabin cruiser for hitting the right field sign more often than any other Met. Throneberry ambled to the microphone at home plate, removed his cap to reveal his freckled bald pate, and began his thank you speech by saying, "I would tell a few jokes, but there are already plenty of comedians around." (Was he thinking of his manager or his fellow players?) Richie Ashburn was honored as the Most Valuable Met with a $5,000 boat of his own. For Marv, even winning would come with a sting.

Whitey's boat was wheeled on the field, but Marv's wasn't; they were afraid the Marvelous One would drop it, quipped one wag.[10] Ashburn's boat was considered a gift by the IRS and thus not subject to income tax. Marv's was allegedly won in a contest and therefore was taxable income. Such was life in the Age of Throneberry.

The New Yorker Yankees concluded their road show with a three-game series at Chicago against Al López's White Sox September 21 to 23. The Pale Hose were out of the race, in fourth place, nine games behind the Yankees. But they were still in a position to play the spoiler. They proceeded to beat the Yankees twice on the southside. The Twins, however, were losing to Robin Roberts and the Orioles on September 21, and dropped 4 and a half behind. The highlight of the Yankee-White Sox series at Comiskey Park was the pitch-

Richie Ashburn, Mets centerfielder and their only All-Star selection. Ashburn (known as "Whitey") was chosen the most valuable Met and awarded a $5,000 boat. Whitey's locker mate, Marv Throneberry, also received a boat (for hitting the "Howard Clothes" sign in right field the most times). Throneberry had to pay taxes on his boat (he won it in a contest). Ashburn didn't (his was a gift and not subject to income tax). Such was life for "Marvelous Marv."

ing duel on Sunday, September 23, between the 23-year-old Bill Stafford and the 42-year-old Early Wynn.

Wynn (called Gus) had begun pitching in the major leagues before the start of World War II, coming up with the Washington Senators in 1939. The stocky right-hander was on the 1954 Cleveland team that won 111 games in 1954 and stopped the New York Yankees championship streak at five. In the second game of the World Series against the New York Giants that year at the Polo Grounds, Wynn was leading, 1–0, going into the fifth inning when he was victimized for two runs by the Giants' Dusty Rhodes in an eventual 3–1 loss.

On September 23, 1962, Wynn and Stafford each pitched ten innings. The Yankees finally broke through with four runs in the final frame to beat Chicago, 5–1. Time was running out for the former Cy Young Award winner.

Wynn would receive one more opportunity the following week at Yankee Stadium to reach the fabled 300-win mark. As for the Yankees, they were off the road for good.

The knowledgeable baseball fan, turning on the TV set, could tell immediately whether he or she was watching a National League or American League game. The key was the different styles of umpiring. At home plate, American League umps peered over the catcher's head, gripping their bulky outside chest protectors. Given their equipment and consequent positioning, they tended to call high strikes. National League umpires, by contrast, wore their lighter chest protectors inside their serge jackets, and thus preferred to look over the catcher's shoulder nearer the batter. Again, given the equipment and positioning, they were more inclined to call low strikes. The arbiters also positioned themselves differently on the field. American League umpires stood outside the diamond on plays at second. The National Leaguers moved in on the diamond grass when a runner reached first base.

In the fall of 1962, however, there was one thing over which both major leagues were in agreement. American League president Joe Cronin announced that his league was joining Warren Giles and the senior circuit in approving a 162-game schedule for 1963. Detroit manager Bob Scheffing, for one, believed that Major League Baseball was making a big mistake. He proposed that the season be shortened to 140 games, the season beginning April 25 and ending September 15, with the World Series concluded well before October 1. The clubs, he reasoned, would make just as much money, if not more, with a shortened schedule. The Lords of Baseball, however, didn't agree with Scheffing. One can understand why. The Bombers had set a new season road attendance of 2,215,659, to surpass the previous year's 1,946, 679. It was a tribute to the drawing power of the M&M Boys. The idea of shortening the Yankee visits wasn't something the American League league owners wished to contemplate. But where was the sense of justice for the tired ballplayer?

City Hall had announced a plan to save the Greek columns surrounding the doomed Pennsylvania Station, soon to be torn down and replaced by the new Madison Square Garden complex. The columns, said New York City's commissioner of parks, Newbold Morris, would be removed to the Battery. There were no plans afoot, however, for saving the Polo Grounds from inevitable extinction. The Mets' final homestand — and apparent farewell to the Polo Grounds — ended with a three-game set against the Chicago Cubs on the weekend of September 21 to 23. The Stengel men had enjoyed their greatest success against the Bruins (they tied the season series at 9–9). On September 21, they won their 38th game with a 5–1 victory over the Cubs. Rookie Galen Cisco went all the way for his first major league victory.

The Mets' loss to the Cubs on Saturday, September 22, was the home club's 116th of the season, setting a modern major league record. Al Jackson took the loss, giving the Mets two 20-game losers (Roger Craig was the other). It was the first time that a club had had two 20-game losers since the Philadelphia Phillies turned the trick in 1938. On an odd note, Richie Ashburn played an inning at second base in relief of Rod Kanehl; at least Whitey wouldn't run into any walls.

The game also marked the Polo Grounds' debut of 17-year-old Ed Kranepool. He was the second youngest player to open at Coogan's Bluff, Mel Ott being five months younger when he made his first appearance in a Giants uniform in 1926. Kranepool was raised by his mother, Ethel, his father having been killed in action during World War II. "I always knew he would be a player," Ethel Kranepool proudly noted. Much, in fact, was expected of the husky six-foot, three-inch, 205 Kranepool, who had broken all of Hall of Famer Hank Greenberg's home run records at Monroe High School. His high school coach, Jim Schieffo, claimed that the youngster "had the fastest hands this side of the Mississippi.[11] The youngster picked up his first major league hit — a double past third in the eighth.

On Sunday, September 23, the Mets beat the Cubs, 2–1, in their last Polo Grounds appearance of the season. There was even an Ott on the field — Bruins outfielder Billy Ott. It was the Mets 39th victory of the season. Bob Miller, the $125,000 bonus pick in the previous October's draft, won his first game of the season after 12 straight defeats. Back in April, the Mets lured curious New York Giants and Brooklyn Dodgers fans to the Polo Grounds with the slogan, "We're Saving a Seat for You!" With a final game crowd of 10,304, the Mets exceeded the Giants' 1957 attendance figures by a substantial margin of 268,607.

As the game progressed, public address announcer Jack E. Lee played a medley of taped musical selections— bridging invented tradition and expectant future. During the first few innings, fans were treated to "That Old House (Ain't Gonna Need This House No Longer)," a tribute to the soon-to-be-demolished Polo Grounds. The middle innings were given over to Rosemary Clooney's novelty hit, "Come Ona My House" (signaling the move to the new Flushing Meadows Stadium in Queens). In the final innings, the loudspeakers whined with the maudlin strains of "Auld Lang Syne." When the final out was recorded, Frank Thomas repeated his 1957 dash to the center field clubhouse, this time accompanied by the Mets' and Cubs' players. A collective sigh enveloped the Polo Grounds— the ballpark that died twice. The fans simply stood silently, as if listening in on Casey Stengel's television interview being conducted below. The interview over, the Old Perfessor, right hand in back pocket, turned and ran in his typical dog trot gait to the center field clubhouse. The crowd filed out to the mystic chords of "Til We Meet Again."[12]

The Bronx Bombers clinched their 27th American League title at Yankee Stadium on September 25 with an 8–3 victory over the Washington Senators. Whitey Ford won his 17th game against eight losses. It wasn't the most well-played contest. Ford surrendered 12 hits in going the route. But the game, which featured 28 hits, six bases on balls, and 20 men left on base, was at least mercifully short, concluding in 2:24. The victory celebration in the visiting clubhouse at D.C. Stadium was a rather subdued affair (one reporter described it as "mild").[13] Only the younger players like Tom Tresh, Phil Linz, and Jim Bouton seemed energized by the moment. Roger Maris (nursing a shoulder injury) was the first one in the showers. Maris, Mickey Mantle, Yogi Berra, and other veteran players changed quickly and left.

What killed an already muted celebration was the news from Chicago that Sonny Liston had knocked out Floyd Paterson in 2:06 of the first round to win the world heavyweight boxing championship. Charles (Sonny) Liston, an ex-con with underworld connections, was universally despised in the press and among the public at large. There were many in the sports world who considered a person like Liston as nothing less than the death of boxing. The New York Boxing Commission branded him a *persona non grata* and had refused to license the championship bout in New York. The bout, which might have been scheduled for Yankee Stadium or the Polo Grounds, was relocated to Chicago. Yankee players like Whitey Ford, naturally sympathetic to the modest and gentlemanly Paterson, were shocked at this turn of events. In yet another way, the world was being turned upside down in 1962. The victory celebration for the Yankees, what there was of it, was over.

Before the New York Mets left town for their last five games of the season, the club announced that Casey Stengel would return as the club's field manager in 1963. His salary was estimated at $85,000, and given the publicity he gave the league, he was worth every penny. Meeting with reporters and dressed in a natty, pin striped blue suit, the Old Perfessor reflected on the present dismal season. "Even I wasn't too excited about this team sometimes," he remarked — an understatement if there ever was one. Casey went on to criticize the Mets' (and indirectly George Weiss') decision to concentrate on veteran players in the expansion draft. "But those fellas can't fool me next year," he warned. "That their old club didn't like them, that they didn't like living in that other city, that their wife wanted to move East. Now I know who can do what."[14] The Mets had a few assets to offer in the trading market, but Casey wasn't about to reveal who they were. After all, they might figure in upcoming trades. One of those assets, Charlie Neal, who had earlier been rumored to be going to San Francisco for Willie McCovey, was no longer on the active roster. A week earlier, he had undergone surgery to remove the growth on his left hand. Neal wasn't the only one missing the final road trip to the Midwest. Also sitting it out were veterans war horses Gil Hodges and Gene Woodling.

The Stengel men had won five games from the Milwaukee Braves in May, but only one after that. They concluded the season series at 6–12, with two consecutive defeats at a chilly County Stadium on September 25 and 26. Several more records were set at Milwaukee — some good and some bad. The good: Warren Spahn beat the Mets in the first game for his 326th lifetime victory, tying him with Eddie Plank for the most among left-handed pitchers. The bad: Jay Hook uncorked a wild pitch in the first inning, the 71st of the season for the Mets and a new league record. In the second contest, the Mets set a new standard for losing, dropping their 118th game of 1962. Roger Craig's personal ledger fell to 10–24. For Casey Stengel, the accumulation of defeats was made even more stinging by the continued success of the Mets' rivals on the other side of the Macombs Dam Bridge. Before leaving town, Casey sent a telegram to Ralph Houk, congratulating him on his second straight pennant as Yankee manager.

During the last weekend of the season, the schedules of the two New York teams were mirror images of each others: the Mets were at Chicago playing the Cubs; the Yankees were at the Stadium entertaining the Chicago White Sox. There were only 595 paying customers at Wrigley Field on September 28, as the Cubs defeated the Polo Grounders, 3–2, marking the 119th loss of the season for Casey Stengel. The Mets came back the next day, winning their 40th and final game of the season, 2–1. Bob Miller, helped by a seventh inning double by Marv Throneberry, pitched a seven-hit complete game, and, more importantly, avoided the embarrassment of losing his 13th game in a row. In the season finale on September 30, 1962, the Mets fell to the Cubs, 5–1 for their 120th loss of the season. Frank Thomas's 34 and final home run of the season was overshadowed by one final embarrassment: the Mets hit into a triple play. Asked later if he had experienced fun that season, Casey dispensed with the Stengelese and answered succinctly: "I would have to say no to that one." Perhaps it was not fun, but old Case had gained an added measure of respect from one of the game's great showman. Stengel, said Bill Veeck, had performed "the most remarkable job in public relations in the history of the game." He was, Veeck added, "one of the last of the great characters."[15]

With another pennant in the bag, the suspense at Yankee Stadium from September 28 to 30 involved Mickey Mantle's chase of the batting title. The Switcher had missed a third of the 1962 season, but by some miracle, seemed to have just enough at-bats to qualify. After the Yankees' last win at Washington on September 26, he was hitting .322, four percentage points behind the leader, Pete Runnels of the Boston Red Sox. On Friday, September 28, Ralph Houk inserted Mantle into the leadoff spot against Early Wynn, who was trying yet again to win his 300th career game. Wynn watched Roger Maris hit his 33rd home run and collected his 100th RBI of the year in the first inning, then settled down. He was leading 3–1 going into the seventh inning, when he was victimized by a two-run homer by rookie Joe Pepitone. The "curve was too high on that kid," Wynn said afterwards.[16] The next inning, four more Yankee runs, including Dale Long's three-run homer, ended Wynn's quest for 300 in 1962. Mickey Mantle came to bat four times, walking once, grounding out weakly once, and popping out twice. With his average down to .319, the batting title was now out of reach.

On Saturday, September 29, the Yankees beat the Chisox once again, 8–6. No one was taking the game very seriously. Whitey Ford started for the Yankees and was replaced by a pinch-hitter in the bottom of third inning. Hitting for Ford was Jim Bouton, an .068 hitter during the season. Then on Sunday, September 30, the Bombers won their 96th game of the season. Mickey Mantle swatted his 30th home run. He finished with a .321 batting average, second behind Pete Runnels' .326. The home run championship went to Harmon Killebrew of the second-place Minnesota Twins. He hit 48, easily outdistancing the runner up, Norm Cash of the Tigers, who had 39. Leon Wagner of the third-place Los Angeles Angels hit 37. Roger Maris' 33 homers equaled his entire output at Yankee Stadium in 1961.

For the New York Mets, hitting into a triple play in the last game of the season had a kind of poetic injustice to it, "a perfect ending" to a miserable inaugural campaign, as described by the man who hit into it, Joe Pignatano.[17] The Mets lost 120 games. Along the way, they racked up losing streaks of nine, 17, 11, and 13 games. The 1962 season, perhaps as a result of the punishing 162-game schedule, had seen an unprecedented number of shutouts and one-run games, 98 in all. In the National League, 16 games ended as shutouts, 26 by just one run. In the American League, there were 19 shutouts and 37 one-run games. The Mets lost more one-run games (18) than any other major league club. In the post-mortem press conference at Wrigley Field, Casey Stengel insisted that the Mets should have won half of those games. One of those games, of course, might have gone their way if only Marv Throneberry had managed to touch first base on his way around the diamond. But the Mets, in spite of Casey's pleas, never seemed to grasp the fundamentals. As he ruefully put it, "It was like spring training all year."

For Richie Ashburn, who was retiring after the season, the Old Perfessor could do no wrong. "I've been in big-league baseball for fifteen years and I thought I knew a lot about the game, but that man knows more than any man I ever ran up against."[18]

The New York Mets, it was assumed, had played their last game at the Polo Grounds. On September 30, the south side of the Macombs Dam Bridge was given over to professional football. The Denver Broncos defeated the New York Titans, 32–10, in an American Football League game. On the north side of the Macombs Dam Bridge, the Yankees, after an injury-ridden season, were preparing to meet a yet unknown National League champion in the World Series.

10

"The Longest Season"

The Bronx Bombers returned to their New Jersey and Long Island homes relatively healthy — and their manager wanted them to stay that way, as they prepared for the 1962 World Series. Ralph Houk's dictum was clear: beware the perils of suburban life; keep away from lawn mowers, hedge clippers, hammers, and small children; avoid barbeque pits, cellar stairs; and "wives who want to demonstrate what they learned in their judo class."[1] The Yankees' stay in suburban New Jersey wouldn't be a long one, in any case. At his Saddle River home, Houk was packing his bags for the trip the West Coast.

The 1962 World Series would begin at the home field of the National League champions. But as of October 1, that venue was still uncertain. The Los Angeles Dodgers and San Francisco Giants finished the regular season tied for first place, with identical 101–61 records. (The Mets' "patsies," the Cincinnati Reds, finished second, three games back). Commissioner Ford Frick announced that a best two-out-of-three-game playoff series from October 1 to 3 would determine the Yankees' World Series opponent.

On Tuesday, October 2, the Bombers took batting practice for an hour and ten minutes at the Stadium, before leaving by bus for Idlewild Airport in Queens. Their original destination was Los Angeles. But after learning that the Giants had taken the first playoff game, the team took a four o'clock flight to San Francisco instead. Touching down in the Bay Area, the New Yorkers were greeted by a small, but partisan crowd of San Franciscans yielding signs that read, "Yankee Go Home." There were some friendly faces in the crowd, however. Roger Maris, to his delight, was greeted by his aunt, her husband Dr. Donald J. O'Neill, and their two children.

For the New Yorkers, home for the next several days would be the Del Webb Town House on Market Street, one of the Yankee owner's many West Coast properties. Ralph Houk said he had no preference as to who the Yankees faced in the World Series, but many of his players were openly rooting for the Dodgers, who tied the playoff series at one game apiece on October 2. In 1962, four of the seven World Series games would be held in a National League park. The players' shares would be more lucrative ($1,800 more) playing at Chavez Ravine, instead of the smaller Candlestick Park. There was also the case of familiarity; Houk's men were already accustomed to playing at Chavez Ravine, the home field of the Los Angeles Angels. A Yankees-Dodgers series would certainly be a study in contrasts: the slugging duo of Mantle, Maris and company, versus the speedster Maury Wills, who had shattered Ty Cobb's all-time stolen base record with 104.

On Wednesday afternoon, October 3, while the Dodgers and Giants were battling it out in Los Angeles, the Yankees conducted an hour and a half practice at Candlestick, their bags already packed for a possible return to Los Angeles. That proved unnecessary, as the Giants defeated the Dodgers to win the National League pennant. The Giants' 6–4 come-from-behind victory brought back memories of the 1951 playoff game at the Polo Grounds and Bobby Thomson's "shot heard round the world." The Yankees kept to the relative safety of the Del Webb Townhouse, since outside, delirious Giants fans took to the streets. A horde of 75,000 waited at the airport for their heroes' arrival at 9 P.M. Pacific Coast Time, clogging up terminals and runways. Jets, unable to taxi on their own power—for fear of blasting bystanders with fumes—had to be towed by tractors to the terminals. Bayshore Highway was backed up for two miles both ways, as delirious fans made their way downtown. The city itself was the scene of pandemonium, Montgomery Street strewn with rubbish. The San Francisco police arrested 11 rowdy revelers.

The 1962 World Series, the first transcontinental contest, was scheduled to begin on Thursday, October 4, at Candlestick Park. The Yankees-Giants World Series rivalry went back 40 years. The Giants, managed by John McGraw, were the masters of the Polo Grounds back then, and the Yankees mere renters in Coogan's Bluff. The McGraw men took the series from the Babe Ruth Yankees in 1921 and again in 1922 (Casey Stengel was a member of the 1922 Giants championship team). The Yankees moved across the Harlem River in 1923, and the balance of power slowly but inexorably move in the direction of the Bronx Bombers as well. The Yankees defeated McGraw's Giants in the 1923 World Series (despite two home runs by Casey Stengel) and beat them three more times afterward, the last in 1951. On the Giants' squad, only the incomparable Willie Mays remained from the 1951 October Classic. Besides Mays, the only Giants present for Bobby Thomson's "shot heard 'round the world" were Whitey Lockman, now the Giants' third base coach, pitching coach Larry Jansen, and Al Dark, the club's manager.

In 1962, Dodger Stadium, Walter O'Malley's new sports palace in Chavez Ravine, was all the rage. Two years earlier, it had been Candlestick Park that captivated the imagination of the baseball world. When it opened in April 1960, Candlestick Park was the second largest stadium in the National League after the Los Angeles Coliseum — which really wasn't a ballpark at all. With a capacity of 42,500, it was the first baseball facility made of reinforced concrete. It was also the first to have a heat radiating system, which as it turned out, was a very good thing for the temperature at Candlestick Point often dropped into the forties at night. The Giants' new playground could accommodate as many as 8,000 cars, something the Yankee owners Dan Topping and Del Webb could only imagine. Unlike the Giants' old home at the Polo Grounds, Candlestick Park was symmetrically laid out: 335 feet down the foul lines and 420 feet to dead center. But Mother Nature sneered at the best efforts of human engineering. The winds gusted across the field, mocking the most prodigious blasts of power hitters and making goliaths out of singles hitters. In order to avoid the worst effects of the winds, the starting time of the first game on October 4 was pushed back to 12:00 noon, Pacific Coast Time.

Game one of the 1962 World Series was a duel between lefties. Ralph Houk announced that Whitey Ford (17–8) would start the first game against the Giants' Billy O'Dell (19–14). O'Dell was well-known to many of the Yankee batters from his days with the Baltimore Orioles. The lefty had been an "in and out" pitcher in the American League, but he had gained confidence in his stuff this past season with the Giants and wasn't afraid of coming in tight on the hitters. O'Dell was fifth in the National League with 199 strikeouts. The Yankees' lineup would have Tony Kubek (hitting .314 since returning from military service) leading off. Bobby Richardson, who hit .302 and set a new major league record with 683 at-bats, would bat second. Mickey Mantle (.321, 30 home runs, 89 RBIs) was the cleanup hitter. Ralph Houk, however, had inserted Tom Tresh into the third spot in the lineup, relegating Roger Maris to the fifth position. Tresh, who made the All-Star squad at shortstop, had flourished in left field after Kubek's return from military service. In his last 44 games, Tom hit .308, finishing with an overall mark of .286, 20 homers, and 93 RBIs. Maris' statistics were not shabby by any means. His average was just .256, but he led the club with 33 round trippers and 100 RBIs. Still, after his record breaking season of 1961, Maris was widely seen as a bust, by fans and sportswriters everywhere. But if Maris was resentful at his loss of status, he didn't say so. Perhaps Bill Veeck was right; Roger liked to be "submerged."

Billy O'Dell gazed up at the cloudless sky and then looked down for the sign from catcher Ed Bailey. At the plate, Tony Kubek felt the cool autumn snap in the air, as he waited for the first pitch of the 1962 World Series. O'Dell fanned Kubek for the first out of the game. But Bobby Richardson singled to right, Tom Tresh followed with a single to center, and suddenly the Yankees had runners at first and second with just one out. Mickey Mantle struck out, but now Mother Nature lived up to her billing as a third character in this World Series. Roger Maris hit a high fly, which the winds picked up and carried all the way to the rail fence in right-center. The Giants' right-fielder, Felipe Alou, got a good jump and put a glove on the ball, but all he had to show for his troubles was a well-scratched forearm. Maris' drive fell for a double, as Richardson and Tresh scampered home with the first runs of the game. Elston Howard failed to bring Maris home, but the Yankees had drawn first blood, and led 2–0.

The Yankees ran onto the field with Whitey Ford following in their wake with his familiar straight-shouldered, deliberate walk. Ford came into the game having pitched 32 scoreless World Series innings, breaking the previous mark held by Babe Ruth, and he extended his streak by retiring the Giants in order in the first inning. The first batter to face Whitey in the second inning was Willie Mays. The Say Hey Kid was Ford's nemesis, six-for-seven against Whitey in All-Star competition. True to form, Mays promptly singled to left. Orlando Cepeda struck out, but Jim Davenport singled to center field, Willie taking third. Ed Bailey then fouled to Bobby Richardson behind first base. Ford was just about out of the inning, when José Pagán laid a perfect bunt down the third base line to score Mays. That ended Ford's scoreless World Series streak at 33 and two-thirds innings. The Giants nicked Ford for another run in the third to tie the game, Willie Mays singling in Chuck Hiller, who had doubled to start the frame. The score was tied: New York 2, San Francisco 2.

Meanwhile, Ford's teammates were suddenly facing a stingy Billy O'Dell. The left-hander settled down after the opening frame, and gave up just two singles in the next five innings. The Yankees finally came alive in the seventh. Clete Boyer, using a heavier bat and exhibiting better pitch selection, had finished with his best season at the plate, hitting .272 with 18 home runs. He swung at an O'Dell slider on the outside corner, a little below the belt, and smashed it clear over the barrier in left field to give the Bombers a 3–2 lead. O'Dell, who pitched 281 innings during the regular season, and was second in the National League with 20 complete games, didn't finish this one. The Yankee chased him with two more runs in the eighth. Roger Maris started things off with a one-out single to right. O'Dell clipped Elston Howard with a pitch, putting men on first and second with one out. Dale Long (playing for the injured Bill Skowron, who wrenched his back in batting practice) singled to right to drive in Maris. It was 4–2 Yankees and the showers for O'Dell. The Bombers scored one more run in the eighth and another in the ninth against the Giants' bullpen for a 6–2 series-opening victory, as a mostly disappointed crowd of 43,852 filed out of Candlestick Park. As Yankee announcer Mel Allen would say, "How about that."

"Good pitching," Whitey Ford explained afterwards in the visitor's clubhouse, "is mainly a matter of getting the batter to hit the pitch you want him to hit, not the one he wants to hit." It wasn't the best game Whitey had ever pitched; he surrendered ten hits in going the route. His curve "wouldn't bite into the breeze" (he attempted only three), but his slider was working well and the cool breeze helped his stamina. Six of the hits registered against him came in the second and third innings when San Francisco scored its only two runs. Whitey held the Giants to four harmless singles after that. As always, he had his troubles with Willie Mays. "Willie hit a different pitch each time," Ford explained. "I finally got him out with a fastball he didn't expect." He quipped, "I was beginning to think he owned me — or at least was a major stockholder."[2]

Mays aside, Whitey had a lot for which to be proud . The win was a record tenth World Series victory. Whitey had also set World Series marks for most total World Series by a pitcher (9), most games pitched (16), most innings (118), and most strikeouts (76). In contrast, Roger Maris had set no World Series marks. But the much maligned right-fielder (with a mighty assist from the Candlestick breezes) had quietly contributed to half of the Yankee scoring. Roger's heroics didn't silence all of his critics. They booed anyway. But he was "happy, no hard feelings toward anybody." It was, he added, "so different from last year. You have no idea. Last year, the pressure was unbearable." Now it was different. "No one expects me to do much." Mays called Roger's first inning double the "key play" of the game.[3]

Going into the second game of the World Series at Candlestick Park on Friday, October 5, there was another Yankee burning to quiet the critics. Ralph Terry had come back from the debacle of the Mazeroski home run to post a sterling 16–3 record in 1961. But World Series success eluded him once again; he suffered the lone Yankee defeat against the Cincinnati Reds. Terry, who led the American League in wins with 23 and hurled the most innings (299) in 1962, would face a revamped Giants lineup. Al Dark sat down Harvey Kuenn, the former American League batting champion now in the twilight of his career, and replaced him in left field with Matty Alou. Matty's older brother, Felipe, remained in right field but was moved up to the second position in the lineup. Matty, a spray hitter, would bat third in front of Willie Mays. Lastly, Dark replaced the hulking but slumping Orlando Cepeda at first base with the even more massive Willie McCovey.

Like Terry, the Giants' starter, Jack Sanford, had something to prove. The 33-year-old Sanford (his uniform number was also 33) had a banner year. He was 24–7 in 1962, with the second most wins in the National League behind the Dodgers' Don Drysdale. But Sanford wasn't a particular favorite of manager Al Dark. The Giants had briefly exposed him to the National

League expansion draft. Sanford might've been one of the premium players available to George Weiss for $125,000, but before Weiss had the chance to take him, the Giants took Sanford off the expansion list. The husky, blond right-hander, who hailed from Wellesley Hills, Massachusetts, had feasted on the Polo Grounders, beating them five times during the season. On Friday, October 5, in the second game of the 1962 World Series versus the New York Yankees, Dark was very happy that he had held on to him.

The temperature was in the mid-seventies, as 43,910 fans watched Jack Sanford take the mound for his third start in seven days (he had worked the second playoff game against the Dodgers). Despite pitching with a slight cold, Sanford hurled a three-hitter, beating Ralph Terry and the Yankees, 2–0. It was the first time the Yankees had been blanked in a World Series game since Warren Spahn turned the trick for the Milwaukee Braves in 1958. The Giants scored all of the runs they needed off Terry in the first inning. Chuck Hiller, the unheralded second baseman who replaced Harvey Kuenn at the top of the order, led off the bottom of the first with a double to right field, as Roger Maris just missed making a spectacular play on the low line drive. Umpire Hank Sauer at first signaled Hiller out, but changed his call when he saw the ball pop out of Maris' glove as he hit the ground. Felipe Alou then sacrificed Hiller to third. Moments later Hiller scored on a ground out by little brother Matty. Al Dark's lineup changes had all come up aces. The Giants' second run of the game against Terry came in the seventh inning on Willie McCovey's home run just inside the right field line.

Later, in a happy Giants clubhouse, a jubilant Sanford declared it "the best game I ever pitched." The fastball, slider, and curve were all working for him. Although he threw mostly fastballs, he also had the New Yorkers swinging at curve balls out of the strike zone. Yogi Berra complained that Sanford gave the Yankees nothing to hit — even when he was behind in the count. Sanford's "waste pitch" was so close that you had to "think twice about letting it go," complained Berra. The only time Sanford was in trouble came in the ninth. Mickey Mantle stung him with a 375-foot double to right-center field ("he really banged it," said Sanford).[4] With Mantle dancing off second and Roger Maris coming to bat, Sanford was worried for the first time in the game. But Maris, almost the hero in the first inning, was now frustrated once again. With the Giants employing a Ted Williams shift (three fielders on the right side of the infield) Maris sent a stinging grounder to the right side. Chuck Hiller made a brilliant stop to throw him out at first and end the game.

For a disappointed Ralph Terry, it was his fourth consecutive defeat in World Series play. He had pitched almost as well as Sanford. If Roger Maris had been able to catch one ball and get a hit on another, Terry, not Sanford, would have been standing in front of reporters with a big grin on his face.

Willie McCovey's homer was especially galling. Terry had set up big Willie with two consecutive change ups, before trying to sneak a slider by him. The pitch — low and inside — "was just where I wanted it to be," lamented Terry. The six-foot, four-inch McCovey didn't hit the ball squarely, but he was so strong that he knocked it out of the park anyway. The memory of the 1960 World Series and Bill Mazeroski's home run was never too far from Terry's mind. "I pitched as good as I know how," he said. "The one Series job I really feel bad about is that relief business at Pittsburgh two years ago when I got clobbered."[5]

Present at the second game of the 1962 World Series was Ralph Terry's former skipper, the present manager of the New York Mets, Casey Stengel. The Old Professor had come up from Los Angeles and declared the battle between Terry and Jack Sanford "a lovely game." Before returning to "momma and the bank," he answered questions about the future of the Mets. He was asked about when the Mets would be in the World Series, prompting a typical circuitous response from the master of gab. "We got trouble with the fans [if we win]," he responded. "Nine hundert tousand" came out to the Polo Grounds in 1962. "How we gonna win when they came out like that to see us lose, I ask ya?"[6]

There was one consolation for Ralph Terry. Just hours after the game, the tall Oklahoman learned that his wife, Tanya, had given birth to their second child, a boy, at their home in Larned, Kansas. That same Friday evening, back in New York City, it was "hootenanny night" at Town Hall. Folk music fans gathered at 123 West 43rd Street in Manhattan to see the Canadian duo Ian and Sylvia, Colorado alto Judy Collins, and a "21-year-old ragamuffin" named Bob Dylan. The young Dylan performed neo-traditional folk songs, "stunning in their wild imagery and human commitment."[7] Dylan, then known as Robert Zimmerman, had grown up in Hibbing, Minnesota. This northeastern Minnesota town at the edge of the Mesabi Range (one of the richest iron ore deposits in the world) was the birthplace of Roger Maris. Dylan was, like so many sons and daughters of the West, trying to make it big in the Big Apple. Maris, who already had all the notoriety he could wish for, was looking to quiet his critics as the Yankees and Giants gathered in the Bronx for the next three games of the World Series.

Ralph Houk had his share of walking wounded as he prepared for the third game of the World Series. Elston Howard had an injured hand and Bill Skowron was day-to-day, depending on the condition of his tender back. Tom Tresh and Clete Boyer, pleasant surprises all year long, were hitting .375 and .333, respectively. Roger Maris was at .286, and perhaps would've hit higher if not for the Ted Williams shift employed by Al Dark. Yet, the antipathy toward Maris in the print media continued unabated. Notwithstanding his play in game one of the series, The *San Francisco Examiner* labeled Maris "the phantom of this opera." That title really should have gone to Mickey Mantle, who was mired in a .125 slump.

As for the Giants, Willie Mays had fattened his average on Whitey Ford and was hitting .375, while Felipe Alou was at .333. The biggest surprise for the Giants in the Series thus far was the robust hitting of the Puerto Rican shortstop, José Pagán, who had a .600 average after two games. His country-man Orlando Cepeda (.306, 35 homers, 114 RBIs during the season), however, was hitless in the Series. There were several theories explaining Cepeda's poor play: an eye ailment, exhaustion (he had played winter ball in Puerto Rico), or, as many believed, he was "no damn good in the clutch." Cepeda's replace-ment at first base in game two, Willie McCovey, was looking forward to play-ing in the Bronx. "I don't see why I should shrivel to death just because I'm playing the Yankees. Playing against them is just like playing ... the Mets."[8]

The New York Mets, having spent a miserable season wallowing in Polo Grounds glories and playing off their persona of lovable clowns, had their sights set on the future. That future was in the Borough of Queens. The Flush-ing Meadows Stadium was more than half completed. Real estate brokers were already counting on the Mets to have a positive effect on property values. The Forest Hills Inn and Apartments, located at the entrance of the Forest Hills Gardens, recently sold for $2,700,000 and were advertised by the new owners as being in proximity to two major attractions: the World's Fair grounds and the Flushing Meadows Stadium. The Mets' debut at Flushing Meadows in April 1963 depended on the completion of a new $93,000,000 road network in Queens, championed by Robert Moses, which included the widening of the Grand Central and Whitestone Parkways, the extension of the Van Wyck Expressway, and the reconstruction of Northern Boulevard.

Not everyone was enthusiastic about the Mets going to Queens. The *Brooklyn Eagle* said it would "allow public reaction decide whether we are to embrace Casey and his athletes as part of the Brooklyn sports picture."[9] Ron Goldfarb, a 15-year-old youngster from Brooklyn Tech, had an ingenious solution. He began a petition to have the team renamed the "Brooklyn Mets." Given the hybrid nature of the club, why not?

On the afternoon of October 7, it was the old tenants of the Polo Grounds, the San Francisco Giants, pitted against their old rivals across the Macombs Dam Bridge, the New York Yankees, in the third game of the 1962 World Series. Thousands of Yankee fans were lined up by 8 A.M., vying for the $2 bleachers seats. As the crowds swelled, River Avenue was littered with empty coffee containers, newspapers, and beer cans. Sally Jacobs was at her station, busy selling Giants hats to Yankee haters. She said, "I never let my sentiments get in the way of my business."[10] Neither did the Yankee owners. Inside the

Stadium, the George Seuffert Band entertained the standing room only crowd of 71,434. Joe DiMaggio was there to throw out the first pitch to huge applause, but the old days of the Polo Grounds weren't entirely forgotten. A dying Blanche McGraw was in attendance; she and Willie Mays were photographed together before the game. Ralph Houk tabbed young right-hander Bill Stafford (14–9) to oppose the Giants' veteran lefty, Billy Pierce (16–6).

Roger Maris had hit 28 fewer home runs than he had in 1961, and knocked in 41 fewer runs. Neither the press nor the fans let him forget it, or his extravagant $70,000 salary. But on this October Sunday in the Bronx, Maris was the man who got things done, as the Yankees regained the series lead from the Giants. Maris' heroics began early. In the bottom of the first inning, with two outs, Tom Tresh singled to center field against Pierce. Mickey Mantle, batting cleanup, then sent a low line drive toward left that Felipe Alou couldn't handle, falling for extra bases. That put runners on second and third with two outs and Maris coming to the plate. Al Dark once again signaled for the Ted Williams shift. But this time, Maris managed to find a seam in the Giants' defense. He singled to right to drive in Tresh and Mantle. It was New York 2, San Francisco 0.

The Yankees continued to threaten against Pierce. But the veteran lefty held on, helped by a nifty Giants defense. Felipe Alou robbed Elston Howard of an extra base hit to left in the second inning. Third baseman Jim Davenport snagged a Bill Skowron line drive in the fifth. The Yankees finally broke through in the bottom of the seventh, with Roger Maris again the catalyst. With the Giants once again bunched up on the right side, he threaded the defense with a single to right. When right-fielder Willie McCovey momentarily fumbled the ball, Roger alertly proceeded to second base. Then came what, in retrospect, was the play of the game. Howard followed Maris to the plate and flied out to Willie Mays in relatively short center. Maris decided to test his underrated speed against Mays' magnificent arm. He tagged up and took off for third. Mays' throw from center was just a bit late reaching Davenport. After Bill Skowron was hit by a pitch, Clete Boyer hit a grounder toward the mound. Pierce fielded the ball and flipped to second baseman Chuck Hiller, who retired Skowron at second, but failed to complete the double play at first, as Maris crossed the plate with the third Yankee run.

Meanwhile, young Bill Stafford was hurling a remarkable game. Both his fastball and curve were working well that afternoon, particularly the fastball. He threw 24 pitches in the first inning, then only 88 more. Stafford allowed two hits through seven innings before surviving a scare in the eighth. He gave up a single to the red-hot José Pagán and then induced Matty Alou to fly out. But Matty's brother, Felipe, batting next, hit a drive through the middle that struck the Yankee pitcher flush in the shin. Stafford recovered to pick up the ball and made the throw to first for the out on Alou — and then doubled up in pain. Still dizzy from the blow, he took some smelling salts, and after a couple of warm-up pitches retired Chuck Hiller for the third out.

Maris' gamble on the base paths loomed large when the Giants rallied against Stafford in the top of the ninth. Willie Mays doubled down the left field line. McCovey grounded out and Orlando Cepeda popped out to Maris in right. Then catcher Ed Bailey nailed a Stafford fastball four rows deep in to the lower right field stands for a two-run homer. Stafford, still smarting from Alou's smash, couldn't put all of his weight on his leg on the pitch to Bailey. Still, with the score now 3–2, Stafford ignored his injury and bore down, retiring Jim Davenport for the last out of the game. Afterward, Ralph Houk admitted that he had gone through a pack and a half of chewing tobacco — half a pack more than during a regular season game. But his faith in his young right-hander was vindicated in the end. The 23-year-old Stafford ended the game with a four-hitter. The losing pitcher, 35-year-old lefty Billy Pierce, was almost as good, surrendering just five hits. Both went the distance in a game that took just 2:06 to play.

As reporters mingled about his locker, Roger explained his bold gamble against Mays in the seventh inning, saying, "I figured I could run faster than he can throw." (In high school Maris ran the hundred in ten seconds flat).

In the wake of the M&M Boys' chase of Babe Ruth's record, there were those who complained that the game had lost much of its excitement with the emphasis strictly on home runs. The game, it was said, lacked its former "cumulative drama"— the base on balls, the steal, the extra base.[11] Ironically, Maris— the man so maligned for ruining the game — in game three provided exactly this kind of excitement.

Ralph Houk figured to chew considerably less tobacco in game four at the Stadium on Monday, October 8. The Yankees were in an enviable position. They led the Giants, 2–1, in the series and were 4–1 favorites to win it all. Influencing the bookmakers, no doubt, was the presence of Whitey Ford on the mound against the supremely talented, but less experienced San Francisco starter, Juan Marichal. A victory by the Yankees in this game set up the possibility of closing out the series on their home field on Tuesday. However, the anticipation of victory was accompanied by considerable carping at the arrogance of Yankee management. Some patrons complained loudly about the conversion of bleacher space into reserved seating. Others groused that the club was selling "standing room on top of standing room." Yet another fan censured the club for trying to commandeer the Macombs Dam Park for additional stadium parking. Owners Dan Topping and Del Webb, all of these critics agreed, were greedy and deserved to suffer. As one disgruntled customer put it, "I hope the Mets take over in New York."[12]

In any case, the mood of inevitable victory was short-lived. On Monday, October 8, 1962, a crowd of 66,607 saw the Giants come back to even the series, 2–2, with a 7–3 victory over the Yankees. Whitey Ford pitched through the first inning without harm, but in the Giant second, Felipe Alou doubled to left field. Orlando Cepeda, back in the starting lineup but still mired in a slump, grounded out to Tony Kubek at short. Jim Davenport struck out. With one more out Ford and the Yankees would be out of the inning. Whitey had a 3–2 count on Tom Haller. The six-foot, four-inch catcher was playing with six stitches on his arm, courtesy of a collision in the playoff series with Los Angeles. But the injury was no impediment this afternoon. Haller swung hard and hit an opposite field drive deep in to the lower right field stands for a 2–0 Giants lead.

The Yankees came back in the bottom of the inning, but their rally felt short. Bill Skowron legged out a triple, having sent Willie Mays scampering around the monuments in deep center field. Minutes later, Clete Boyer flied to Harvey Kuenn in left to end the threat. The game continued in favor of the Giants, 2–0, with both teams squandering opportunities. In the top of the fifth, the visitors loaded the bases against Ford but failed to score. In the bottom of the inning, a Yankee rally was squashed when Bobby Richardson hit into a double play.

Juan Marichal had pitched four scoreless innings when he came up in a sacrifice situation in the fifth. He hurt his right index finger trying to lay down a bunt, and had to leave the game. The Yankees proceeded to nip Marichal's replacement, Bob Bolin, for two runs to tie the game. Ralph Houk then made a fateful move. Anxious to pad the score, he had Yogi Berra bat for Whitey Ford. Berra walked to fill the bases. But Bolin retired the side without further damage. The Yankees and Giants remained tied at 2–2.

The Giants then blew the game open in the seventh. Jim Davenport drew a walk from Yankee reliever Jim Coates. Tom Haller struck out. Matty Alou, pinch-hitting for José Pagán, doubled to left, Davenport going to third. Now, a series of moves and counter moves ensued. Ed Bailey, a left-handed hitter, was announced as a pinch hitter for ex–Yankee World Series star Don Larsen. Ralph Houk responded by replacing Coates with lefty Marshall Bridges. Dark called back Bailey and sent in the right-handed swinging Bob Nieman. As a rookie with Bill Veeck's Browns in 1951, Nieman had set a major league record by hitting home runs in his first two at-bats in the major leagues. But the now experienced veteran wouldn't have a chance to swing the bat. He was walked intentionally, and Ernie Bowman was sent in to run for him. Bowman was something of a lucky charm. The Giants had won 44 of the 45 games he had played.

Bowman had proved to be the good luck charm once again. With the bases full of Giants, Bridges retired Harvey Kuenn on an infield popup for the second out. This brought the light-hitting Chuck Hiller to the plate. Back in June, trade rumors had swirled regarding a possible trade between the Giants and Mets that would have sent Willie McCovey to New York for Mets second baseman Charlie Neal. McCovey remained a Giant and Hiller was entrusted with second base. The Giants would be glad they did not make the trade. The young second sacker took a called strike from Bridges and then a ball low and outside. With the count 1–1, Bridges tried to jam him, but the ball stayed over the plate and Hiller sent it sailing over the head of Roger Maris into the lower right field stands. His grand slam home run, the first in World Series play in 42 years, gave the Giants a 6–2 lead. Each club scored one run in the ninth frame, making the final score, Giants 7, Yankees 3. With the World Series tied at two games apiece, the Yankees wouldn't be closing the series at home after all.

On Tuesday, October 9, storm clouds descended on the Bronx. The day was cast in darkness. Motorists inched their way over the Macombs Dam Bridge to Yankee Stadium, headlights on, windshield wipers straining for visibility. At the subway stop, riders pushed through the heavy rains, racing for the entrances. Once inside, the Yankee faithful waited — and waited — exhibiting the patience of Mets fans waiting for a win. A heavy drizzle pelted the Stadium into the afternoon, as fans pulled out umbrellas or improvised with newspapers. Many surrendered their seats to the rain and stood under overhanging billboards along the center field wall. George Seuffert, usually positioned in front of the center field flag pole, retreated with his band of music makers to the mouth of the tunnel exit. At 2:11 P.M. the announcement came from Commissioner Ford Frick: the fifth game of the 1962 World Series was postponed until Wednesday, October 10. There was chaos everywhere. Out-of-towners worried about premature eviction from their New York hotels. New travel arrangements had to be made with the airlines. Kids who had played hooky from school to attend the game had to come up with a new set of excuses. One teen had already "buried more grandparents than laws of genetics allowed."[13]

Rain or shine, Roger Maris managed to be in the middle of controversy. The booing continued unmercifully — from both Yankee and Giants fans. But Roger also brought troubles on his own head. Asked about a fly ball he might have caught, he answered petulantly, "I'm not going to run into a brick wall for anyone." He wasn't the only ballplayer reluctant to risk his personal safety, but others managed to keep their thoughts to themselves, or like Casey Stengel, they would have given it a humorous twist. Maris usually said the first thing that came to mind. Writing in the *San Francisco Chronicle*, Charles McCabe said of Maris, "He handles public relations with the adroitness of

Commodore Vanderbilt." (Vanderbilt was famous for his crude ways.) Others agreed with the scribe. "The guy can play ball," said one fan, "but Holy Moses!" Some New Yorkers were actually rooting for the Yankees to lose. "The Giants in six," whispered Toots Shor.[14] Maris, unlike Casey Stengel, wasn't a patron at Toots' saloon.

With an extra day off, Ralph Houk had an opportunity to rest his walking wounded and contemplate the loss that would force the Yankees back to San Francisco for the conclusion of the series. The Giants exposed several chinks in the Yankees' pitching armor. The Bombers didn't have the Ford-Arroyo combo, which had made the club so formidable in 1961. At age 33, Whitey Ford may no longer have been up to the rigors of pitching 18 innings with just four days rest. Marshall Bridges had enjoyed a terrific first half of the season filling in for Arroyo, but he tailed off in the last two months. Meanwhile, the Giants' pitching staff, despite losing the services of Juan Marichal, was still more than a match for the Yankees. At bat and in the field, the two teams looked even as they went into the fifth game of the 1962 October classic. Wednesday began with a light drizzle; but thankfully, by 11 A.M., the skies had cleared and the fans had begun to squeeze through the turnstiles to the welcoming green pastures of Yankee Stadium. The 63,165 fans on hand that afternoon cheered lustily as Jack Sanford and Ralph Terry squared off for the second time in the series.

For the first seven innings, game four was basically a replay of game two at San Francisco. Ralph Terry pitched beautifully, giving up just two runs. But Jack Sanford was even better, surrendering a mere run on just three hits while striking out ten. Terry kept the big bats of Mays, McCovey, and Cepeda silent, but was victimized by the singles hitters in the Giants lineup. Chuck Hiller cuffed him for an RBI double in the third inning and José Pagán hit a solo homer off him in the fifth. The Yankees, meanwhile, capitalized on some San Francisco miscues. In the fourth inning, Tom Tresh doubled and subsequently scored on a Sanford wild pitch — a slider that spun into the dirt. A passed ball brought in the second Yankee run in the sixth inning, Bobby Richardson sliding under Sanford's glove as catcher Tom Haller protested in vain.

With the score 2–1 in the Giants' favor, and Jack Sanford apparently in command, the Yankees rose up in dramatic fashion in the eighth inning. With one out, Kubek singled to right. Richardson followed with a single to left, placing runners on first and second with one out. Up came Tom Tresh. Tom's father, Mike Tresh, the former major league catcher, was watching with his wife and daughter-in-law Cherie in his seat behind home plate. But the elder Tresh was too nervous to sit still, so he got up and stood by the nearest exit. From this vantage point, he watched his son take Sanford's first pitch outside for a ball. Al Dark popped out of the dugout and came to the mound for the first time in the game. He had no intention of taking Sanford out, Dark later said. "I just wanted to slow him down."[15] Dark returned to his perch, and Sanford looked in for the sign. The Giants' right-hander threw a fastball that started low and then rose up in the strike zone. Tresh seized on it and drove it over Matty Alou's head into the right field seats, several rows back. With one swish of Tresh's bat, Sanford's dominance over the Yankees was gone. The score was suddenly New York 5, San Francisco 2.

Terry had one last scare in the ninth. Willie McCovey, who had cuffed him for a home run in game one, came to the plate. This time, Terry held Big Willie to a single. After Felipe Alou struck out, Tom Haller hit a drive to left-center field that Mickey Mantle couldn't reach. It fell for a double, scoring McCovey. The score was Yankees 5, Giants, 3. José Pagán then grounded out. Now, with two outs, Ed Bailey came up as a pinch-hitter. Bailey hit a drive to right field that looked at first as if it might be a home run. Terry had given up 40 gopher balls during the regular season — but not this time. He watched intently, hands on his hips, as Roger Maris faded back and caught the ball several feet in front of the right-field stands.

And so, the Yankees were going back to San Francisco leading the series, 3–2, with a chance to close out the Giants on Friday, October 12, at Candlestick Park. As the fans trouped out, the public address system (somewhat cruelly) serenaded the Giants with the old waltz, *After the Ball*:

> Many a heart is aching
> If we could read them all
> Many a heart is breaking
> After the ball.[16]

It was indeed a bitter loss for the Giants. Dark called it the "worst game in a long time." We "gave away too many outs." Sanford, looking pale and drawn after a week of battling the Dodgers, the Yankees and the flu, croaked that he "came in too high with a slider to Tom Tresh." As the Giants stewed, back in the Yankee clubhouse a jubilant Terry telephoned his wife Tanya in Kansas. She had just returned from the hospital on Saturday after delivering a second son, Frank Gabe. Among the crush of press corps, photographers, and the merely curious in the Yankee clubhouse, was a familiar face from the past — the New York Met's Casey Stengel. Approaching Ralph Terry, the Old Perfessor extended his hand and rasped, "Glad to see you finally got the win, kid." Terry's eyes glistened as he responded, "I'm sorry I didn't win it for you."[17] As sweet as victory was, the Mazeroski home run was still there to haunt them both.

Joe DiMaggio called the 1962 October Classic the best pitched series he had ever witnessed; the statistics, in fact, confirmed the pitchers' dominance. After five games the Yankees had outscored the Giants, 17–16. New York's composite ERA was 3.07 and San Francisco's was 3.44 — high perhaps, by today's standards, but then again, these pitchers were facing tough lineups. The composite box score looked like this after five games:

	Innings			
	1–3	4–6	7–9	Total
NY	2	4	11	17
SF	6	1	9	16

Tresh was the New York hitting star at an even .400. The rest of his teammates were either ordinary or simply awful: Kubek (.286), Skowron (.273), Howard (.214), Richardson (.190), Maris (.188), and Mantle (.111). San Francisco, meanwhile, received robust hitting from Pagán (.500) and Haller (.364), and average or mediocre hitting from everybody else: Hiller (.278), Felipe Alou (.278), Mays (.238), McCovey (.182), and Cepeda (.000). The Yankees, who had averaged eight home runs a World Series in the past, had only two, one each by Tresh and Boyer. The Yankee fans booed Maris, but they weren't particularly happy with Mickey Mantle either — and they let him know it. A heckler seated in center field had baited him all afternoon, at one point shouting, "Hey Mantle, everybody came out to see who was better, you or Mays, now we wonder who's the worst." An inning later, when Mantle returned to the field after another fruitless time at bat, the same heckler greeted him with the verdict: "Hey, Mantle, you win."[18]

In 1962 a kid from Brooklyn could push his bike onto the now defunct 69th Street ferry, cross over to the other side, and ride around Staten Island just for the fun of it. That relatively innocent, bucolic world was about to change. As the World Series was being played in the Bronx, the 693-foot tower on the Staten Island side of the Verrazano Narrows Bridge was reaching 90 percent completion. When the tower on the Fort Hamilton, Brooklyn, side was finished, and the 4,260-feet span stretched across New York harbor, the Verrazano would be the longest suspension bridge in the world, surpassing San Francisco's Golden Gate Bridge. On October 11, the Yankees were hovering over the red top of the Golden Gate as their plane made its descent into San Francisco.

As the New York Yankees and San Francisco Giants were traveling from coast to coast, a decision was being made that would have a profound effect on the future of all twenty major league teams. The Major League Baseball Players' Association had decided to throw in the towel and give up the second All-Star Game for 1963. In exchange, the major league owners agreed to address the players' concerns regarding travel conditions, namely: the scheduling of all night plane rides following getaway games; the scheduling of doubleheaders after night game; and the scheduling of doubleheaders on consecutive days. The decision to do away with the second All-Star Game was a blow to the pension fund but the physical and mental strain of coast to coast travel had become too much for the players to bear — perhaps even inspiring the Gene Conley/Pumpsie Green escapade. The next year's *single* All-Star Game would be held at Metropolitan Stadium in Bloomington, Minnesota. The 1964 All-Star Game was awarded to New York and would be played at the Flushing Meadows Stadium — that is, of course, if it was completed on time.

The Yankees arrived in the Bay Area, most of them dressed in neatly tailored business suits with matching ties. Yogi Berra had taken his wife, Carmen, to San Francisco the first time around; many other players had followed suit. But on this second trip to the Coast, only California residents Tex Clevenger and Bud Daley brought their wives. Roger Maris, as with most of his teammates, was going straight home after the series. The club checked into the Del Webb Townhouse; but Ralph Houk left soon after to attend a press conference at the Palace Hotel. Attired in a blue suit and tie, puffing on a black cigar, the Major patiently answered questions for an hour or so. But the manager of the pennant-winning Yankees wasn't the star of the press conference. As he was leaving, Casey Stengel was coming in. Suddenly, the room came alive. The Old Perfessor, manager of the worst team in baseball history, proceeded to regale the writers with stories of yesteryear until they simply ran out of copy.

The Del Webb Townhouse formed part of a string of western motels built by the Yankee owner. Webb may have been the Yankees "silent partner," but there was no denying his influence on post–World War II American culture. "You can debate who it was exactly [who] won the West," one observer remarked, "but it's obvious who owns it."[19]

The Yankees' stay at Webb's hostelry was going to be longer than they expected. As the players were unpacking their bags, the weather bureau was tracking a violent storm bearing down from Oregon. The storm, as predicted, descended on San Francisco on Friday, October 12, with raging fury. Heavy rains and 60-mile-per-hour winds lashed the Bay area, ripping down power lines, flooding streets, and bottling up traffic. The sixth game of the 1962 World Series was postponed — the first time that the Series had been rained out in *both* teams cities since 1911. On Saturday, October 13, the weather was no better, causing a second postponement in a row. While Willie Mays and his Giants teammates enjoyed the comforts of home, the Yankees players struggled with jet lag. Due to the three-hour time difference between the east and west coasts, many found themselves waking up between five and six o'clock in the morning. Far from their New Jersey and Long Island homes, they scrambled to fill up the time: shopping, sightseeing, watching movies, playing cards, reading, or, more often than not, staring blankly at a TV screen. Mickey Mantle was glued to the Texas-Oklahoma football game. Hygiene was becoming a problem; Bill Stafford, anticipating a short stay, had brought only one suit. Yogi Berra took Tony Kubek to the movies to watch a seafaring story. It was one of the worst films Kubek had ever seen, but Yogi, a Navy veteran from World War II, begged to differ.

There were 72 days until Christmas as the 1962 World Series endured its third consecutive cancellation — the fourth of the Series overall — on Sunday, October 14. Although the rains and winds had abated, there remained the difficult task of clearing the waters from Candlestick Park. The field's playing surface, beneath the few feet of grass, consisted of a layer of adobe clay. This made quick drainage almost impossible. Faced with these difficult field conditions, head groundskeeper Matty Schweb contrived an ingenious solution. He had his men spread a chemical concoction called Agri-Zyme on the field in an effort to bring the earth worms out of their holes, and allow the field to drain at least a little.

By Sunday, Ralph Houk decided that the Yankees had sat around long enough. He took his players on a 160-mile round trip to Modesto, west of San Francisco in the San Joaquin Valley, for an afternoon of batting and fielding practice. Mickey Mantle and Whitey Ford had just sat down to a huge breakfast at 9:30, when they learned that the team bus was getting ready to leave without them. They left their meals untouched and rushed to join their teammates. At Modesto, practice was conducted at Del Webb Field (Modesto being a former Yankees affiliate). Five thousand spectators watched the players as they limbered their muscles for the first time in four days. The San Francisco Giants, along for the ride, followed them onto the field. Back in New York, the football Giants played their first home game, losing to the Pittsburgh Steelers, 20–17. (In deference to baseball's predominance as the National Pastime, they had spent the first month of the NFL season on the road). On the other side of the continent, helicopters flew over Candlestick Park for two hours, hovering just six feet off the ground, in an effort to improve playing conditions for the next day's game

On Monday, October 15, the sky was cloudless as 43,948 fans settled back to watch lefties Whitey Ford and Billy Pierce take the mound in the oft-postponed sixth game of the 1962 World Series. Pierce was a familiar figure for the Yankees, having faced him many times during his long tenure with the Chicago White Sox. Pierce had a poor 25–37 lifetime record against New York. But in 1962 he was undefeated (12–0) at Candlestick Park, including a victory over Sandy Koufax in the first playoff game against the Los Angeles

Dodgers. The bookmakers, with Ford on the mound, were staying with the Yankees, making them 3–1 favorites to take the series.

Both Ford and Pierce frustrated the teams' sluggers in the initial inning. In the top of the first, Mickey Mantle just missed hitting a home run off Pierce. In the bottom of the inning, the Giants' Chuck Hiller beat out a one-out single to short against Ford. Felipe Alou reached on a rare error by Clete Boyer, but Ford ended the rally by inducing Willie Mays to hit into a double play. The game, for all practical purposes, was decided in the Giants' fourth. With one out, Felipe Alou singled off Boyer's glove. Ford walked Mays, putting runners on first and second. Whitey then attempted a pickoff play at second on Alou. Later, he claimed that he hadn't meant to throw the ball; it had simply slipped out of his hand. Intentional or not, the ball sailed into center field and died in the wet outfield grass. Before Mantle managed to retrieve it, Alou had rounded third and come in to score. Jolted by the throwing error, Ford proceeded to yield singles to Orlando Cepeda and Jim Davenport, giving up two more runs. San Francisco was now in front, 3–0.

In the Yankee fifth, Billy Pierce challenged Roger Maris once too often with the curve ball. Roger connected with a Pierce delivery and socked it for a home run, cutting the San Francisco lead to two. But the Giants came storming back in the bottom of the inning against Ford to ice the game. Harvey Kuenn, Chuck Hiller, Felipe Alou, and Orlando Cepeda all singled, producing two runs for a 5–1 advantage. Cepeda's RBI single knocked Ford out of game. The Bombers then scored a run in the eighth on a double by Clete Boyer and a single by Tony Kubek. But it was too little, too late. The Giants won, 5–2, to tie the series and force a seventh game. It was a frustrating defeat for the Yankees, anxious as they were to end the series and return home after what seemed like an eternity in San Francisco.

Ford gave five runs and nine hits in absorbing his fourth World Series loss, a record. Pierce pitched magnificently for the Giants, giving up just three hits on the afternoon. He struck out only two and walked two in earning his 13th victory in a row at Candlestick Park.

The Yankees' frustration spilled out into the locker room after the game. Elston Howard didn't think Pierce was as sharp as he had been back in New York. He was just "laying the ball in there and daring us to hit it ...as big as a grapefruit," said Ellie.[20] Ralph Houk, criticized for removing Ford too quickly in game four, defended his decision to let Ford hit in the fifth. All could agree on least one thing: the game was mercifully short. It was over in two hours flat. Casey Stengel, on hand for the proceedings, was once again the center of attention for copy-starved sportswriters. The Giants, Casey claimed, had used the awful playing conditions to their advantage. "Had those Yankees mired up their ankles," he chortled. But it wasn't the fortunes of his former team that Stengel was there to promote; it was that of the New York Mets. Surveying the playing field, he announced, "If those teams down there don't want any of those players, I'll take 'em for my Mets." As the writers laughed, he exhorted them to "put that down in your papers." His team could use a "little advertisin."[21] And who was a better pitchman than the Old Professor?

It was the eve of the final game of the 1962 World Series. Willie Mays was in bed by 8:30 in his San Francisco penthouse apartment. Jim Davenport was babysitting his five kids while his wife went shopping. Al Dark was home in nearby Atherton pondering the next day's moves. They and the rest of the Giants would sleep in their own beds. The New York Yankees were spending one last night as guests of owner Del Webb. Time crawled by. Yogi Berra and Whitey Ford signed autographs in the lobby on the way to dinner. No one talked very much. Mantle and Maris were hiding out in their rooms, not answering phones. The usually calm Ralph Houk, his nerves frayed from the long stay on the West Coast, lashed out at the New York press corps. Noting the time (9:30 P.M.), he barked, "I don't want you talking to our players at this time of night. Who are trying to help out?"[22]

It would be Ralph Terry versus Jack Sanford for the third time in the series. The bookmakers, having witnessed outstanding pitching by both men, called the seventh game of the 1962 World Series even.

A 35-mile-per-hour wind was blowing in from dead center field as Jack Sanford took the mound on Tuesday, October 16, for the series finale. In a reprise of the two previous meetings, he and Terry were soon locked in a pitchers' duel. For four innings they allowed nothing but zeroes on the Candlestick scoreboard. In the Yankee fifth, Bill Skowron managed a single off Sanford. Clete Boyer followed with another single. Sanford then committed the baseball equivalent of high crimes and misdemeanors: he walked rival pitcher Terry to load the bases. A double play ball by Tony Kubek scored Skowron. The scoreboard now read, New York 1 Giants, 0. Meanwhile Terry held the mighty Giants hitless until the seventh when he yielded a single to Sanford. In the eighth inning, the Oklahoman retired the first two men . In stepped Willie Mays. Terry delivered and Mays sent a drive screaming into the extreme left field corner. Tom Tresh rushed over and made a spectacular over-the-shoulder catch. Had the ball fallen in, Mays would have scored the tying run on a subsequent triple by Willie McCovey. But McCovey died on third as Terry snuffed out the Giant rally by striking out the "Baby Bull," Orlando Cepeda.

Ralph Terry had given up just two hits going into the bottom of the ninth inning when the Giants staged one final, gallant rally. Matty Alou, batting for Sanford, dragged a bunt to the right side of the mound, which neither Terry nor Bill Skowron could retrieve in time. At this point, Yankees fans with long memories would have been reminded of the seventh game of the 1960 World Series. Pitcher Jim Coates' failure to cover first base quickly on an infield dribbler by Roberto Clemente in the eighth allowed the Pirates to rally to tie the game and eventually win it the next inning on Mazeroski's home run. Now, two Octobers later, Matty remained on first as his brother, Felipe, and Chuck Hiller struck out. Terry had one more out to go—and the batter was Willie Mays. Matty Alou took off from first as a drive from Mays' bat whistled past him down the right field line. It looked like at least a double for Mays and a run batted in, tying the game at 1–1. But Matty Alou never received the chance to cross the plate. Roger Maris rushed over, fielded Mays' ball cleanly, and made a perfect peg to the cutoff man, Bobby Richardson. The Giants' third base coach, Whitey Lockman, saw the ball headed for Richardson's glove and raised his arms high over his head, holding Matty at third.

Yet, Terry was still not out of the danger. The next batter was Willie McCovey. In game two, McCovey had reached Terry for a home run, sending the Yankee pitcher toward his fourth consecutive World Series failure. In game five, Terry had managed to silence big Willie's bat and win his first game in the October Classic. Now, they were about to square off for what likely was the last time in the Series. The tension was heavy as McCovey came striding to the plate. Alou at third and Mays at second represented the tying and winning runs—and a world championship for the Giants. Ralph Houk, who earlier had signaled for Bill Stafford and Bud Daley to warm in the bullpen, slouched his way to the mound. After a brief word with Terry, he departed.

The tall Oklahoman, left alone on the mound, looked in for the sign from Elston Howard, and then reared and fired. McCovey let loose with a tremendous drive that the wind took and pushed foul, short of the right field fence. Terry recovered his breath, wound up and delivered again. This time McCovey unlimbered his large frame and sent a screamer slashing through the right side of the Candlestick infield. Within seconds the ball landed chest high in Bobby Richardson glove. The chunky second sacker bowed slightly, as if thanking providence, while the crowd watched in stunned silence. At 2:29 P.M. Pacific Coast Time, the longest World Series in history was finally over. The New York Yankees had won their 20th world championship, defeating the San Francisco Giants in the seventh game, 1–0.

The *New York Post*'s Leonard Schecter described the Yankees' locker room as usually being as "exciting as the inside of a bank vault"—but that wasn't the case this afternoon in San Francisco. After seven games in 17 days, including four rainouts and two cross-country journeys, the Yankees were proving to be quite human after all. Corks from Paul Masson vintage bottles bounced off the ceiling; anyone within distance of the celebration was being anointed with champagne. The center table at the visitors' clubhouse was filled with cold cuts, but nobody was eating. There was simply too much tension, frustration, and pure ennui to unleash. "This is the best I ever felt," said Mickey Mantle wryly, "and the worst I ever played." The sense of relief was etched in

the pale, drawn face of Ralph Houk. It was the "toughest [game] I ever have managed," he said simply. A reporter asked Houck if he was tempted to put McCovey on in the ninth? The Major answered, "Terry said he'd prefer to pitch to him and it was alright with me." Bobby Richardson noted that if McCovey's drive "had taken off, I might have been trouble." But instead it sank, coming in "like a bullet shoulder high."[23]

Ralph Terry, of course, was the center of attention. "This was the greatest game I ever pitched in my life," he told reporters—an understatement if there ever was one. No, he wasn't perturbed by losing the no-hit game when Sanford singled in the sixth inning. Nor did he let the hecklers in the stands get to him. When McCovey came up to the plate in the last of the ninth, he heard the catcallers yelling, "Here comes the home run ...remember Mazeroski, Terry." He endured the taunting and persevered. "Thank God for the second chance," he sighed.

Ralph Terry, the Yankee right-hander. In game seven, with two outs, and the tying and winning runs on base, Terry faced San Francisco Giants slugger Willie McCovey. From the stands, Terry heard: "Here comes the home run ... remember Mazeroski." Terry retired McCovey on a line drive to second baseman Bobby Richardson. Roger Maris had earlier made a key fielding play to prevent the tying run from scoring.

Terry recalled being upset on the plane ride back from Pittsburgh after the 1960 World Series, while drowning his sorrows with five martinis. During that awful trip home, Casey Stengel dropped by his seat and asked Terry what he had thrown to Mazeroski. "A curve ball low and away," the young pitcher replied. Stengel nodded and said, "As long as you were trying to pitch him right, It's OK."[24] Terry never forgot those words. The old man could've chewed him out and made him feel small. Instead, Stengel treated him with kindness and understanding.

In October 1961, Casey had come storming back to New York to manage the Mets, determined to exact revenge on Dan Topping for firing him, after the Mazeroski home run had ended the Yankees' World Series hopes. In 1962, revenge had come in the shape of public adulation, winning the hearts of New Yorkers and fans everywhere, despite losing a record 120 games. The seventh game victory in the 1962 World Series by Ralph Terry provided a heavy dose of consolation as well.

Despite its dramatic climax, the 1962 World Series lacked one thing, according to Prescott Sullivan of the *San Francisco Examiner*: an easily identifiable goat. This is true; Ralph Terry, who had served that purpose so well in 1960, had been redeemed, as had (in a way) Casey Stengel. But Terry and Stengel weren't the only ones receiving a measure of absolution on this sunny, windswept afternoon in San Francisco. So did Roger Maris. Everyone remembers Bobby Richardson's catch of Willie McCovey's drive. But it was Maris' pickup and throw on Willie Mays' drive just prior to McCovey's at-bat that represented the key fielding play of the inning—and the game. Had the ball fallen and died on the wet grass on either end of the play, Matty Alou would've have scored the tying run easily. But as with any situation involving Maris, things were never quite so simple. After the game, controversy swirled around the question of whether Giants third base coach Whitey Lockman should have sent Alou home. The *San Francisco Examiner*'s Curly Grieve deemed the decision to hold him a "conservative one." Joe DiMaggio also thought that Alou might've made it. But others disagreed. Writing in the *San Francisco Chronicle*, Al Rosenbaum asked the question—"Could Matty have scored?" He answered it in the negative: "Alou didn't have a chance." Both managers agreed with Rosenbaum. "It would have been suicide," said Al Dark. "He would have been out by a mile," said Ralph Houk. Matty himself protested, "I had no chance to go."[25]

Only a perfect pickup and throw prevented the San Francisco Giants from extending the game into extra innings and perhaps sending the Yankees back to the Bronx in defeat. But after a season characterized by outsized expectations and colossal underachievement and bitter disappointment, after the constant booing and editorial vitriol—not entirely undeserved—the 28-year-old from North Dakota had come through in the end. Maris hit only .174 in the Series, far less than Tom Tresh. But he had played a major role in three of the Yankees' four victories, including the crucial first, third, and seventh games of the October Classic, giving the Yankees the edge in each.

Someone said of the finale, "It was more than a game. It was like a Greek tragedy."[24] Ralph Terry had gotten to play the hero at last; he was voted the most valuable player of the series, winning the coveted Corvair from *Sport* magazine. But Maris, flawed and frayed, came out of his tent and had his moment of glory as well.

Redemption for Roger Maris, however, would have to be a private matter. The press wouldn't award that distinction publicly. The World Series had not changed the perceptions of Casey Stengel and Roger Maris very much. The Associated Press, ignoring the 120-loss season, actually gave Casey some votes for Manager of the Year; UPI, ignoring Maris' 30-plus home run, 100-RBI season and a laudable World Series performance, awarded him the "top flop award." But then again, why should this be surprising? The 1962 baseball season was once again a world turned upside down.

Epilogue

Reunion Day

Summer arrived early in 1973, brushing aside spring with the back of its sweaty palm and clamping a fiery grip on New York City. During much of June, July, and August, temperatures hovered around 90 degrees. At one point, the steel mechanism in the Macombs Dam Bridge swelled, jamming the span's mechanism. For several hours, traffic was at a standstill across the Harlem River between Manhattan and the Bronx. Anyone with time or means—or who was not glued to the TV set watching the Senate Watergate hearings—had left the city and headed east to Jones Beach on Long Island, or south to the Jersey Shore, or north and west to the Catskills and the Poconos. Thousands of others waded in the public pools at Flushing Meadows Park and other city aquatic centers.

Saturday, June 9, was a typical sunny, hot, and humid day, but not everyone was wading in the waters or scaling the mountains. That afternoon in Queens, a crowd of 69,138 witnessed the 105th running of the Belmont Stakes. "Secretariat," ridden by Ron Turcotte, galloped the one and a half mile course in 2:24, winning by an astounding 31 lengths and becoming the first Triple Crown winner in 25 years. Just hours before Secretariat sprinted into horse racing legend, former members of the 1962 New York Mets gathered at Shea Stadium, along with ex–Dodgers and Yankees, to celebrate the club's 12th annual Old Timers Day. Although always bittersweet, the 1973 reunion was an especially poignant occasion. The former players and 47,800 fans in attendance had come together to pay homage to the memory of Gil Hodges.

Gil Hodges retired as a player on May 5, 1963, his surgically reconstructed knee unable to bear the weight of another grueling baseball campaign. Gil had always been tabbed as managerial timber, and so it came to be. He managed the Washington Senators in the American League from 1963 to 1967, before returning to the National League to take over the New York Mets in 1968. The following year, that astounding year of 1969, he led the "Amazin'

Mets" to a surprising World Series victory over the heavily favored Baltimore Orioles. Gil managed the team for just two more seasons. On April 4, 1972, he collapsed and died of a heart attack following a round of golf in West Palm Beach, Florida. He was just two days short of his 48th birthday. Hodges was buried in Holy Cross Cemetery in his beloved Brooklyn. Yogi Berra, the ex–Yankee player and manager, and most recently a Mets coach, replaced him.

Gil Hodges' former teammates on the 1962 Mets club — including Roger Craig, Rod Kanehl, Félix Mantilla, Frank Thomas, Jay Hook, Al Jackson, Jim Marshall, Ken McKenzie, Joe Pignatano, and Richie Ashburn — gathered around home plate for the formal retirement of his uniform number. Mets general manager Bob Scheffing made the presentation of his number 14 jersey to Joan Hodges, as her four children looked on. "You are the greatest fans in the world," Joan told the crowd.[1]

A two-inning exhibition game followed the ceremony, pitting the Old Mets against a combined Yankees/Dodgers squad that included Joe DiMaggio, Whitey Ford, Pee Wee Reese, Carl Furillo, Jim Gilliam, Johnny Podres, and Ralph Branca. DiMaggio was the "designated hitter," the DH introduced for the first time that year in the American League as a way of adding offense — and fan interest — to a game, which by now, had been supplanted by professional football as the National Pastime.

In the two-inning game, the Old Mets defeated the Old Yankees/ Dodgers squad, 1–0. The next day, the *New York Times'* headline jokingly read: "Alumni of Mets showing improvement with age." Managing the old Mets, as he had in 1962, was Casey Stengel. The Old Perfessor had stayed on for another season at the Polo Grounds in 1963, before moving on to the finally completed Flushing Meadows Stadium — named Shea Stadium after Bill Shea — in 1964. Whatever the venue, Casey's teams continued to lose spectacularly, averaging 110 loses a year. With the World's Fair next door and the Stengel name still being magic, the Mets continued to attract large crowds. In their first year at Queens, they drew 1,732,597. The 1964 pennant-winning Yankees, managed by Yogi Berra, attracted just 1,305,638 to the Bronx. But the romance had to end sometime. On July 25, 1965, Casey fell down and broke his hip at a late night party at Toots Shor's. He never returned to the dugout. The following year, in a special election, he was inducted into the Baseball Hall of Fame.

On that June day in 1973 the Old Perfessor, aged 83, donned the Mets' uniform one more time. He was escorted onto the field by a young black hostess wearing a pinstriped shirt and matching striped cap. Miss Rheingold, along with Casey part of the concerted attempt at invented tradition in 1962, was but a memory by now.

The only other member of the 1962 Mets to be elected to Cooperstown was Richie Ashburn. After hitting .306 in 1962 and making the All-Star team,

Robin Roberts, the Philadelphia Phillies' great, in a Yankee uniform. Released by the Phillies, ignored by the Mets, signed and let go by the Yankees, Roberts landed with the Baltimore Orioles, for whom he was the American League Comeback of the Year Player in 1962. Casey Stengel received votes for Manager of the Year. Roger Maris was chosen the "flop of the year." Proof of a world turned upside down.

Whitey retired to become a TV-radio color commentator for the Philadelphia Phillies. He joined the veteran Byrum Saam, but was best remembered for his partnership with Harry Kalas beginning in 1971. Whitey and the silver-tongued Kalas carried on a banter that delighted generations of Phillies fans. Ashburn, who never played in Shea Stadium, very nearly died in the ballpark. On September 9, 1997, he collapsed after a game between the Mets and Phillies and succumbed from a heart attack at age 70. Two years earlier, he had been inducted into the Baseball Hall of Fame.

Richie Ashburn was at heart a Philadelphia Phillie, like Robin Roberts. Roberts, ignored by the Mets and released by the Yankees, won the Comeback Player of the Year Award in 1962 with the Baltimore Orioles.

Unlike Richie Ashburn, Rod Kanehl was and would always be a Met, one of the Amazin Ones, the gang of improbable heroes who turned the New York baseball world over in 1962. On that Old Timers Day in June 1973, Kanehl played second base and right field in the two innings at Shea , once again showing his versatility, if not grace. Kanehl's career with the Mets proved to be a short one. He played two more seasons for Stengel in 1963 and 1964, before being released by George Weiss in 1965. "They gave away my uniform number even before spring training started," he ruefully recalled.[2] By 1966 Rod Kanehl was running a contracting business in Springfield, Missouri, and playing semi-pro ball out of Wichita with a team called the Dreamliners. Charlie Neal, Kanehl's former double play partner, served as both player and bus driver.

George Weiss not only got rid of Kanehl, but also the best of the Mets' players. Roger Craig played on the Cardinals' team that defeated the Yankees in the 1964 World Series. Frank Thomas was on the Phillies' team whose September collapse allowed the Cardinals to clinch the pennant on the last day of the 1964 season. Félix Mantilla, traded to the Boston Red Sox, had three productive years in Beantown, reaching career highs in average (.315), home runs (30) and RBIs (92). Jim Hickman made the National League All-Star team in 1970 with the Cubs, achieving personal highs in home runs (32), RBIs (115), and average (.315). George Weiss never received much for these players—nor for Al Jackson or Jay Hook.

That first year, banners were festooned across the Polo Grounds bearing the names of Rod Kanehl , Marv Throneberry, and Elio Chacón. On a late June night in 1966, there were no banners to be seen at Shea Stadium. The Mets were slowly starting to shed the image of lovable losers that they had burnished during the second half of the 1962 season. The farm system was starting to produce real young talent. Gil Hodges returned in 1968, and, although an original Met and darling of the fans, he never became the butt of anyone's jokes. By 1969, the National League pennant flag was waving over Shea Stadium. The Mets became a team that was expected to win, not lose. And win they did. On June 9, 1973, they were mired in fifth in place in the Eastern Division. (Major League Baseball never gave up its 162-game season, preferring two six-team divisions, and making the season even longer than it was in 1962.) But led by Yogi Berra, the 1973 Mets came back to win the National League pennant and play in another October Classic, this time against Charles Finley's Oakland Athletics.

The ultimate symbol of Mets futility, Marv Throneberry, was absent from the Old Timers Day, celebration but not from the TV screen. Marvelous Marv was capitalizing on his Mets notoriety by doing beer commercials for Miller Lite; Rheingold Beer was all but defunct by now. "I don't know why they asked me to do this commercial," he ponders on screen.

In fact, other than the uniform, there was little to connect the present Mets with the Stengel men of 1962. That was the case, except for Ed Kranepool. The 17-year-old rookie hung around for 18 years, playing on both the worst and the best of Mets teams. But Gil Hodges, Miss Rheingold—the stuff of invented tradition in 1962 — were gone. And so was the Polo Grounds; an apartment complex now occupied the site of the old ballpark on Coogan's Bluff.

Yankee Stadium, celebrating its 50th year in 1973, still stood proudly on the other side of the Macombs Dam Bridge. On August 11, it opened its gates for the annual Old Timers Day. On hand for the festivities were Babe Ruth's widow, Claire, and Yankee immortals Joe DiMaggio, Bill Dickey, and Phil Rizzuto. Casey Stengel was present as well. He was introduced before Mickey Mantle and after Joe DiMaggio. When his name was intoned by public address announcer Bob Sheppard, Stengel, dressed in a striped sports jacket and dark pants, gently picked up both his trouser legs, performed a little jig, and skipped onto the field to join Mickey between second and third base

Rod ("Hot Rod") Kanehl, a former Yankee farmhand, was a jack of all trades and master of none for Casey Stengel in 1962. A Polo Grounds favorite for his hustling play, Kanehl was released in 1965. "They gave away my uniform number even before spring training started," he ruefully recalled. Kanehl returned for Old Timers Day at Shea Stadium on June 9, 1973, for the retirement of Gil Hodges' number 14. Gil died the year before, at age 48.

The one and a half inning exhibition pitted the Casey Stengels against the Ralph Houks. Members of the 1962 Yankees, the franchise's last world championship team, were scattered between the two squads. The Stengel men included Tom Tresh, Bill Skowron, Johnny Blanchard, Héctor López, Whitey Ford, and Ralph Terry. Besides Tresh, who played on both sides, the Major's squad boasted Bobby Richardson, Mickey Mantle, Elston Howard, and Bob Turley.

The Stengels dropped a 2–0 decision to the Houks. Casey managed in mufti perhaps the pain of his firing by Dan Topping in October 1960 never quite disappeared sufficiently for him to don the Yankee pinstripes once again. But his reputation as baseball ambassador remained intact as he received a thunderous ovation from the Yankee Stadium crowd.

Over a decade had gone by since Ralph Terry retired Willie McCovey on the vicious line drive to Bobby Richardson, bringing a dramatic finish to the 1962 World Series— the last world championship for the Yankees of the sixties. By 1968, Mantle, Ford, Richardson and Kubek were all gone from the Bronx. Howard, Skowron, Boyer, and Maris had all been traded away. Bill Stafford and Jim Bouton had developed sore arms, and Terry became ineffective. Tresh's potentially brilliant career was derailed by a knee injury.

Mickey won his third MVP award in 1962. He then went into a long decline, which ended with his retirement in 1968. Roger hung up his spikes the same year, after playing on two consecutive pennant winners with the St. Louis Cardinals in 1967 and 1968. He never again hit as many as 30 home runs in a season after 1962.

Maris wasn't present at Yankee Stadium on August 11 for the Old Timers' Day festivities; he didn't feel quite at home in the Bronx. The memories of 1962 — the media frenzy and the controversy over the asterisk, the attacks on him as the embodiment of practically everything wrong with the modern game — were simply too hard to overcome. But Roger's name was still very much in the news in 1973. The Braves' Hank Aaron was making his steady assault on Babe Ruth; record of 714 lifetime home runs. As Aaron continued on his quest, many pundits and fans recalled Maris' own battle to overcome the Babe — with an added racial tone. Blacks had made great strides in major league baseball since the spring training camps were integrated in 1972, but Buck O'Neil never graduated to the managerial position he justly deserved.

Two hours before the Old Timers Day festivities began at Yankee Stadium on August 11, 1973, a sudden gust of wind hit the 1964 American League pennant hanging from the façade in the upper right field stands, tearing a large hole in it. This act of God symbolized the sad fate of the Yankees in the late 1960s and early 1970s. The Bombers didn't wave another championship flag after 1962. Ralph Houk, who retreated to the general manager's office in 1964, was succeeded in the dugout by Yogi Berra. After the 1964 World Series loss to St. Louis, Yogi was fired and replaced by Johnny Keane, the manager of the world champion Cardinals. Under Keane, the Yankees sunk to the bottom of the American League standings, prompting the return of Houk in 1966. By the following year, Gil Hodges had returned to New York, signaling a new chapter in the history of the New York Metropolitan Baseball Club.

The rivalry between the two New York clubs was measured in more than wins and losses. It was also a question of winning and losing the hearts and minds of the metropolitan area fans. In 1962 the Yankees drew 1,493,574 fans to the Stadium; afterwards, attendance steadily declined. In 1972, the Yankees drew just 966,368 fans to the Bronx, the lowest attendance figures since World War II. Meanwhile, the Mets had topped two million fans each year from 1969 to 1972; the latter season, 2,134,185 customers passed through the turnstiles at Shea Stadium.

The Old Timers' reunion in August 1973 was the last of its kind. Yankee Stadium underwent a $27 million renovation in 1974 and 1975, the Bombers taking residence at Shea Stadium for two seasons before returning to renewed glory in 1976. Under the leadership of their energetic young owner, George Steinbrenner, the Yankees invested heavily in the free agent market, winning back to back world championships in 1977 and 1978.

In the 1980s it was the Mets who ruled New York; since the mid–1990s, it's been the Yankees. The rivalry spawned in that amazing year of 1962 continues. The wheel will turn yet again.

Chapter Notes

Abbreviations for Frequently Used Sources:

BD	Baseball Digest	NYP	New York Post
LIP	Long Island Press	NYT	New York Times
ND	Newsday	SEP	Saturday Evening Post
NEN	Newark Evening News	SI	Sports Illustrated
NYDN	New York Daily News	SM	Sport Magazine
NYJA	New York Journal American	TSN	The Sporting News
NYHT	New York Herald-Tribune		

Preface

1. Conversation with Jim Bouton, April 23, 2011.

Prologue

1. Yogi Berra and Ed Fitzgerald, *Yogi* (Garden City, NY: Doubleday, 1961), p. 176.
2. *NYHT*, March 16, 1961.
3. *St. Petersburg Times*, February 1, 1961; *Pittsburgh Courier*, February 4, 1961.
4. *St. Petersburg Times*, February 3, 1961.
5. *Pittsburgh Courier*, April 1, 1961.
6. *SI*, March 5, 1962; Casey Stengel and Harry T. Paxton, *Casey at the Bat: The Story of My Life in Baseball* (New York: Random House, 1962), p. 223.

Chapter 1

1. *NYT*, October 3, 1961.
2. *SEP*, December 9, 1961; *Esquire*, May 1, 1961.
3. *TSN*, October 11, 1961.
4. *Ibid.*, September 25, 1961.
5. *Ibid.*, October 18, 1961.
6. *SI*, March 6, 1961.
7. *NY JA*, October 12, 1961.

8. *NYT*, October 13, 1961.
9. *Ibid.*, October 27, 1961.
10. *Ibid.*, November 9, 1961.
11. *NYHT*, January 11, 1962.
12. *TSN*, November 22, 1961.
13. *NYT*, April 10, 1960.
14. *BD*, October-November, 1961.
15. *NYT*, December 13, 1961.
16. *TSN*, December 13, 1961; *Esquire*, May 1, 1961.
17. *NYT*, September 15, 1961.
18. *TSN*, December 27, 1961; *Esquire*, May 1, 1961.
19. *NYT*, July 2, 1961.

Chapter 2

1. *NYT*, December 29, 1961.
2. *Ibid.*, February 20, 1962.
3. *Ibid.*, January 4, 1962.
4. *BD*, October 11, 1962.
5. *Jet*, January 11, 1962.
6. *NYT*, January 3, 1962; *NYHT*, January 10, 1962.
7. *NYT*, January 31, 1962.
8. *Ibid.*, January 18, 1962.
9. *Ibid.*, January 10, 1960.
10. *Pittsburgh Courier*, January 27, 1962.
11. *NYT*, January 27, 1962.

12. *NYT*, January 28, 1962.
13. *NYHT*, February 2, 1962.
14. *NYHT*, February 25, 1961; *St. Petersburg Times*, February 26, 1961.
15. *NYT*, February 18, 1962.
16. *Atlanta Daily World*, February 7, 1962.
17. *NYT*, February 19, 1962.

Chapter 3

1. *NYT*, February 21, 1962.
2. *Ibid.*, February 20, 1962.
3. *Ibid.*, February 25, 1962.
4. *Ibid.*, March 5, 1962.
5. Stengel, *Casey at the Bat*, p. 238.
6. *NYHT*, March 1, 1962.
7. *Ibid.*, March 2, 1962.
8. *BD*, March 5, 1962.
9. *NYT*, March 11, 1962.
10. *Ibid.*, March 22, 1962.
11. *NYHT*, March 18, 1962.
12. *Ibid.*, March 19–21, 1962.
13. *NYHT*, March 23, 1962, *NYT*, March 23, 1962.
14. *NYHT*, March 25, 1962.
15. *NYT*, March 27, 1962.
16. *SI*, August 8, 1966.
17. *Philadelphia Inquirer*, March 19, 1962.

Chapter 4

1. *NYT*, April 9, 1962.
2. *NYHT*, April 10, 1962.
3. *ND*, April 11, 1962.
4. *NYT*, November 21, 1960; *SI*, April 28, 1961.
5. *NYHT*, April 11, 1962.
6. *NYT*, April 13, 1962.
7. *NYDN*, April 13, 1962; *Pittsburgh Post-Gazette*, April 14, 1962.
8. *LIP*, April 14, 1962.
9. *ND*, April 17, 1962.
10. *NYJA*, April 26, 1962; *Philadelphia Inquirer*, April 26, 1962.
11. *TSN*, December 20, 1961.
12. *NYJA*, April 17, 1962.
13. *Ibid.*, April 18, 1962.
14. *BD*, July 1962.
15. All stadium descriptions contained herein are based on *SI*, April 10, 1961.
16. *NYT*, April 23, 1962.
17. *Pittsburgh Post-Gazette*, April 23, 24, 1962.
18. *NYT*, April 25, 1962.

Chapter 5

1. *NYJA*, April 29, 1962.
2. *Pittsburgh Press*, April 15, 1962.
3. *NYHT*, May 2, 1962.
4. *NYT*, May 4, 1962.
5. *NEN*, May 5, 1962.
6. *NYT*, May 8, 1962.
7. *Chicago Tribune*, May 4, 1962.
8. *NYT*, May 11, 1962.
9. *Ibid.*, May 6, 1962.
10. *NYHT*, May 8, 1962.
11. *SI*, August 8, 1966.
12. *NYT*, May 17, 1962.
13. *NYHT*, May 18, 1962.
14. *SI*, April 10, 1961.
15. *NYT*, May 20, 1962.
16. *NYJA*, April 26, 1962.
17. *NYT*, May 28, 1962.
18. *Ibid.*, April 7, 1962.
19. *NYHT*, May 29, 1962.
20. *Ibid.*, May 31, 1962.

Chapter 6

1. *NYT*, June 3, 6, 1962.
2. *NYDN*, June 1, 1962.
3. *BD*, August 1963.
4. *Los Angeles Times*, March 23, April 19, 1962.
5. *NYDN*, June 14, 1962.
6. *Ibid.*, June 10, 1962.
7. *Ibid.*, June 13, 1962.
8. *NYT*, June 17, 1962.
9. *Ibid.*, January 26, 1963.
10. *NYDN*, June 27, 1962.
11. *Cleveland Plain Dealer*, June 18, 1962.
12. *Detroit Free Press*, June 16, 1962.
13. *NYT*, June 25, 1962.
14. *Ibid.*, June 27, 1962.
15. *Los Angeles Times*, July 1, 1962.

Chapter 7

1. *NYT*, July 2, 1962.
2. *TSN*, July 21, 1962.
3. *NYT*, June 15, 1960.
4. *Ibid.*, June 21, 1960.
5. *Washington Post; Pittsburgh Courier*, July 12, 1962.
6. *NYT*, July 11, 1962.
7. *TSN.*, October 27, 1962.
8. *NYHT*, July 19, 1962.
9. *Boston Globe*, July 17, 1962.
10. *NYDN*, July 26, 1962.

11. *NYT*, July 22, 1962.
12. *Boston Globe*; *NYDN*, July 29, 1962.
13. *NYT*, Jul 31, 1962.
14. Bill Veeck, *Veeck as in Wreck* (Chicago: University of Chicago 1962; 1976), pp. 254–55.

Chapter 8

1. *TSN*, August 18, 1962.
2. *NYT*, August 5, 1962.
3. *SI*, August 26, 1962.
4. *PPG*, July 8, 1960.
5. *NEN*, May 14, 1962, *NYT*, August 5, 1962.
6. *NYHT*, August 3, 1962.
7. *TSN* August 4, 1962.
8. *NYT.*, August 4, 1962.
9. *SEP*, August 11, 18, 1962.
10. *Minneapolis Star*, August 7, 1962.
11. *NYHT*, August 11, 1962.
12. Ibid.
13. *TSN*, August 4, 1962.
14. *SI*, June 5, 1961.
15. *TSN*, August 11, 1962.
16. *Ebony*, June 1962.
17. *Pittsburgh Courier*, July 28, 1962.
18. *NYT*, August 30, 1962.
19. *Ibid.*, August 31, 1962.

Chapter 9

1. *NYP*; *NYT*, September 5, 1962.
2. *NYP*, September 13; *Minneapolis Star*, September 18, 1962.
3. *NYT*, September 4, 1962.
4. *Sport*, August 1962.
5. *NYT.*, September 11, 1962.
6. *Ibid.*, September 16, 1962.
7. *Ibid.*, September 19, 1962.
8. *SI*, August 20, 1962.
9. *NYT*, September 18, 1962.
10. *Ibid.*, September 21, 1962.
11. *NYHT*; *NYT*, June 29, 1962.
12. *NYP*; *NYT*, September 24, 1962.
13. *Minneapolis Star*, September 26, 1962.
14. *NYT*, September 25, 1962.
15. *Ibid.*, September 4, October 1, 1962.
16. *Chicago Tribune*, September 29, 1962.

17. *NYP.*, October 1, 1962.
18. *NYT*, August 26, 1962.

Chapter 10

1. *NYP*, October 2, 1962.
2. *San Francisco Chronicle*, October 5, 1962.
3. *NYT*, October 5, 1962.
4. *Ibid.*, October 6, 1962.
5. *NYP*, October 7, 1962.
6. *San Francisco Examiner*, October 6, 1962.
7. *NYT*, October 6, 1962.
8. *San Francisco Examiner*, October 6, 7, 1962.
9. *BD*, October 15, 1962.
10. *NYHT*, October 14, 1962.
11. *BD*, September 1962, *NYP*, October 8, 1962.
12. *San Francisco Chronicle*, October 8, 1962.
13. *NYT*, October 12, 1962.
14. *San Francisco Chronicle*, October 5, 10, 1962.
15. *NYT*, October 11, 1962.
16. *NYHT*, October 14, 1962.
17. *NYP*, October 14, 1962.
18. *San Francisco Examiner*, October 12, 1962.
19. *NYP*, October 15, 1962.
20. *NYT*, October 16, 1962.
21. *San Francisco Examiner*, October 16, 1962.
22. *San Francisco Chronicle*, October 16, 1962.
23. *NYP*, September 30, 1962, October 17, 1962; *NYT*, September 17, 1962.
24. *NYP*, October 19, 1962; *BD*, January, 1963.
25. *San Francisco Examiner*, *Francisco Chronicle*, October 17, 1962.
26. Ibid.

Epilogue

1. *NYDN*, June 10, 1973.
2. *SI*, August 8, 1966.

Bibliography

Statistical Materials

Baseball Almanac (online)
Baseball Encyclopedia, 8th edition, (1990)
Baseball Register, 1962

Baseball Register, 1963
New York Mets Official 1962 Yearbook
New York Yankees Official 1962 Yearbook

Newspapers (Local)

Long Island Press
New York Daily News
New York Herald-Tribune
New York Journal-American

The New York Post
The New York Times
Newark Evening News
Newsday

Newspapers (National)

Baltimore Sun
Boston Chronicle
Boston Globe
Chicago Tribune
Cincinnati Post
Cleveland Plain Dealer
Detroit Free Press
Kansas City Star
Los Angeles Express
Los Angeles Times
Miami Herald

Milwaukee Journal
Minneapolis Star
Philadelphia Examiner
Pittsburgh Post-Dispatch
Pittsburgh Press
St. Louis Post-Dispatch
St. Petersburg Times
San Francisco Chronicle
San Francisco Examiner
Washington Post

Newspapers (African American)

Amsterdam News
Atlanta Daily World
Chicago Defender

Los Angeles Sentinel
Pittsburgh Courier

Periodicals

Baseball Digest
Ebony
Esquire
Jet
Look

Saturday Evening Post
Sport
The Sporting News
Sports Illustrated

Books

Allen, Maury. *Roger Maris*. New York: Donald I. Fine, 1986.

Berman, Marshall. *All That Is Solid Melts into Air: The Experience of Modernity*. New York: Simon & Shuster, 1982.

Berra, Yogi, and Ed Fitzgerald, *Yogi*. Garden City, NY: Doubleday, 1961.

Bjarkman, Peter. *The New York Mets Encyclopedia*. Champaign, Ill.: Sports Publishing Company, 2001.

Brosnan, Jim. *Pennant Race*. New York: Harper and Brothers, 1962.

Caro, Robert A. *Robert Moses and the Fall of New York*. New York: Knopf, 1974.

Creamer, Robert. *Stengel: His Life and Times*. New York: Simon & Schuster, 1984.

Einstein, Charles. *Willie's Time: A Memoir of Another America*. New York: Berkeley Books, 1979.

Frommer, Herbert. *New York City Baseball: The Last Golden Age, 1947–1957*. New York: Macmillan, 1980.

Golenbock, Peter. *Dynasty: The New York Yankees, 1949–64*. Englewood Cliffs, NJ: Prentice-Hall, 1975.

Jackson, Kenneth T. *Crabgrass Frontier: The Suburbanization of the United States*. New York: Oxford University Press, 1985.

Jacobs, Jane. *The Death and Life of Great American Cities*. New York: The Modern Library, 1993.

James, Bill. *Historical Baseball Abstract*. New York: The Free Press, 2001.

Stengel, Casey, and Harry T. Paxton. *Casey at the Bat: The Story of My Life in Baseball*. New York: Random House, 1962.

Veeck, Bill. *Veeck as in Wreck* Chicago: University of Chicago, 1962.

Whyte, William H. *City: Rediscovering the Center*. Philadelphia: University of Pennsylvania Press, 2009.

Index